The Conservation
of Enemies _____

Recent Titles in
Contributions in Political Science
Series Editor: Bernard K. Johnpoll

Eurocommunism: The Ideological and Political-Theoretical Foundations
George Schwab, editor

American-Soviet Relations: From 1947 to the Nixon-Kissinger Grand Design
Dan Caldwell

The First Amendment Under Siege: The Politics of Broadcast Regulation
Richard E. Labunski

Political Culture, Foreign Policy, and Conflict: The Palestine Area Conflict System
Basheer Meibar

The Politics of Wilderness Preservation
Craig Willard Allin

Nationalism: Essays in Honor of Louis L. Snyder
Michael Palumbo and William O. Shanahan, editors

Compromised Compliance: Implementation of the 1965 Voting Rights Act
Howard Ball, Dale Krane, and Thomas Lauth

City of the Right: Urban Applications of American Conservative Thought
Gerald L. Houseman

The American Governorship
Coleman B. Ransone, Jr.

Strategic Studies: A Critical Assessment
Colin S. Gray

The Conservation of Enemies
A STUDY IN ENMITY

Frederick H. Hartmann

CONTRIBUTIONS IN POLITICAL SCIENCE, NUMBER 68

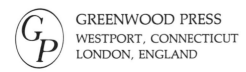

GREENWOOD PRESS
WESTPORT, CONNECTICUT
LONDON, ENGLAND

Library of Congress Cataloging in Publication Data

Hartmann, Frederick H.
    The conservation of enemies.

    (Contributions in political science, ISSN 0147-1066 ;
no. 68)
    Bibliography: p.
    1. International relations. I. Title. II. Series.
JX1391.H33   327.1'1   81-6343
ISBN 0-313-23063-6 (lib. bdg.)   AACR2

Library of Congress Catalog Card Number: 81-6343
ISBN: 0-313-23063-6
ISSN: 0147-1066

First published in 1982

Greenwood Press
A division of Congressional Information Service, Inc.
88 Post Road West
Westport, Connecticut 06881

Printed in the United States of America

10 9 8 7 6 5 4 3 2 1

CONTENTS

Part V: The Conservation of Enemies

ILLUSTRATIONS

PREFACE

This book reflects my conviction that the really important mistakes in foreign policy and national security policy begin with the way the problems are viewed. Above all, the errors are intellectual, and the most serious errors focus on how the fact of enemies and the phenomenon of enmity are visualized.

The book's special emphasis on enemies reflects the fact that I have for some years taught U.S. military students at the mid-career, professional, and graduate (war college) level, and I am very much aware of how such students normally approach such questions. For understandable reasons, they tend to begin with the enemies arrayed against the United States and the capabilities they possess: what we would confront if war began, and how we would have to counter it. Especially because they realize how difficult it is to amass or retain superiority over such enemies, however, they easily become interested in the more basic question of whether an uncomfortable number of enemies with a disconcerting amount of capability has to be accepted as a "given."

The title of this book has been chosen after much deliberate thought. Some might argue that the book should really be called "the conservation of *enmity*," since I throughout address enmity as a constant that, allocated and reallocated within the system through a series of policy choices, results in increasing or decreasing the number of enemies confronted. Observing international affairs and foreign policy through such a looking glass is highly illuminating, whether or not the proposition is true in some ultimate sense.

A few may also consider the title a mere play on words, but I have found in lecturing around the United States that the "conservation of enemies" is a phrase that to most listeners clearly conveys my concern about the dangers of accumulating enemies, gratuitously or casually. It starts the listeners thinking about the linkage between goals, perception, and opposition encountered, and that is the thought process I want to encourage.

My thanks go to a generation of students at the Naval War College, Newport, Rhode Island, who insisted on probing more deeply, even if in a friendly way. I also thank my students and colleagues at the University of California at Berkeley in 1979-1980, who helped me sharpen these thoughts, and the Hoover Institution at Stanford, California, which gave me a place to work and a great library to use. My daughter Lynne suggested the material on linguistics in Chapter 7 and my wife Reggie helped to edit the entire manuscript to its present (more modest) size. Finally, I want to express my gratitude to the Center for Advanced Research of the Naval War College for partial support in the initial research stage.

Part I ——————————

A STUDY IN ENMITY

1

DEFINING THE PROBLEM

"Enemy — emphasizing the idea of hostility."

The Random House Dictionary

Enemies and enmity are such a normal part of the nature of things that they have received little systematic attention. Wars, in which enemies fight each other, have been examined individually and as an institution. Crises, in which enemies seek by "management" of their tensions to avert violence, have become highly popular of late as subjects for research. Deterrence, as the psychological interaction of enemies eyeing each other's nuclear arsenals, has its share of attention. Certain other questions have been comparatively neglected, however, such as where enmity itself comes from, how much enmity is "normal" in the contemporary world of nation-states, how its extent and intensity are affected by the perceptions of policy makers, and how much it can be controlled by conscious policy design. Yet unless enmity exists apart from human will, it is possible to control its dimensions as well as its manifestations. It can be contoured and shaped, at least down to some "normal," residual amount. If it cannot be eliminated, it should be possible to reduce it to acceptable dimensions, provided its nature is understood.

As a phenomenon, enmity exists on three separate levels. On the most obvious and violent level is the eruption called war. One level less drastic are crises that must break out into war unless they are "managed." Deep under the crust of daily events, however, is a third level, which goes under a variety of names but in which events on the second and first level find their origin. Like a volcanic eruption, which is due to forces largely unseen, eruption of the system into crisis or war is a signal of failure in what we shall call *contouring or controlling enmity.* While this book will explore aspects of each level, as well as inquire whether enmity itself is an innate and inescapable part of the system, the greatest emphasis will be on this third level.

In speaking of enemies and enmity, the question naturally arises as to whether it is worthwhile to distinguish one from the other. "Enemies" refers to those who are hostile, and is therefore a question of number; "enmity" denotes the hostility itself, and is therefore a question of degree. These are, strictly speaking, not the same. Nations do not collect "half-enemies," but they may confront nations whose enmity toward them is tempered by other concerns. Strictly speaking, to say "enemies" is to say "hostile sovereign units." In discussing enemies, we shall try to remain faithful to an operational definition: that enemies are nations (a) against whom one contemplates the possible use of force, as indicated through contingency planning, or (b) against whom fighting has occurred. In contrast, to say "enmity" is to refer to the degree to which opposed interests predominate in a bilateral relationship. This distinction is an important one because it focuses attention on the relationship between the policies pursued by the "actors" in their multilateral context and the enemies confronted by particular parties as a result. In turn, both "enemies" and "enmity" can be distinguished from "tension level," using that term to mean the fluctuating "expectation of violence" in the system as a whole.

Exploration of the subject of enemies and enmity, once begun, leads in many directions. Part I will deal with theories about the sources and dimensions of enmity and with the way policy, which itself rests on the perception of a problem, influences the dimensions of enmity. With this foundation, Part II will deal with factors affecting policy decisions, including perception. Part III, my cardinal principles model, will provide a convenient vehicle for examining the external environment to which policy must react as well as the internal limitations cultures impose on any government's appraisal of the external environment. Also noted is what that model prescribes as policy content, provided its particular view of reality is accepted. My point, however, is not to urge the validity of the model so much as to demonstrate the role of any model in defining the parameters of what is perceived.

Part IV then examines three other universal models, the environments they describe, and the policy actions they prescribe. The aim is to bring out clearly the contrasting policy results of various perceptions of the problem faced.

Finally, Part V provides a three-part summing up. First, the universal models are systematically compared; next, the relationship of strategic (weapons-related) theory to these models and to policy issues is examined; then a concluding chapter ends with a brief analysis of the main trends in U.S. foreign policy in handling enemies and enmity. It examines whether the United States in its policies (and its preference in models) has exceeded the norm for enemies and enmity.

That is the practical point of writing this book: to cast light on why the United States, from an intellectual point of view, followed the policy path that led to Vietnam. While many important issues were raised by that war, including whether it was fought properly, surely the most important question is whether it should have been fought at all. How did the United States come to perceive the problem as it led to the policy decision to fight that enemy in that war?

The title of this book, *The Conservation of Enemies*, is deliberately chosen to emphasize an attitude toward enmity. What it is meant to suggest above all is that nations that behave rationally do not by choice or by error collect more enemies at any one time than they can safely confront. The phrase is meant to combat the tendency to assume that enmity has to be accepted, even though ever increasing, rather than limited by policy choice to a more modest and acceptable degree. Conservation of enemies in this sense means not taking more than one's share. It is a generalization about policy making.

But something more is meant besides — something much more controversial. Recall that the older phrase, conservation of energy, refers to the principle in mechanics that the *total* energy of any material system is a quantity that can neither be increased nor diminished by any action between the parts. It can be redistributed in various forms, but not changed in amount. It is fruitful and provocative to consider the state system, with any given and set number of members, from this same perspective. There is no need here to assert this as a truth, only to suggest it as a point of view from which to contemplate the data, much in the sense in which George Abell, the astronomer, has written: "Science strives to find representations that accurately describe nature, not absolute truths."[1] Conservation of enemies is intended to provide a representation by which we may try to describe nature.

If a constant amount of friction (enmity) that can be redistributed through policy actions is assumed, it is possible to visualize a process or game in which the players each seek to transfer excessive enmity to other players. Crises can be thought of as confrontations reflecting excessive enmity not otherwise successfully redistributed. Conservation of enemies in this sense is therefore a generalization about the international relations system and how it operates. But the nature of that system is itself in dispute. Are enemies "made" or "born"? Is there a condition in which enemies would cease altogether to exist?

Many optimistic analysts think of international relations as an interaction by states that, if properly adjusted by all or most of the nation-states, can lead to a radical elimination of the strains and stresses and hates and jealousies so prevalent in the system. To those who hold this belief, the problem is the way human beings have organized their environment. Enlightened cooperation is seen as leading to a resolution of the world's major ills. On energy, for example, an agreement wise in its features would make supplies available on a universally equitable basis. On food, a fine balance between production and consumption would be brought about that would eliminate hunger. At least one of the models examined in Part IV shares this mind-set. Its advocates are not likely to greet enthusiastically the idea of conservation of enemies.

A second view of the future of international relations looks not so much to the elimination of strains and stresses as to their even distribution and balance within the system. This second view reflects a conception of the nature of man that was well expressed in the *Federalist* papers, where ambition is seen as best countered by rival ambition.[2] On weapons, for example, this theory envisages distribution in such a manner that all are armed for adequate defense but none for assured aggression. On rival alliance blocs it looks to the creation of a situation in which each nation is confident of its own strength but not of its superiority. This second view, in addition to being compatible with the idea of conservation of enemies, finds sympathetic echoes in another of the models we shall examine in Part IV.

Obviously, the first view is highly optimistic about the nature of humanity. It assumes absolute progress in overcoming evils and the likelihood that people will remake the world by doing away with its shortcomings. By contrast, the second set of views is guardedly optimistic about the nature of humanity. It is far from pessimistic or cynical, but it would not attempt to eliminate shortcomings so much as to defuse or counterbalance them through persistent effort.

There is also at least a third view of the nature of humankind, of the future of international relations, and of the roots of enmity. This third view is essentially apocalyptic; it looks forward in fear and trembling, or with unconscious gloating, to a nuclear Götterdämmerung. It holds that no positive choices are available and that in the end human beings will be overcome by the evils they have perpetrated.

Most of us would dismiss this utterly pessimistic third view, in which the idea of conservation of enemies becomes redundant; we would probably subscribe instead to either one or the other of the remaining views or some combination of the two, believing, for instance, that hunger could be eliminated but not fear of aggression. Obviously, this whole area is one in which it is necessary to be careful in reaching judgments.

Despite the hopes and dreams of a legion of liberal reformers, recorded history certainly sheds doubt that the millenium, when enemies will vanish, can easily be brought about. Writing about conflict and war more than four hundred years before Christ, Thucydides made a claim to future usefulness that twenty-four centuries have failed to refute. He wrote:

It will be enough for me . . . if these words of mine are judged useful by those who want to understand clearly the events which happened in the past and which (*human nature being what it is*) will, at some time or other and in much the same ways, be repeated in the future.[3]

Thucydides is eloquent testimony to the enduring nature of enmity among organized political units. What is much more difficult to establish from historical records, which are often fragmentary, is whether things have gotten better or worse since his time or have remained essentially unchanged.

It is hard to discern whether human beings are more "barbarous" today, whether their inhumanity is greater or less than in earlier ages. If we compare Hitler's extermination center at Dachau with Nero's habit of lighting his garden at night with burning Christians, we can say that one method of destruction is technologically more up to date—but can we conclude that the extermination center shows a decline or growth in inhumanity?

Tacitus writes of his own day that Rome was a "delirium of hate and terror; slaves were bribed to betray their masters, freed men their patrons. He who had no foe was destroyed by his friend."[4] Tacitus's account of the slaughter, as three successive Roman emperors perished in the one calendar year of A.D. 69, lives up to his statement. Yet Hitler clearly excelled in the quantity of the horrors he perpetrated. Suetonius, writing of the reign of Tiberius (A.D. 14-37), said, "No day passed but someone was executed." True, too, of Stalin not long ago and of Idi Amin more recently.

A full reading of Suetonius's history, *The Lives of the Twelve Caesars*, inclines the balance of virtue more in favor of our own day. There are tales in Suetonius that retain some shock value even in this jaded age. Even of "good" Augustus, Suetonius writes:

That he was a common adulterer his very friends do not deny, but they excuse him forsooth, saying that he did it not upon filthy lust, but for good reason and in policy to the end that he might more easily search out the plots . . . by the means of women and wives. . . ."[5]

Consider the implications of this casual comment for the nature of Roman society! It was a society in which, we are told, Caligula sprinkled gold dust instead of sawdust on the floor of the circus arena; a society of which Juvenal said, "Luxury, more ruthless than war, broods over Rome. . . . No guilt or deed of lust is wanting since Roman poverty disappeared."[6]

All these authors are describing Rome during, or just before, the early Christian era.

Thucydides, writing in the fourth century B.C., told how his own people, the Athenians, dealt with the Melians. In the diplomatic negotiations that Thucydides describes, the Athenians say at one point: ". . . you know as well as we do that, when these matters are discussed by practical people, the standard of justice depends on the equality of power to compel and that in fact the strong do what they have the power to do and the weak accept what they have to accept."[7] Stalin might have said that; it is more difficult to establish how consistently in the last twenty-four hundred years people have acted on such assumptions. What we do know, from Thucydides' own words, is that "the Melians surrendered unconditionally to the Athenians, who put to death all the men of military age whom they took, and sold the women and children as slaves. . . ."[8] These actions were taken coldblood-edly, as a policy matter, to set an example to the Athenians' wavering allies.

Machiavelli, who lived from 1469 to 1527, penned views that seemed par-ticularly shocking to his own age, partly because political writings in his own time were lost in clouds of sentimentality and idealism, describing a Golden Age that in fact had already decayed. Also, Machiavelli was at-tempting to describe the rise of the modern nation-state system, at a time when older norms had lost their validity but newer norms had not acquired authority. Diplomacy was still a hit-or-miss, ad hoc system involving the use of special envoys. Sometimes these envoys were thrown into prison or even killed. Even less drastic receptions had unpleasant and uncertain aspects. The idea of a system of permanent embassies with inviolability and extraterritoriality, even the custom of respecting the person of the diplomat, was still evolving.[9] International law in the modern sense did not exist. When the Protestant Reformation then destroyed much of the moral and political authority of the Pope, very serious problems were created. Com-paring then and now in terms of such institutional devices to mitigate hostilities, there is no question that the modern age shows to better advan-tage.

The available evidence shows certain historical periods of more than ordinary turmoil. There were periods when extraordinarily cruel acts occurred, even frequently. It is much more difficult, however, despite the most careful study of the evidence, to conclude that there is any given trend. The earlier writers are not around to tell us what they would have thought, by comparison, of later ages, and the later writers have problems with the always partial data from earlier ages, data that are difficult to understand in themselves.

Apparently — and remember that Western knowledge is primarily oriented toward Western civilization — there were peaks of particular violence in earlier ages, when the hostility of individual to individual, and their cruelty, were most pronounced. In Roman times it came when luxury had sapped Roman republican virtues; in the Middle Ages, for complex reasons, it came at the time of the Crusades; again, in the late-Renaissance period of Machiavelli and Hugo Grotius (Grotius lived from 1583 to 1645), it came because of the transition from one international system to another. It is not possible to conclude that violence and enmity steadily increased or decreased, but only that there have been particular peaks of violence and aggression.[10]

These are some of the reasons the issue cannot be disposed of by saying that the future will be the simple extension of the past, but there is also another reason. Enormous cultural and technical changes have taken place, particularly in the last two hundred years. Slavery, common and accepted with little question for thousands of years, is generally proscribed today, anywhere in the world. This represents a substantial revolution in behavior. Nuclear power is capable of transforming the world, quite literally, either in a positive or a negative sense. Characteristics now accepted as human nature are not likely to remain constant if and when the conditions of life alter radically.

No amount of past evidence, even if more conclusive than what we have, can be proof of how it will be in the future. In 1940 E. H. Carr expressed the frustration he felt with the point of view of either a complete "idealist," who would be a reformer, or a complete "realist," who would accept things as is. He went to the heart of the matter, pointing out that realism, by being content to concern itself with what *is*, thereby neglects what *could be*.

Most of all, consistent realism breaks down because it fails to provide any ground for purposive or meaningful action. If the sequence of cause and effect is sufficiently rigid to permit the "scientific prediction" of events, if our thought is irrevocably conditioned by our status and our interests, then both action and thought become devoid of purpose. . . . Such a conclusion is plainly repugnant to the most deep-seated belief of man about himself.[11]

Machiavelli, Marx, and Lenin all thought individuals could decisively influence events. Carr quotes Lenin, the apostle of scientific "inevitability," as saying: "At the decisive moment and in the decisive place, you must prove the stronger. . . ."

Carr's point is that the future may indeed be drastically different from the past, especially if people will it to be so. They may not have done it in the past, but that is no proof that they will not do it at some time in the future. If the future may be different, there can be no certainty about how much change is possible. It is not possible to conclude that enmity as a phenomenon *must* persist in the future as in the past, or at least to the same degree.

Even a cursory look at primitive societies shows us that people are capable of shaping very divergent and contrasting environments. Erich Fromm, citing evidence compiled by such noted anthropologists as Ruth

Benedict and Margaret Mead, shows how difficult it is to generalize with any accuracy about primitive peoples. Of thirty primitive tribes studied, Fromm reports details for three, each typical of a quite contrasting way of life. Fromm's summary of the data is especially helpful because he looks at all three from the standpoint of aggressiveness versus peacefulness.[12] As he points out, there is no overall anthropological work devoted to this question.

Fromm characterizes the Zuñi Indians (system A) as a virtually non-competitive society in which "individuals who are aggressive, competitive, and noncooperative are regarded as aberrant types."[13] Material things are not highly valued, and personal authority is disparaged. A good man is one who has a generous heart, an accommodating disposition, and a "pleasing" address.

In system B (the Manus Islanders),

the main aim of life is . . . the attainment of personal success through economic activities. . . . All their energy is completely devoted to material success, and they drive themselves so hard that many men die in their early middle age; in fact it is rare for a man to live to see his first grandchild. . . . Energy is so completely devoted to the overriding aim of success that personal motives of affection, loyalty, preference, dislike, and hatred are all barred.[14]

But there is little destructiveness or cruelty—just unrelenting and fierce competition.

The people in system C (the Dobu Islanders) are close to Hobbes's description of the human being in a state of nature. In interpersonal relations everyone is distrusted as a possible enemy. "Even marriage does not lessen the hostility between the two families."[15] The greatest achievement and most admired virtue is *wabuwabu*, "which stresses one's own gains at the expense of another's loss. The art is to reap personal advantage in a situation in which others are victims."[16] (As Fromm points out, this is quite different from the idea of the market exchange, where, in principle, each is satisfied.) Fromm quotes Ruth Benedict's report that the Dobu approach to killing a man is first to convince him you are his friend. Benedict writes: "The Dobian lives out without repression man's worst nightmares of the ill-will of the universe. . . . All existence appears to him as a cut-throat struggle. . . ."[17]

The comparison of these three systems does seem to show clearly that there are no grounds to believe that civilized people are more or less aggressive than primitive people. All varieties of aggressiveness are found in primitive societies.

We cannot, however, conclude from these extraordinary divergencies of behavior that modern mankind's environment and the way people choose to act are matters of completely free choice. All three of these primitive societies were in a real sense isolated communities, two of them islanders. The external world, with its tendencies and problems, did not impinge on them much. So while the primitive society data here are very interesting and show surprising variations in human behavior, they provide only partial answers for the modern world.

Carr, after arguing that we must not overlook the potentiality for change, also makes the inverse observation. He points out that we can attach only limited credibility to the likelihood of behavior occurring in the future that is radically different from that prevailing in the past, unless there is more than wishful thinking involved. Carr is correct. No one can deny that enmity, present in Thucydides' day, still exists in a very real way in the contemporary world and that there are no signs of its demise. Until that outlook changes, the idea of conservation of enemies is worth exploring.

With these preliminary thoughts in mind, let us look at the phenomenon of enmity as treated in literature, history, and the behavioral sciences.

NOTES

1. George Abell, *Exploration of the Universe*, 2d ed. (New York: Holt, Rinehart, Winston, 1969), p. 16.

2. Alexander Hamilton, James Madison, and John Jay, *The Federalist* (Avon: Conn.: Heritage Press, 1973). See no. 51, p. 348.

3. Thucydides, *The Peloponnesian War*, trans. Rex Warner (Baltimore: Penguin Books, 1954), p. 48. Italics added.

4. Cited in William Barclay, *The Letter to the Romans*, rev. ed. (Philadelphia: Westminster Press, 1975), p. 31. The wording in the Wellesley translation is similar. See Tacitus, *The Histories*, trans. Kenneth Wellesley (New York: Penguin, 1964), pp. 2, 3.

5. Suetonius, *The Lives of the Twelve Caesars*, trans. Philemon Holland (New York: Heritage Press, 1965), p. 121.

6. Juvenal, *Satires*.

7. Thucydides, *The Peloponnesian War*, p. 402.

8. Ibid., p. 408.

9. See James G. Frazer, *The Golden Bough* (New York: Macmillan, 1922), p. 226 for the way the ambassadors of the Byzantine Emperor Justin II were received by the Turks. See also p. 229 for the way envoys to the Tartar khans were treated.

10. See the comparable conclusions reached by a very different methodology in J. David Singer and Melvin Small, "Conflict in the International System, 1816-1977: Historical Trends and Policy Futures," chap. 4 in Charles W. Kegley, Jr., and Patrick J. McGowan, eds., *Challenges to America: U.S. Foreign Policy in the 1980s* (Beverly Hills, Calif.: Sage, 1979).

11. E. H. Carr, *The Twenty Years' Crisis, 1919-1939* (London: Macmillan, 1940), p. 117.

12. Erich Fromm, *The Anatomy of Human Destructiveness* (New York: Fawcett Crest, 1973). His survey of these systems is on pp. 193-204.

13. Ibid., p. 196.

14. Ibid., pp. 199-200.

15. Ibid.

16. Ibid., p. 202.

17. Ibid., p. 204. Quoted from Ruth Benedict, *Patterns of Culture* (New York: New American Library, Mentor, 1934).

2

ENMITY AS A PHENOMENON

[I]n every individual the readiness to fight is greatest in the most familiar place, that is, in the middle of its territory. . . . In nearing the center of the territory the aggressive urge [i.e., willingness to fight] increases in geometrical ratio to the decrease in distance from this center. This increase . . . is so great that it compensates for all differences ever to be found in adult, sexually mature animals of a species. If we know the territorial centers of two conflicting animals, such as two garden redstarts or two aquarium sticklebacks, all other things being equal, we can predict, from the place of encounter, which one will win: the one that is nearer home.

Konrad Lorenz[1]

We have seen that classical authors, like Thucydides, have tended to assume that enmity is a natural and permanent part of things. The religious classics give the same impression: Psalms 72:9, for example: "His enemies shall lick the dust." Or the Koran: "We delivered you from your enemy, and We made a covenant with you on the holy mountain's side   " (Surah XX, verse 80). The great Hindu classic, the Bhagavad-Gita, discovered in the eighth century, has as its theme a fratricidal conflict between the sons of two brothers. The Book of Mormon (Alma, 51, verses 17-20) tells of how Moroni's army slew four thousand to promote the standard of liberty. The words of Matthew in the New Testament of the Bible (5:44), "Love your enemies, bless them that curse you," begin with the assumption of hostility, whatever the hope of some eventual transformation.

The literary emphasis is much the same. Voltaire, much admired in his time for his insight and wit, said, "I have never made but one prayer to God, a very short one: 'O Lord, make my enemies ridiculous.' And God granted it."[2] And Nietzsche rather sourly wrote of "unconscious gratitude for a good digestion (sometimes called 'brotherly love')."[3] The same thought has been suggested less cynically by other authors—that health, wealth, and comfort, although they may also cause indifference, at least do not encourage hostility and may be the source of good will in an individual. If generosity is dependent on abundance, however, the resource and population projections for the years ahead indicate a poor outlook for it.

In the pages ahead is speculation from many disciplines as to whether human beings as individuals are incurably aggressive or whether such qualities are reflections of the environment in which human beings exist. Even if the individual personality in its natural state is highly pacific, it must be viewed along with the ingrained tendency of people to cluster in groups. One feature stemming from this proclivity for organizing into groups is reasonably understood and its psychological effects tolerably well agreed upon.[4] The consensus is that responding to needs such as defense and subsistence by organizing groups necessarily creates a sense of alienation from those left outside the group. Here we have one important societal root of the phenomenon of enmity: the hostility of organized group versus organized group.

The American Declaration of Independence of July 4, 1776, begins with the words:

When in the course of human events, it becomes necessary for one people to dissolve the political bonds which have connected them with another, and to assume among the powers of the earth, the separate and equal station to which the Laws of Nature and of Nature's God entitle them. . . .

Two points are worth noting here. The first is that many of the eighty thousand Tories who ultimately fled the colonies to take refuge in Canada or England believed to their last breath that it was not a case of "one people" versus "another" but of the members of one people at war with itself. "He who is not with me, is against me" had become a line of demarcation drawn down the middle of a previously united people. The second point is that when two groups were formed from the one, conflict and war soon followed. Whether they initially intended it or not,[5] those colonists who united to form the United States soon found themselves also united against King George; they were united *for* something, and therefore *against* something.

To be a member of a group or tribe or nation is to *not* be a member of whatever association is its alternative. Membership represents choice and is therefore, and inevitably, a sign of division as well as a sign of unity. To cling to one is to be separated from the other and, often enough, to suspect the other of hostile or opposed intent. Groups may cooperate, especially if they distrust third groups even more, but the out-group is always by definition alien. Nowhere is this more marked than with national groups. Even groups founded on love, such as the Christian faith itself, have shown in their later history this tendency toward hostility, at times far from the ideal.

In reporting the history of his times in the second century, Tertullian quotes pagan appraisals of the Christians that reveal how well the ideal was still observed after the time of St. Paul: "How these Christians love one another. Every man once a month brings some modest coin, or whenever he wishes and only if he does wish, and if he can — for nobody is compelled."[6] These funds went to the needy.

The bonds of affection remained strong among the early Christians. Schisms were not yet the serious problem they became later, and they believed in their faith enough to die for it. Pliny the Younger, writing in 112 to the Emperor Trajan in Rome for guidance, has left us an eloquent testimony to the exceptional spiritual unity and strength of these Christians. Pliny, as a provincial governor in remote Bithynia, expressed his unease and bewilderment at the heroism and lack of hate he found when he tried to stamp out the Christian "heresy."[7]

It is partly because these martyrs were stubborn in their faith that Christianity spread to become, in essence and virtually acknowledged as such, the state religion of the Roman Empire. Far from persecuting all Christians, Constantine (who would be baptized, as was then common, on his deathbed) personally presided over the Council of Nicaea in 325. The reason that council had been called, however, was to attempt to recreate doctrinal harmony, to put an end to the controversy over the doctrine of the Trinity, which was waxing bitter. In 333 Constantine moved strongly against the Arian heresy. He ordered that "if anyone shall be caught concealing a book by Arius, and does not instantly bring it out and burn it, the penalty shall be death; the *criminal* shall suffer punishment immediately after conviction."[8] By now, Christians were putting Christians to death for heresy.

When we compare Trajan with Constantine from this perspective, we see little difference except in the target of the persecution. Each of the two Roman emperors put his enemies to death, the first to eliminate Christianity, the second to eliminate orthodox Christianity's enemies.[9] By the time of Constantine, love and forgiveness had already faded considerably into the background.

Pope Urban II's famous sermon at Clermont in 1095, in which he preached the First Crusade, gives us an insight into conditions a thousand years after St. Paul. The sermon comes down to us in a variety of texts. William of Malmesbury's early-twelfth-century version purports to reflect Urban's general thrust and tone, which are quite remote from the early Christian emphasis on love and forgiveness. The enemy is now the adherents of a rival religion.

Can anyone tolerate that we do not even share equally with the Moslems the inhabited earth? They have made Asia, which is a third of the world, their homeland. . . . They have also forcibly held Africa . . . for over 200 years. . . . In this land you can scarcely feed the inhabitants. That is why you use up its goods and excite endless wars among yourselves.[10]

Urban was speaking in the context of the vast increase in Western population in the eleventh and twelfth centuries, which pressed inexorably on food supplies.

Large masses moved east in response, plus many nobles. Jews were often terrorized to raise funds, and some were killed: five hundred at Worms and a thousand at Mainz in 1096. When Jerusalem fell in 1099, Moslems and Jews—men, women, and children alike—were killed. When Constantinople fell in 1204, the soldiers were allowed three days to pillage. These facts make dismal reading, but a few more are needed to complete the picture of what has been possible when people have dealt with enemies, even in the name of a faith preaching love, forgiveness, and reconciliation.

The Protestant Reformation, which began in 1517, led eventually to one of the most savage and prolonged wars Europe ever suffered, the Thirty Years' War, from 1618 to 1648. This struggle, which in one sense marked a relapse of moral standards, also in another sense marked their rebirth, for it inspired the first codification of modern international law. Hugo Grotius, in his *De jure belli ac pacis (On the Law of War and Peace)* in 1625 said that there was throughout the Christian world

a lack of restraint in relation to war, such as even barbarous races should be ashamed of; I observed that men rush to arms for slight causes . . . and that . . . there is no longer any respect for law, divine or human; it is as if, in accordance with a general decree, frenzy had openly been let loose for the committing of all crimes.[11]

Singling out the Christian faith in this way is not to suggest that Christians have been especially filled with hostility toward those who differed with them. The Moslem trail of blood is probably more impressive altogether; the Moslems believed that in dispatching the infidel who rejected the "true faith," they were acting in complete accordance with their beliefs. The Old Testament history of the Jews also makes for bloody reading, and Hindus and Moslems in our own day continue to slaughter one another.

The point in following Christianity's trail is to show how, even with love and forgiveness of enemies as an article of faith, Christians as human beings, hating their enemies, have killed them over many centuries.

If this is so, it ought to be apparent that modern schemes to eliminate hostility by such methods as a world federalist convention or a spontaneous popular agreement to some form of universal law have to overcome some very deeply rooted tendencies in human behavior to oppose and oppress out-groups.

In Richard A. Falk's relatively recent book, *A Study of Future Worlds*, a much more optimistic view prevails. He wants to equip "central institutions" with "police" capabilities, while depriving national institutions of military capabilities. Since, says Falk we are not so naive as to anticipate the disappearance of conflict or tensions, we foresee the need for a series of reliable and readily available settlement techniques that could take over the role presently filled by the war system. Such substitutions would involve the development of workable adjudicative and conciliatory mechanisms, *with means to assure their implementation*.[12]

How does Falk propose to accomplish this? By force? By consensus (by doing away with groups)? Falk's answer is to begin the "transition process" in the "political arena" with "efforts to reorient national outlooks. . . ."[13] The aim is "for governmental leaders to attain a high degree of consensus on world order problems and goals."[14] The consensus should focus on "the need to achieve ecological equilibrium while simultaneously giving high priority to the equity imperative,"[15] overcoming poverty.

Falk's answer is social consensus: constructive argument followed by rational agreement. His argument recalls Emery Reves's more eloquent book, *The Anatomy of Peace*, which captured the popular imagination in 1945. The overriding lesson of history, said Reves, is that "conflicts and wars between social units are inevitable whenever and wherever groups of men with equal sovereignty come into contact."[16]

What was required, said Reves, was "transferring parts of the sovereign authority of the existing warring national institutions to universal institutions capable of creating law and order in human relations beyond and above the nation-states."[17]

In the eighth century B.C., Isaiah, in *his* vision, wrote that "in the last days" all the nations "shall beat their swords into plowshares, and their spears into pruninghooks; nations shall not lift up sword against nation, neither shall they learn war any more." This solution for conflict and hostility was acceptance of God's will. Where Falk's rational consensus would deal in logical and dispassionate fashion with mankind's problems and divisiveness, and Reves advocated a universal law, Isaiah saw the overcoming of the sin of pride as the solution.

All three, each in his own fashion, called for the elimination of groups that, by virtue of their apartness, suspect and fear those outside the group. Modern reformers in particular, who base their case on logic and the obviousness of the problems and, therefore, on the inevitable need for some rational solutions, do not look back very much. E. H. Carr told us why: they have to believe that the future will be different from the past.[18]

Our world is in great need of peace and unity and far from having even the promise of them. There is virtually no evidence to bolster Isaiah's hopes, let alone the hopes of Falk and Reves. Again, as Carr cautions us, this does not mean that the future must reflect the more dismal aspects of past experience; yet, as Thucydides insisted, the future is more likely than not to see the behavior of the past repeated, including most particularly hostility and war.[19] We must begin from that point and not rush too hastily into projections of a more perfect future.

One major argument about hostility and enmity, as we can see from both Falk and Reves, is whether the source of enmity is really environmental or instinctive. Is it formation of rival groups that creates the hostility, or does that habit simply reinforce an innate tendency to be hostile?

In Konrad Lorenz's pioneering work on animal behavior, *On Aggression*, he has made a number of extremely interesting although controversial assertions bearing on these issues. As a biologist, Lorenz is convinced of the reality of instincts. He calls "the aggression drive" a "true, primarily species-preserving instinct" that, because it is spontaneous, is also extremely dangerous. He makes this point in opposition to what he calls the "completely erroneous view that animal and human behavior is predominantly reactive and . . . can be altered, to an *unlimited* extent, by learning. . . ."[20]

After writing at length about the territoriality of fish and birds, Lorenz turns to groups of people. He describes the rituals developed by species to prevent unnecessary conflicts, particularly what he calls "submissive gestures" such as the virtually universal human signal of nonhostile intent conveyed by offering the right (or weapons) hand. Lorenz makes the important point that, while certain such gestures are quite widespread among human beings, culture and tradition produce great variations in the manner in which they are used.

Local traditions of good manners, in different subcultures, demand that a quantitatively different emphasis be put on . . . expression movements. A good example is furnished by the attitude of polite listening which consists in stretching the neck forward and simultaneously tilting the head sideways, thus emphatically 'lending an ear.' . . . In some parts of northern Germany it is reduced to a minimum, if not absent. . . . Between cultures in which this convention is different, misunderstandings are unavoidable. By East Prussian standards a polite Japanese performing the 'ear-tending' movement would be considered to be cringing in abject slavish fear, while by Japanese standards an East Prussian listening politely would evoke the impression of uncompromising hostility.[21]

This emphasis on cultural diversity as a root of enhanced hostility between groups is one to which Falk and Reves give only minor attention.

Late in his book, Lorenz provides a fuller idea of his total perspective when he makes much the same point as Carr about realism, but with more unrestrained optimism. To Lorenz the human race is "the most ephemeral and rapidly evolving of all species." He has by then shown different principles of organization among species, describing, for instance, the "anonymous herd" and the rat who will not harm his own group but will ruthlessly destroy "foreign" rats. He links species like that of the goose, the members of which feel personal bonds of affection with others in their group, to aggressive behavior patterns toward "foreigners." He points to a squad or platoon in a war: to the typical self-sacrifice shown for one soldier by another, which enables them to survive against the common foe.

In the higher species, including human beings, Lorenz argues that aggression against those *outside* the group is the complement to the bonds uniting those *inside* the group. He calls this behavior instinctive, but he seems to mean that it represents very deep-seated reactions (previously learned?), which may continue to exist long after they cease to serve a genuine function and which can in such cases be held partially in check by redirection of aggressive tendencies. It is here that Lorenz sees the hope for the future.

Lorenz is arguing that reactions of hostility leading to war are counterproductive in a nuclear-armed world and that, therefore, as evolution continues, the human race will adapt to new circumstances. But will it change quickly enough? As every student of evolution assures us, many species, like the dinosaur, became extinct because they could not adapt in time.

In his last chapter Lorenz gives an optimistic view of humans, but in the chapter before that he conveys a more pessimistic outlook, where he writes of "militant enthusiasm." He calls militant enthusiasm "a true autonomous instinct," which "engenders a specific feeling of intense satisfaction."[22] Militant enthusiasm arises when the individual's "social unit" appears "to be threatened by some danger from outside," especially by a hated enemy. Add "an inspiring leader figure" and "the presence of many other individuals, all agitated by the same emotion" and one can expect conflict.[23]

Psychologists generally make a quite different argument. As a group they tend to reject the formerly popular notion that human beings possess instincts, including an instinct to be aggressive, to fight, and to make war. They no longer accept as legitimate the question clearly posed years ago by Sigmund Freud as to whether the human species would "succeed in mastering the disturbance of their communal life by the *human instinct of aggression* and self-destruction."[24] Psychologists also just as strongly resist the arguments of many biologists, especially those arguments drawn from apparently instinctive fish and animal behavior, which have made such an impact on the popular imagination. Psychologists are not convinced by the "territorial imperative," as Robert Ardrey called it, which Ardrey describes as follows:

We may also say that in all territorial species, without exception, possession of a territory lends enhanced energy to the proprietor. Students of animal behavior cannot agree as to why this should be, but the challenger is almost invariably defeated, the intruder expelled. In part, there seems some mysterious flow of energy and resolve which invests a proprietor on his home grounds. But likewise, so marked is the inhibition lying on the intruder, so evident his sense of trespass, we may be permitted to wonder if in all territorial species there does not exist . . . some universal recognition of territorial rights.[25]

As in other professional groups, there are important differences of opinion among biologists themselves. Some point out that while territorial animals do act as Ardrey reports, only a relatively few animals are territorial. Even where the evidence of aggressive behavior is clear and unambiguous, and not in contest among biologists, it is necessary to proceed with caution in drawing conclusions about aggression. For example, studies of animals in the London Zoo showed pronounced aggression among baboons in captivity: eight of sixty-one males died by violence. Erich Fromm reports a detailed study of baboon behavior in the Zürich Zoo, compared to the behavior of baboons living wild in Ethiopia. The study showed "that the incidence of aggressive acts in the zoo was nine times as frequent in females and seventeen and a half times as frequent in adult males as it was in wild bands."[26] Fromm adds, significantly: "Captive animals, although they are well fed and protected, have nothing to do . . . hence they often become bored, dull, and apathetic."[27]

This condition of boredom that breeds violence seems to be at the opposite extreme from the instability during particular historical periods marked by great violence and aggression. There aggression seems to stem from the very lack of settled conditions. Perhaps both extremes produce the same responses.

Because Fromm's book, *The Anatomy of Human Destructiveness*, is such a seminal work, and because it surveys most of the literature bearing on human destructive tendencies, it may help to indicate where Fromm, as a psychoanalyst, stands and how he sees the main argument about the nature of a human being as it bears on the phenomenon of enmity.

Fromm argues that many biologists, with their preoccupation with instinctivism, see the individual in too simple fashion, as really lacking free will. People are what their instincts make them; therefore their behavior is biologically determined. Similarly, Fromm argues that many or most psychologists (the behaviorists) have become prisoners of a view of individuals as the reflection of their environment, equally lacking free will. People are what their "neighborhoods" make them, so their behavior is environmentally determined:

The man of the instinctivists lives the past of the species, as the man of the behaviorists lives the present of his social system. The former is a machine that can only produce inherited patterns of the past; the latter is a machine that can only produce social patterns of the present. Instinctivism and behaviorism have one basic premise in common: that man has no psyche with its own structure and its own laws.[28]

Both instinctivistic and behavioristic theory have a common and serious defect, says Fromm. Both

exclude the *person*, the behaving man, from their field of vision. Whether man is the product of conditioning, or the product of animal evolution, he is [seen as] exclusively determined by conditions outside himself; he has no part in his own life, no responsibility, and not even a trace of freedom.[29]

These two groups, which reduce human beings to mechanical responses, argue as anyone would have to argue who thought that the state system *determined* nation-state behavior, as if it dictated action and reaction from some central console. Those who believe that national decision making is foreordained by the nature of the bureaucracy or by concerted pressure groups would also have to use this mechanistic argument. These are points we shall come back to in Chapters 5 and 6.

Fromm closes his indictment of these mechanistic approaches with a final sentence, that if one accepts these views, man is "a puppet, controlled by strings — instinct or conditioning."

Fromm, like Carr, points to and rejects the extreme formulations. Carr puts his argument against the rigidities of extreme realism or extreme idealism in the form of a paradox: that what *is* is already changing to what *can be*. The future will not be a simple projection of the past, but neither is infinite change to be anticipated — or even significant change, short of substantial alterations in the environment. Fromm points to the reality of choice, rejecting the notions of both complete freedom and no freedom. Human nature (whatever it may be) and the social and physical environment in which human beings exist (whatever its characteristics) set the limits within which the choices can be made, but human behavior is *determined* neither by instincts nor environment. Neither of these more flexible views fits comfortably with what Falk and Reves argue from *their* perspective.

The basis for political organization in the world is still the system of sovereign nation-states, which in its modern form first began to take shape in the sixteenth century. Today its members are about 150 in number. Their ability to assure their citizens' happiness, prosperity, or even domestic peace and tranquillity is uneven; Falk and Reves would say none of them can. The reason for Falk's attitude is that this condition leaves much to be desired from an optimal world basis. Falk is not the first, as we have shown, to argue in effect that the human race, being rational and confronted by major transnational problems like pollution and energy resources and distribution, let alone nuclear weapons, needs to change its ways by changing its attitudes. Falk is also not the first to argue that national frontiers, which once safely shut out alien problems — as the somewhat romantic reconstruction of past history tends to put it — are no longer impermeable.[30] If it ever represented reality, the view Arnold Wolfers once characterized as the "billiard ball" model of international relations no longer commands much support. Wolfers described that model as one in which "every state represents a closed, impermeable and sovereign unit, completely separated from all other states."[31] The billiard ball model describes a system in which every state takes care of its own needs, complete unto itself for essentials.

In *A Tramp Abroad* and *Innocents Abroad*, Mark Twain tells of the innocent days of a century ago, when passports were hardly needed or used, when passage across frontiers was much simpler than it is today for most borders. States were hardly "closed" in that sense. It is true that from a security point of view, in the earlier age, when transportation and communication facilities were far less advanced, the very logistics of mounting an armed threat at a distance or on a large scale discouraged such efforts. But one can overstate the point.

Whatever the reality of the billiard ball model, Reves is quite correct in his statement, quoted earlier, that history shows that "conflicts and wars... are inevitable whenever and wherever groups of men with equal sovereignty come into contact."[32] The consequences of that fact, which was true in Thucydides's era too, have changed vastly in scale. De Tocqueville may have thought in his time that one day Russia and the United States would become important to one another, but even a half century ago it seemed unlikely. Yet today Moscow controls the nuclear warheads that could obliterate so many million American lives, and Washington is in a position to retaliate. This transformation of the world in so many ways makes the problems much more urgent, but it in no way makes the solutions easier or more likely than before. Presumably these changed conditions will in the long run alter human behavior — but in what way and when? Like a Gresham's law of politics, fear may drive rationality off the market. Things may get worse.

There is one quite clear trend that discourages optimism. The problems confronting individual states are hard enough to solve per se; they have become even more difficult because the number of national groups (separate, sovereign actors) has also greatly increased. The number of units that govern themselves and control the use of armed forces has grown steadily since Reves wrote in 1945: it is now about two and half times what it was then.

From an ecological and technical point of view, the world has grown steadily smaller and each state is less able to go its own way in isolation. The logic of this development, as Reves and Falk both argue, is that people will change their way of governing themselves and organize universal institutions capable of dealing with universal problems, in that way controlling enmity. However, since this prediction was made by Reves, the prevailing trend has been exactly in the opposed direction: sovereignty (the ability to decide not to cooperate or agree) has been extended to ever more, and smaller and less viable, units. From the point of view of pure numbers, it becomes ever more difficult to reach agreement on anything — even, for instance, on outlawing air piracy.

There is, of course, no intrinsic reason why such a large number of sovereign units, if they perceive mutual advantage in an agreement, cannot all agree. Numbers in themselves pose no insuperable logical obstacle to agreement. For instance, if the issue is simple enough, and universal enough — such as the seizure of American diplomatic personnel in Iran in 1979 — it is still possible to achieve unanimity in the UN Security Council. Nevertheless, as human experience clearly shows, the greater the number, the more difficult an agreement.

From a mathematical point of view, the more separate armed forces and governments are able to disagree with one another, the more conflicts will probably develop. Confronted with the number of contested frontiers, it is hard to remain optimistic.

So the trends in the world are at cross-purposes: problems logically needing universal solutions are being discussed within a more and more fragmented political system. This increase in fragmentation, in separateness, with national group divided from national group by separate state apparatus, is a built-in source of enmity in the international arena. As — or should we say "if"? — the world continues to be divided into smaller and smaller units, the psychological and other effects of separation are going to ensure that the problem of enmity continues, under conditions making it highly dangerous to everyone.

To sum up, there are no grounds at this point to decide conclusively whether enmity is purely environmental in its origin or whether an instinctive enmity is amplified by organization into separate groups. The only certainty is that the very division of group versus group, now carried further than ever, creates the psychological grounds for a systems-originated enmity that shows every sign of enduring in our lifetime.

If we consider hostility to be "natural" rather than as a malfunctioning of the system, however, how *much* of it is "normal?"

NOTES

1. Konrad Lorenz, *On Aggression* (New York: Harcourt, Brace & World, 1966), pp. 35-36.

2. Voltaire, Letter to M. Damilaville, May 1767.

3. Friedrich Wilhelm Nietzsche, *The Twilight of the Idols,* "Morality as the Enemy of Nature," p. 3.

4. See Otto Klineberg, *The Human Dimension in International Relations* (New York: Holt, Rinehart, Winston, 1964), especially pp. 33-48. Also, George W. Kisker, ed., *World Tension: The Psychopathology of International Relations* (New York: Prentice-Hall, 1951).

5. See Samuel B. Griffith II, *In Defense of the Public Liberty* (Garden City, N.Y.: Doubleday, 1976).

6. Quoted in Paul Johnson, *A History of Christianity* (New York: Atheneum, 1977), p. 75.

7. Ibid., p. 71.

8. Ibid., p. 88. Italics added.

9. One is reminded of the chilling scene in Fyodor Dostoyevsky, *The Brothers Karamazov*, in which the Grand Inquisitor decides to put Jesus to death as a troublemaker. In any edition, see pt. 2, bk. 5, chap. 5.

10. Quoted in Johnson, *Christianity*, p. 244.

11. Grotius, *Prolegomena*, par. 28; trans. in *Classics of International Law*, vol. 2, no. 3 (Washington, D.C.: Carnegie, 1925), p. 20. The "truce of God," however, was often highly effective in limiting warfare prior to the Protestant Revolution, especially under the stronger popes.

12. Richard A. Falk, *A Study of Future Worlds* (New York: Free Press, 1975), pp. 11-12. Italics added.

13. Ibid., p. 283.

14. Ibid., p. 287.

15. Ibid.

16. Emery Reves, *The Anatomy of Peace* (New York: Harper, 1945), p. 253. The gist of the argument is on pp. 253-70.

17. Ibid, p. 255.

18. E. H. Carr, *The Twenty Years' Crisis, 1919-1939* (London: Macmillan, 1940), pp. 14-15.

19. Thucydides, *The Peloponnesian War*, trans. Rex Warner (Baltimore: Penguin Books, 1954). See discussion in chap. 1 of this book.

20. Lorenz, *On Aggression*, pp. 49-51. Italics added to preserve Lorenz's actual meaning.

21. Ibid., pp. 81-82.

22. Ibid., p. 271.

23. Ibid., pp. 272, 273.

24. Sigmund Freud, *Civilization and Its Discontents* (New York: Norton, 1962), p. 92. Italics added. This edition includes footnotes added in 1931, in revision.

25. Robert Ardrey, *The Territorial Imperative* (New York: Dell, 1971), p. 3. Roger Fisher, in his *Basic Negotiating Strategy* (London: Allen Lane, Penguin Press, 1971), makes a closely parallel point from the field of international law.

26. Erich Fromm, *The Anatomy of Human Destructiveness* (New York: Fawcett Crest, 1973), p. 127.

27. Ibid., p. 130.

28. Ibid., p. 94.

29. Ibid., pp. 95, 96.

30. See the influential book by John Herz, *International Politics in the Atomic Age* (New York: Columbia University Press, 1959), for a careful argument of this view.

31. Arnold Wolfers, *Discord and Collaboration; Essays on International Politics* (Baltimore: Johns Hopkins University Press, 1962), p. 19.

32. Reves, *The Anatomy of Peace*, p. 253.

3

THE DIMENSIONS OF ENMITY

They love him most for the enemies he has made.
                    Seconding speech nominating Grover Cleveland, 1884[1]

Even the most casual survey will tell us that some nations have a history of encountering or indulging in international violence far in excess of the median. Enmity is not standard in amount throughout the system. If this is so, what accounts for the variations? Are there objective factors that control the amount of enmity? Certain locations, or certain kinds of frontiers, for example? What single variable, if any, is most clearly associated with increased and decreased amounts of enmity or with increased or decreased numbers of enemies?

For most nations — and even the revolution in transportation and communications has not changed this in fundamentals — it is those nearby nations that share common frontiers that are most suspected. It is they against whom war plans will often be drawn. As Thomas Fuller put it in 1732, "Nobody can live longer in peace than his neighbor pleases," because the neighbor is by definition accessible. Some are more accessible, of course, than others. The Danes have a proverb: "These three make bad neighbors: great rivers, powerful lords, and wide roads."

There is one fundamental difference here between individuals and nations. An individual who dislikes the place in which he or she lives can move. As William R. Castle put it in his *Dragon's Teeth in South America*, it "is discouraging to try to be a good neighbor in a bad neighborhood" — but nations have no choice. They have to begin their assessment of danger from a hard-headed analysis of who their neighbors are and what their attitudes seem to be. Easily crossed land frontiers are the most hazardous, and it follows that a nation with much of its 360-degree periphery composed of such frontiers is in a situation of maximum danger. The peril is compounded if the governments or the attitudes prevailing among its neighbors are hostile.

Before World War I, in a famous memorandum about the balance of power to which we shall return later, Sir Eyre Crowe commented:

History shows that the danger threatening the independence of this or that nation has generally arisen, at least in part, out of the momentary predominance of *a neighboring State* at once militarily powerful, economically efficient, and ambitious to extend its frontiers or spread its influence.[2]

Crowe, speaking of neighbors, lists three factors to be taken into account in assessing a neighbor's potential hostility: a military force sufficient to be formidable, an "efficient" economy, and ambition.

That neighbors are often enemies and almost always mutually suspicious is easily demonstrated. It is no accident that the Poles hate and fear the Russians. Between them there has never been a "natural" frontier with any staying power. That they are "allies" in the Warsaw Pact is what the Germans call "theater" and we would call a farce. Ancient, mutual antagonism between neighboring England and France furnished the theme for innumerable Shakespearian plays. Later, Franco-German antagonism helped to mitigate Franco-British hostilities. Argentina and Chile, neighbors even though not easily accessible to each other, remain on bad terms. In the days of China's weakness in the nineteenth century, the neighboring Russians took over a half-million square miles of Chinese territory. So did the United States annex neighboring Mexican territory. Zaire recurrently finds itself invaded from the nations that share its frontiers. Relations between Israel and its neighbors have been generally hostile. The Swiss, in their long struggle for independence, fought their neighbors many times.

Perhaps it is simpler to illustrate the point in reverse. We can ask how many nations harbor hostility, to the extent of contemplating possible war, with states that are *not* neighbors. How many nations "export" troops to some distant battlefield, and how usual is this? The former colonial powers provide some examples, as they built up their empires; we also have the examples of the expeditionary forces used in two world wars and some earlier cases from the Crimean War and the Napoleonic wars. There is the example of the UN and its forces in the Korean War. We can also cite the modern-day Cubans and their adventures in Africa. But the list is not very long, and the sending of forces to fight far away rarely commands much public sympathy.

If neighbors are no unmixed blessing, landlocked states have the worst case. A contemporary atlas will show only seventeen such states. If we add Zaire and Iraq, each with a minute access to open waters, the total of nineteen is only approximately one out of eight or nine states. Eliminating from this group those who have had "protectors" (France for Chad, India for Nepal and Butan, for example), we are left with ten. Of these, except for

Botswana, every one in recent times has been torn by violence, civil war, coups, and other bloodshed. (Even Chad, in 1981, suffered violence.) At the other extreme, powerful island states like England or Japan have fared quite well.

But once leave these extremes and it becomes difficult to reach meaningful conclusions. One great problem stems from European colonialism, which removed vast areas from independent participation in the system. While it imposed foreign rule over millions of square miles of Africa and Asia, it also sheltered them for many decades from invasion by third parties. Similarly, Africa's occupation from head to foot contrasts with Latin America's almost total immunity from invasion in the nineteenth century. The explanation for the immunity of Latin America lies, of course, in England's deliberate decision to prevent Spain from reestablishing control in Latin America, amplified by America's declaration of the Monroe Doctrine.

Another possibility is to correlate violence across frontiers traditionally in dispute. Data on boundary disputes is not easily available. Obviously it involves politically sensitive issues, and governments are reluctant to make public judgments about the frontiers of other nations. It should come as no great surprise that the special international boundary study published by the U.S. Department of State on December 1, 1967, is somewhat vague.[3] The categories used include indefinite boundaries, disputed boundaries, and boundaries requiring some disclaimer on U.S. official maps.

Even then, a relatively casual comparison of what this map shows and the actual recent history of boundary disputes and claims shows a divergence. For example, the map ignores Bolivia's still-voiced claim to an opening to the sea, although it includes the dispute between Argentina and Chile. Again, many problem areas are shown for Africa, but Libya's frontiers are not one, even though Libya has disputed its frontier with Chad. The Iraqi-Iranian frontier, the scene of violence in 1980-1981, is not shown as a problem (and officially it had been "settled" under the Shah). Chinese frontiers with Vietnam, the occasion for a Chinese resort to force in 1979, are not shown as in dispute, although all other Vietnamese borders are shown with disclaimers. The Chinese-Mongolian border also carries a disclaimer, and the northwestern frontier of Mongolia with Russia is marked as indefinite, but the real extent of the dispute over the Sino-Soviet frontier is not evident from this map. Japan, which has a serious dispute with the Soviets over some islands north of Hokkaido in the Kurils, is not shown with any dispute. A later State Department map, dated August 1979, is not very changed from the description just given. (The main difference is that all Vietnamese borders are no longer shown in dispute.)

So this map in either version is very conservatively drawn, and it leaves out certain obvious areas of contention — but what it really tells us is that, while some apparently "agreed" frontiers flame up, some "disputed" frontiers cause no resort to violence. We cannot predict active enmity in any reliable way from observing such data.

If we turn to statistical data on conflict, we do not find simple patterns. J. David Singer and Melvin Small have carefully compiled data for 144 nations involved in 239 wars between 1916 and 1965.[4] In the period they cover, they show 35 wars for 24 nations in the Western Hemisphere. Europe's 47 nations totaled 144 wars, while Africa's 32 nations had 4 wars. The 16 nations in the Middle East had 28 wars, and the 25 nations of Asia also had 28. These statistics indicate enormous deviations in experience.

Singer and Small review Richardson's earlier findings. Richardson found that 48 percent of opposed belligerents in wars (1820-1929) had fought against one another previously, whereas only 29 percent had been wartime allies before fighting one another.[5] Using fewer wars and a longer time span, Singer and Small, after excluding one-time cases, looked at the behavior of 136 pairs:

There were 95 pairs . . . with some experience as opponents, but 77 of them also fought at least once on the *same* side. Moreover, 44 of these wartime alliances followed at least one occasion on which the partners had fought *against* one another. And of the 60 pairs whose first interaction was as enemies, 42 subsequently fought as allies. . . . As for consistent friendships, . . . 41 of the 136 pairs with some partnership experience never fought against each other, the remaining 95 did. . . .[6]

They conclude: "Most nations, despite occupying essentially the same piece of real estate and embracing essentially the same ethnic stock, show a remarkable flexibility in 'selecting' their partners and adversaries."[7] This seems eminently true, but it means that none of the variables we have considered so far has a determining effect or a constant value universally. From these facts Singer and Small go on to say that the small number of traditional enmities offers some hope for the future: "If most nations find it possible to cooperate with almost any other ones in wartime, such cooperation in the avoidance of war may not be as impossible to achieve as the pessimists might have us believe."[8] This seems less obviously certain.

A little reflection will suggest other possibilities. For example, a nation that persists with its traditional enemies while acquiring new ones will soon have too many (the principle of the conservation of enemies). In Chapter 4 we shall illustrate this very point in a case study of England and Germany just at the end of the nineteenth century. A nation, if it is prudent, will ration itself as to the enemies it can afford to "accept." The very old proverb, "my neighbor's neighbor is my friend," is apropos. It warns us again not merely to look at statistics but to look at the map. The meaning of a particular shared frontier can only be determined in the light of a 360-degree analysis of the total frontiers of the two states involved. (The meaning of any front line is heavily dependent on what is occurring at the flanks and rear.) Conditions along that 360-degree total frontier may be the supreme variable even though it is not the first one to occur to our minds.

Catullus, in the first century B.C., warned of a purely frontal preoccupation: "Everybody has his own delusion assigned to him: but we do not see that part of the bag which hangs on our back."⁹ Since the world is round, as Columbus pointed out, a preoccupation with *one* frontier (or *one* other state) may lead to dangerous consequences.

So, in considering the dimensions of enmity, we are led to some tentative conclusions. So far as can be established, there is no natural or normal amount of enmity that *all* nations encounter. Variations abound. When enmity becomes overt, it is highly likely to involve neighboring states, if only because territorial disputes or ambitions are in the nature of things directed against neighbors. When this occurs, the pairing off or side-taking will vary, as Singer and Small indicated. The probable reason is the one just given: different conditions at the flanks or rear will dictate different stances toward the nation to the front.

Our investigations in this chapter have concentrated on physical or quantifiable factors. It would obviously be highly useful if we could identify degrees or amounts of enmity with particular objective conditions, in some dependable way. But not one of the variables we have examined will serve either as a universal or as an automatic explanation of enmity. The human role in creating or avoiding enmity through conscious policy decisions looms even larger as a result.

But if conscious human behavior is a significant variable in itself, can we achieve more control over its effects?

NOTES

1. Edward Stuyvesant Bragg, Democratic National Convention, Chicago, July 9, 1884.

2. G. P. Gooch and H. Temperley, eds., *British Documents on the Origins of the [First World] War, 1898-1914*, 11 vols. in 13 (His Britannic Majesty's Stationery Office, London: 1926-1938), vol. 3, app. A, p. 403.

3. See world map entitled *International Boundaries and Disclaimers*, issued by the Geographer, Office of Research in Economics and Science, Bureau of Intelligence and Research, U.S. Department of State, December 1, 1967. The latest updating, August 1979, is entitled *Guide to International Boundaries*. The routine practice of the Geographer is to issue a numbered series for specific bilateral frontiers on a regular basis. No. 161, for instance, published on February 9, 1977, is on the Belize-Mexico boundary, while no. 163, of March 7, 1978, is on the Syria-Turkey boun-

dary. No. 163 makes no mention about any dispute, such as is shown on the December 1, 1967, world map.

4. J. David Singer and Melvin Small, *The Wages of War, 1816-1965, A Statistical Handbook* (New York: Wiley, 1972).

5. Lewis F. Richardson, *Statistics of Deadly Quarrels* (Pittsburgh, Pa.: Boxwood Press, 1960), pp. 196-99.

6. Singer and Small, *Wages of War*, p. 345.

7. Ibid.

8. Ibid.

9. Catullus, *Odes.*

4

ACQUIRING ENEMIES:
A CASE STUDY

A man cannot be too careful in the choice of his enemies.

Oscar Wilde[1]

So far we have discussed enemies and enmity on an abstract basis. To begin the study now of how the policy role varies the enmity encountered, we shall become very concrete. Using a case study, we shall focus on two nations, Great Britain and Germany. The period is the closing years of the nineteenth century and the beginning of the twentieth, the last three decades before World War I. These two nations, initially friendly, ultimately became bitter enemies and it is that transformation and how it occurred which is instructive. This particular case provides an especially rich, provocative, and relevant illustration because it involves significant policy changes directly and clearly affecting the enmity each nation confronted.

Factually, the situation was as follows. As our period begins, Britain, long accustomed to hold aloof from other than temporary alliances, was in "splendid isolation," that is, without a guaranteed ally, except possibly Portugal, in the whole world. With worldwide commitments, Britain was either overextended or approaching that condition. Its major great-power enemies were France and Russia.

France was enemy number one by long tradition. Ever since William of Normandy had conquered Britain, the affairs of France and England had been intermixed, with antagonisms springing up in their train. War followed war. By the eighteenth century the Anglo-French conflict had become reflected in the New World, as in the Seven Years' War (1775-1763) and in the French aid to the Americans in the American Revolutionary War (1775-1783). French Minister Vergennes's secret appraisal of French interests in the American War of Independence stated bluntly: "England is the natural enemy of France—and she is a rapacious, unjust and faithless enemy. The invariable object of her policy is the destruction of France, or at least her abasement, humiliation and ruin." It followed that France "should seize every possible opportunity to enfeeble the might and power of England," including aid to the Americans.[2] Shortly afterward, England fought Napoleon, at times almost alone. Then, in 1854, for rather unusual reasons, England and France became temporary allies in the ill-fated Crimean War. That exception to the pattern was not considered to inaugurate any lasting change. What made it a reasonable collaboration from the British viewpoint was that the Crimean War was against Russia, Britain's enemy number two.

Russia first achieved prominence as a rival to Britain in modern times by its determination to make gains at the expense of the weak Ottoman Empire. As this Turkish "Sick Man of Europe" slowly relinquished its grip upon the Balkans, Britain found itself trying to prevent an overturn of the balance of power. After about 1875, when colonial imperialism became again for some decades a popular pursuit among European powers, colonial competition between the British and the Russians occurred across important parts of Russia's southern frontier, especially between Afghanistan and Persia (Iran). In 1885, when Russian local forces fought the Afghans and occupied part of the border, Prime Minister William Gladstone asked Parliament for £11 million to fight the war. The incident was smoothed over, just as earlier tension in 1875 and later tension in 1898 was handled short of war. But the rivalry and the antagonism were still there. Britain's relations with the rest of Europe, while not close, were at least not unfriendly.

Then, in 1899, the British became involved in a faraway local struggle in South Africa that ultimately was to affect British decision making on a worldwide basis. The Boer War began, and while that conflict lasted, from October 12, 1899, to May 31, 1902, the British were not only quite overextended, but they also found themselves about as popular in fighting the Boer farmers as the United States proved to be in world opinion decades later during the Vietnam War. German Kaiser Wilhelm's gestures of support to the Boers were especially and bitterly resented by the British.

Until roughly the time of the Boer War, Germany was not considered a threat by the British. Bismarck, in directing the wars of German unification against Austria (1866) and then France (1870), had taken great care not to antagonize the British. His master stroke was ostentatiously to revitalize guarantees of Belgium's neutrality just before the Franco-Prussian War and then to release France's written demands for the Lowlands to the correspondent of the London *Times*, which printed them for all the world to read. Sir Austen Chamberlain's famous remark in the House of Commons on March 24, 1925, quite accurately addressed British sensitivity over this area: "All our greatest wars have been fought to prevent one great military power dominating Europe, and at the same time dominating the coasts of the

Channel and the ports of the Low Countries." Britain would probably have stayed neutral in the wars of German unification in any event, since it was obvious that Germany was not seeking to overturn the balance of power but rather had the more limited goal of uniting most of the German people. In making France's demand public, Bismarck's action made English neutrality certain.

In the next twenty years, although relations varied some, no acute tensions arose between the two nations. Even when Bismarck sanctioned the beginnings of a modest German colonial policy in 1884, the friction was restrained. There is little doubt that Bismarck considered colonial affairs (where British interests were directly affected) as purely secondary for Germany. As he said to a colonial enthusiast: "Your map of Africa is very fine, but my map of Africa is here in Europe. Here is Russia and here is France and here we are in the middle. That is my map of Africa."[3] William Leonard Langer suggests a second aspect of Bismarck's policy on English and colonial affairs: "By sending the English to Egypt and thus embroiling them with France he established a control over English policy which he never again lost."[4] The essential key to Bismarck's policy toward England, however, is that he already had an enemy in France; France was never very likely to be supported by England except under extraordinary conditions, and Bismarck took care to avoid those conditions. Bismarck took equal care, despite his alliance with Austria of 1879, to maintain a link with Russia so that Russia would not ally with France.

Bismarck put the point succinctly to Saburov, the Russian ambassador in Berlin, in January 1880. He stressed

the importance of being one of three on the European chess-board. That is the invariable objective of all cabinets and of mine above all others. Nobody wishes to be in a minority. All politics reduce themselves to this formula: to try to be one of three, as long as the world is governed by an unstable equilibrium of five Powers.[5]

If this was supposed to be an "invariable objective," and one that Bismarck acted on, as Figure 1 shows, it was also one for which Wilhelm and the chancellors he appointed to follow Bismarck had far less understanding or sympathy. Hardly was Bismarck retired (fired) by Wilhelm in 1890 when the Reinsurance Treaty, the critical link with Russia, came up for renewal. This treaty was absolutely necessary to keep Russia tied to Germany. Yet Wilhelm, after some vacillation, declined to renew it, despite Russia's eagerness to continue the link. Although he first assured the Russians he would renew the treaty, Wilhelm in fact, after a confused sequence of events, let it lapse automatically on June 18, 1890.[6] Within a half-decade Moscow and Paris became allies, as Russia sought a second-best alternative.

Figure 1. European Alliances and Alignments, 1887-1890 (conventional format).

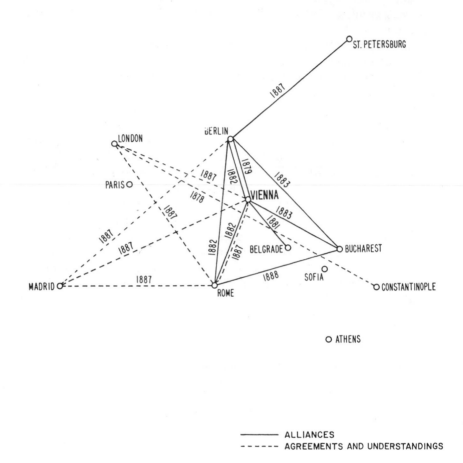

——————— ALLIANCES
- - - - - AGREEMENTS AND UNDERSTANDINGS

In rejecting the Reinsurance Treaty, Wilhelm accepted the argument of his advisers that it was incompatible with other German pledges (especially toward Rumania) and therefore compromised German honor. Wilhelm did not take naturally to the complex, although rational, situation that Bismarck had contrived by simultaneously agreeing with Russia that Germany would not support an Austrian attack on Russia and agreeing with Austria that he would defend Austria against any Russian attack.

The strategic effect of the policy change toward Russia was to make Anglo-German relations truly critical for Germany. To encourage such close relations, the Germans could build on the strong cultural ties between the Anglo-*Saxon* British and the Germans, including the fact that the English and German ruling houses were related by blood. Kaiser Wilhelm's predecessor, his father, Frederick III, had been married to a daughter of Queen Victoria. Wilhelm's own mother, therefore, was English, and the King of England was his uncle.* When Kaiser Wilhelm made a great state visit to London on July 4, 1891, and the newspapers were full of speculation about Britain joining the Triple Alliance of Germany, Austria-Hungary, and Italy, no one was astonished. The idea was perfectly compatible with Britain's general posture. Indeed, in the first six months of 1894, Lord Rosebery for Britain *did* negotiate to establish just such a connection. Such efforts were to continue as late as 1901.

While these German actions made sense for Germany, they do not readily square with the typical stereotypes about British foreign policy. After all, was not Britain the famed "holder" of the balance of power, as Henry VIII had so graphically asserted by having himself painted with the scales of Europe in his hand? Was not England the very balancer of the balance? How could Britain seriously consider joining the *stronger* of the two alliance groupings in Europe — the other being the newly created Franco-Russian Alliance of 1894?

The answer lies in the identity of the weaker group. Both of its members were Britain's enemies. While it is true that Britain had historically tended to aid the weaker side of the balance, a good part of the reason was that France had perennially been on the stronger side.

This was the situation as the nineteenth century closed and the Boer War began. Consider now, especially in view of German security needs, what German Chancellor Bernhard von Bülow wrote to Kaiser Wilhelm on January 21, 1901:

Your Majesty is quite right in perceiving that the English must come to us. They have just lost a lot of hair in Africa, America appears unsteady, Japan unreliable, France full of hate, Russia perfidious, public opinion in all countries hostile; . . . now it gradually dawns on the British consciousness that they cannot, by their own strength alone, hold their world empire against so many opponents.[7]

---

*The British royal family, German by descent, only took the English family name "Windsor" in this century as a result of the Anglo-German antagonism discussed in this chapter. The name "Wettin," family name of Albert of Saxe-Coburg-Gotha, consort to Queen Victoria, was given up by King George V in 1917, an example followed by the rest of the royal family.

What Bülow was advocating was raising the price for Britain's admission to the protection of the Triple Alliance of Austria, Italy, and Germany.

Britain had indeed accumulated too many enemies and too many hostages to fortune. Bülow's analysis of what the military call the "threat" Britain faced was accurate in every detail except for the policy alternatives available to Britain. Bülow described Britain's problem well enough, but he saw only one of the possible responses to that problem.

In 1895, as British relations with Germany began to become difficult, Britain's leaders were already making a parallel inventory. Sir Edward Grey, British foreign secretary in the critical decade that culminated in World War I, wrote that British imperial successes had created widespread hostility and envy, motivating

a general tendency to vote us a nuisance and to combine against us. I am afraid we shall have to fight sooner or later, unless some European apple of discord falls amongst the Continental Powers, but we have a good card on hand to play and I think a bold and skillful Foreign Secretary *might detach Russia* from the number of our active enemies without sacrificing any very material British interests.[8]

Russia was to be detached, but not for another twelve years. In the meantime, though, Britain took some steps to reduce its problem and augment its resources. In 1902 Britain made an alliance with Japan. In the previous year Britain had settled the argument with the United States over the Panama Canal issue in the Second Hay-Pauncefote Treaty, which abrogated the Clayton-Bulwer Treaty and, in effect, gave in to U.S. demands for a free hand on the isthmus.

These events confirmed a trend begun in 1897, when Britain had reversed its refusal to accept the arbitration the United States insisted on in the Venezuela boundary dispute. Proud Britain had swallowed its pride and even put up with Secretary of State Richard Olney's bombastic note of July 20, 1895, which asserted that "today the United States is practically sovereign on this continent, and its fiat is law upon the subjects to which it confines its interposition." In view of critical developments elsewhere, adjustments were required. The Americans were only of secondary importance compared to the deteriorating relations with France, culminating in late 1898 with the Fashoda crisis in the Sudan. Higher priority had to be accorded to the 1896 furor over Kaiser Wilhelm's famous telegram to Paul Kruger, the president of the (Boer) South African Republic, after a British-Boer fracas called the Jameson Raid.

So, under the impact of a series of disagreeable events, the British began actively sorting out and reducing the dimensions of their problem. Extremely important in this series were the consequences of Wilhelm's decision to build a vast German high seas fleet, which above all else destroyed Anglo-German friendship. Initially the British were slow to recognize the implications of the German naval bills of 1898 and 1900, but by October 1902 the British cabinet was discussing quite seriously Earl Selborne's warning that "the German Navy is very carefully built up from the point of view of a new war with us."[9] The German naval expansion plans, announced in 1897, were to be completed by 1904. The plan was to add twelve battleships (making a total of nineteen), ten heavy cruisers (for a total of twelve), and twenty-three light cruisers (for a total of thirty).

In a memorandum of January 1, 1907, Sir Eyre Crowe, the senior career official in the British Foreign Office, showed the shift in the British outlook:

The vain hopes that in this matter Germany can be "conciliated" and made more friendly must definitely be given up. It may be that such hopes are still honestly cherished by irresponsible people, ignorant, perhaps necessarily ignorant, of the history of Anglo-German relations during the past twenty years.[10]

As the British mulled over their problem, and despite their attempts to solve it with the Japanese alliance and the American settlements, plus the conclusion of the Boer War, that problem took a further, even drastic, turn for the worse. The outbreak of the Russo-Japanese War initiated a chain of events, with its ramifications in the Dogger Bank incident (described in the next few pages), that was shortly to bring Britain up to the very brink of a war with both Russia and France.

These events during the Dogger Bank crisis were the stuff of high drama, from beginning to end. Had they run their course unchecked, World War I would have broken out a decade sooner and with an entirely different set of allies on each side than was the fact in 1914.

Recall now the alliance ties. There was the 1882 Triple Alliance of Germany, Austria-Hungary, and Italy, dominated by Germany. Second, there was the 1893-1894 Franco-Russian alliance directed against Germany. Finally, Britain had its 1902 alliance with Japan, which provided that Britain would fight alongside Japan if Japan faced *two* powers.

The Russo-Japanese War began on February 8, 1904, with a Japanese surprise attack on the Russian fleet at its naval base at Port Arthur in the Far East. Two days later war was officially declared. Russia began preparations to augment its naval forces in Asia with hastily collected ships from the Baltic fleet in varying conditions of operational readiness. Improperly disciplined, this fleet set off for war in October 1904, with the admiral in command hoping to achieve some order during the long sea voyage.

Toward dusk on the night of October 21, 1904, alarmed at reports that Japanese torpedo boats were lurking ahead, the Russian fleet in the North Sea steamed warily and nervously southward toward the English Channel.

The Russians, passing through the area known as the Dogger Bank, suddenly saw a line of vessels ahead maneuvering with green and red rockets, in wide sweeps. Russian standing orders for night engagements prescribed that gunfire would be controlled and directed by the great searchlights of the admiral's flagship. But as the undisciplined Russian fleet bore down on the "enemy," various searchlights flashed around in search of targets and firing began in an indiscriminate fashion. Before long, shells were indeed landing on the Russian ships — shells fired by other Russian ships. The "enemy" torpedo vessels were in fact British fishing trawlers, one of which was sunk and several lives lost. As the Russians plowed southward in panic, the British survivors reached port.

Prime Minister Arthur James Balfour's biographer, his niece, Blanche E. C. Dugdale, wrote without exaggeration, "This fantastic mistake brought Great Britain and Russia to the verge of war."[11]

The war that hung in the balance was quite unwelcome to Great Britain. One issue it raised was whether, if Britain fought Russia in Europe while Japan fought Russia in Asia, France (as Russia's European ally) could remain neutral. The Franco-Russian alliance did not *require* France to fight England; but England was the old enemy. Perhaps more important was a second issue: if France allowed Russia to be defeated, Germany would be unrestrained in its rear as it faced toward France. Could France then survive? Could France afford the risk of permitting that situation to develop? Even if the French failed to act, would the British really benefit by assisting Japan to defeat Russia, and thus strengthen quite directly Britain's emerging new enemy, Germany?

French Foreign Minister Théophile Delcassé, going through much this sequence of thoughts, now intervened and suggested a peaceful settlement. The Russians, embarrassed, consented; the British, soon realizing the real nature of the incident, agreed as well. At hand, luckily, was the perfect instrument: the Hague Convention for the Pacific Settlement of International Disputes of 1899. It provided for "international commissions of inquiry" to settle disputes "involving neither honor nor vital interests, and arising *from a difference of opinion on points of fact.* . . ."[12]

The Hague Convention was the perfect instrument, because Britain's choice had narrowed drastically by the time Delcassé moved. When it became obvious to the British that they were confronting Russian ineptitude rather than callousness or hostility, they could, if they had wished, still have forced a confrontation. But that meant either humiliation for the Russians or a war that left Germany neutral and everyone else involved. There was far more advantage to the British if, through such a device as the Hague Convention, they helped hide Russia's blunder by establishing the "points of fact," that is, by hiding the obvious in a long-winded report that would take a long time to write.

The five-nation commission of inquiry that was established consisted of naval officers from Britain and Russia, France, Austria-Hungary, and the United States. It reported on February 25, 1905, that Russia had to bear the blame and pay damages, but it also went into counterbalancing detail. It dwelt on the lack of Russian intent to cause harm and the Russians' conviction, based on intelligence reports, that the Japanese were actually on the Dogger Bank, waiting to trap them.

So was war averted. The British, sobered by these developments, determined to continue their efforts to revamp the diplomatic situation they confronted. They had not long to wait before a new challenge effectively decided the issue. That challenge came from Germany, and it began a series of six crises that ended in World War I.

Again the chronology has to be kept in mind. When the Russo-Japanese War began in February 1904, some eight months before the Dogger Bank incident, the British had decided to begin defusing their colonial competition with France. These negotiations had culminated in April 1904 with the so-called Anglo-French Entente. This agreement had given Britain free rein in Egypt and France free rein in Morocco, but the Dogger Bank incident had threatened to destroy this still quite tentative drawing together of two old enemies. When that did not happen, Germany determined both to test the new entente and to contest the French plans to take over Morocco. Kaiser Wilhelm, on the initiative of his advisers, went to Tangier and advocated independence for Morocco. This confrontation was to lead in turn to the Algeciras Conference of 1906 — which was a disaster for the Germans, while it strengthened Anglo-French cooperation. What Algeciras began continued as a pattern in the crises that followed.

Algeciras had an additional effect. It persuaded Britain to reactivate the 1895 idea of coming to some arrangement with Russia. Lord Salisbury, in a note to Russia of January 25, 1898, had actually offered to divide Asia from Alexandretta to Peking into a Russian and a British sphere of interest. Russia had rejected that overture, but now, having lost a war and undergone a short revolution, Russia was in a mood to cooperate. Accordingly an Anglo-Russian Entente was concluded on August 31, 1907. It divided Persia (Iran) into three spheres of influence: a northern one under Russian control, a southern one dominated by the British, and a middle neutral zone. The status of Afghanistan as a buffer state under some British influence was reaffirmed, and both parties recognized Chinese claims to Tibet. And just as the Anglo-French Entente had been followed by a crisis, so, too, was the Anglo-Russian Entente — by the Bosnia-Herzegovina annexation crisis of October 1908. Despite British diplomatic support, the Russians had to yield, and Austria-Hungary (Germany's ally) "won" in the sense that it kept the provinces. But Austria had already been there in military occupation for decades, so no territory really changed hands.

The significance of this second of six crises leading to World War I was that it stiffened the two opposing blocs, with Britain now effectively joined to its old enemies in diplomatic array against Germany and Austria-Hungary (plus, nominally, Italy). By 1908 the diplomatic revolution was complete.

One other prime result of this Russian diplomatic defeat was that the Russians promised themselves that never again would they be humiliated. This pledge, tested in 1914 with the final crisis of the six, was one very good reason why war occurred then.

For our purposes it is not worthwhile examining all six crises in detail, but it is instructive to note the momentum they represented, which culminated in the most grievous war of modern times. The relevance of these events to this book grows out of the pressures that, accumulating on Britain primarily through German actions, persuaded Britain to initiate a diplomatic revolution that reduced its enemies to manageable proportions by eliminating France and Russia from the list. Unfortunately, the increasing rigidity of the alliance system, especially after the 1907 entente (Figure 2), increased the overall tension in the system as well.

One conclusion that emerges from this example of policy making is that a "threat analysis," such as Bülow made when he said that France was "full of hate" (for England), that Russia was "perfidious," and so on, ought to be *followed* by an analysis of alternative courses of action — in this case, of actions open to the British. Instead, Bülow began by describing Britain's presumed single alternative — which proved to be the one alternative Britain decisively rejected. Bülow to the contrary, Kaiser Wilhelm had not been "quite right in perceiving that the English must come to us." The British chose a different alternative altogether.

A second conclusion is that this case study shows how near a thing it was that events turned out the way they did. The Dogger Bank incident clearly demonstrated the dangers of indecision. At the same time, that incident provided fresh incentive for the deliberate revamping of the strategic situation Britain faced. It finally brought the British to analyze the national interests of the French and Russians, compared to their own, in the colonial domain. It made the British ask themselves whether some rearrangement of priorities of interests, and some substitution of interests, might not tip the total balance of relationships from hostility to neutrality to friendship. In making this analysis, the marked British tendency toward pragmatism and away from sentimentality accelerated a revision of attitude (and policy) of quite far-reaching proportions.

It was in this pragmatic spirit four years later that the British also weighed the advantages and disadvantages of continuing colonial rivalries with Russia. By mutually changing policy, Britain and Russia reduced their mutual antagonism, leaving each freer to face the remaining threat.

**Figure 2. Triple Alliance vs Triple Entente, 1907
(conventional format).**

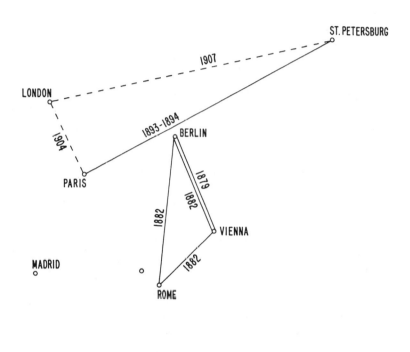

ALLIANCES
AGREEMENTS AND UNDERSTANDINGS

That is what the British actions demonstrate. What the German actions demonstrate under Wilhelm II is less simple to describe. Until Bismarck's "retirement" in 1890, German policy, while complicated, was also quite pragmatic. Bismarck's memoirs, while not to be taken entirely at face value, do indicate the consistent quality of his strategic thought. When the crushing defeat of Austria in 1866 permitted Prussia great gains if it chose to insist on them, Bismarck steadfastly opposed. He explained the point as follows: "If Austria were severely injured, she would become the ally of France and of every other opponent of ours; she would even sacrifice her anti-Russian interests for the sake of revenge on Prussia."[13] And, if Austria were dismantled, what would take its place? Bismarck's farsightedness is very well brought out in his analysis of Austro-Russian-German relations in the 1880s and 1890s. Beginning from the fact of the Austro-German alliance, in his memoirs he points to the necessity of maintaining "the bridge which leads to St. Petersburg" as a counterweight to what would otherwise be Austria's natural tendency "to enlarge her claims."[14] Bismarck adds: "We cannot abandon Austria, but neither can we lose sight of the possibility that the policy of Vienna may willy-nilly abandon us."[15] He meant that Austria had Balkan ambitions that in no way served German interests. Bismarck's remarks were published in the 1890s, but they described perfectly the situation that developed in the summer of 1914 and drew Germany inexorably into war.

When Wilhelm took active control, it was the pragmatism in German thinking that largely evaporated — at least in the sense of German leaders understanding the strategic political situation and the nature of the forces at work. It would not be correct to say that under Wilhelm II Germany was bent on *increasing* its enemies; it would come closer to the German attitude to say that Wilhelm saw no real connection between his policy and the growing number of Germany's enemies.

At the time, Wilhelm and his nation quite failed to appreciate the fact that they were driving the British into a fundamental reappraisal. They thought, if anything, that they were forcing the British to seek an alliance with them, as Bülow's remarks indicate. The whole psychological appraisal the Germans made in these years betrays an enormous insensitivity. Consider how they handled the Second Moroccan crisis (another of the six leading to World War I). The British ambassador's dispatch of August 25, 1911, reports the German explanation for the threatening move they had made: "that it was not recognized in England that the dispatch of a ship to Agadir, which had been the Emperor's idea, was really meant *to make it easier* for the French Government to defend any compensation they might be ready to give...."[16] The British ambassador commented, "I could not help saying that it seemed to be a somewhat dubious method of facilitating the negotiations. ..."[17]

Somehow the Germans had convinced themselves that throwing their weight around would make it easier for their opponents to concede a contested point. As late as 1938, Sir Harold Nicolson remarked that "the German heroic conception of life leads to what I may call a warrior conception of policy and diplomacy."[18] Nicolson's assessment hardly typifies Bismarck or Adenauer, but it would have seemed a sound characterization to almost any British leader in Wilhelm's time.

Consider Kaiser Wilhelm's public appraisal of German actions in the 1908 crisis: that Germany had taken Austria-Hungary's side "in shining armour at a grave moment."[19] At the end of the Algeciras Conference in 1906, the Kaiser sent a telegram to the Austro-Hungarian foreign minister, thanking him for having been "a brilliant second on the duelling ground."[20] Kaiser Wilhelm's habitual wearing of a military uniform was not just a clue to his personal preferences; it tells something about the psychological outlook of the Germany of his time.

Prince Bülow tells us in his memoirs that the Kaiser did not seem to realize just how serious and definitive a policy change he had made in 1890 by turning the Russians away. Bülow comments: "The more inimical to Germany was the feeling in England, the more did the Kaiser lean towards Russia. As a final goal he had a formal German-Russian alliance in view." Bülow "repeatedly explained to him" how the failure "to renew the Bismarckian Reinsurance Treaty . . . had made it difficult to reinstate the old conditions that had existed between Germany and Russia."[21]

But Wilhelm had Bülow draw up a treaty text. Signed at Björko in July 1905 by the Czar and the Kaiser, it had to be tabled because of the problems it would have created on every side. Wilhelm by then was proposing the creation of a German-Russian-French front against England. There was, of course, little hope by this date of merely restoring close relations with Russia. The further idea of France being willing to join Germany in a common front against England had no basis at all.

Wilhelm's Germany lacked a certain stability. Newly powerful and almost unaware of the disturbances that ensued, Wilhelm's Germany flexed its muscles and built a large navy to supplement an already very large army. It thought in terms of glory and honor and not always very far ahead.

England and Germany ultimately became enemies as their perceptions of each other strayed further from what we would today call a reciprocally realistic view. The British frequently drew wrong conclusions from the erratic German actions, but the German error in perception was much greater than the British error. Germany's actions were frequently designed for one set of results but brought about a quite contrary situation. Nor was there real consistency of approach or judgment by Germany after Bismarck's fall.

But how do we make this judgment? What we mean is that the British actions, while arising from mistaken assumptions about German motivation, were nonetheless realistic in increasing British security—specifically, by decreasing the number of enemies to acceptable proportions through deliberate policy changes. By contrast, the Germans were not only mistaken as to British attitudes but erred grossly as to British alternatives. This double failure created an increasingly dangerous security situation for Germany, replete with enemies on either flank (France and Russia), and a third and peripheral enemy in England. To say the least, the German actions represented inadequate intellectual consideration of the problem.

Ironically, the Germans were to try to compensate for this disastrous failure in diplomacy by creating an intricate mobilization scheme (the Schlieffen Plan), which proposed to shuttle German troops first to the Western front to defeat France, and then to the Eastern front in time to meet the more slowly mobilizing Russians! It would have been far easier to have avoided the problem of a two-front war in the first place.[22]

What this case study demonstrates is how two nations over a period of years came to see each other as enemies, where before that perception did not exist. The actions of each nation, acting in response to this perception, resulted in shifts in alliance partners as well. England made a net reduction in the amount of enmity it faced; Germany made a net increase. What should be added is that the player in control of the interaction that produced this net change was really Germany—which was also on balance the loser. Germany can be said to have led off (offensively), while Britain responded (defensively). By 1901 the results for Germany were already poor; by 1907 they were disastrous.

Unless one believes that the poor results for Germany and the much better results for Britain were due to some other discernible factor, one would conclude that they came from skill and that the British were more careful in the selection of enemies. The British both prioritized enemies and kept the list small, while Germany vacillated among potential enemies and let the list grow. In choosing policy alternatives, Britain far outperformed Germany in "conserving" enemies.

NOTES

1. Oscar Wilde, *The Picture of Dorian Gray*, 1891.

2. Quoted in Samuel B. Griffith II, *In Defense of the Public Liberty* (Garden City, N.Y.: Doubleday, 1976), p. 256.

3. Eugen Wolf, *Vom Fürsten Bismarck* (Leipzig, 1904), p. 16, as quoted in Gordon A. Craig, *Germany, 1866-1945* (New York: Oxford University Press, 1978), p. 117.

4. William Leonard Langer, *The Franco-Russian Alliance, 1890-1894* (New York: Octagon Books, 1967), reprinting the original 1929 Harvard University Press edition), p. 20.

5. Rothfels, *Bismarck und der Staat: Ausgewählte Documente*, 2d ed. (Stuttgart, 1954), p. 135. Quoted frequently, in this case in Craig, *Germany*, p. 115.

6. The best detailed account is in Langer, *The Franco-Russian Alliance*, pp. 27-60. Craig, *Germany*, pp. 230-32, takes a somewhat different view from Langer.

7. *Die Grosse Politik der Europäischen Kabinette, 1871-1914*, J. Lepsius, A. Mendelssohn-Bartholdy, F. Thimme, eds., 39 vols. (Berlin: 1922-1927), vol. 17 (no. 4983), p. 20.

8. Quoted in Zara S. Steiner, *Britain and the Origins of the First World War* (New York: St. Martin's Press, 1977), p. 40. Italics added.

9. Monger, "End of Isolation: Britain, Germany and Japan, 1900-1902," *Transactions of the Royal Historical Society*, 5th ser., xiii, 1963, p. 82, as quoted in Steiner, *Britain*, p. 31. See also David Thomson, ed., *The New Cambridge Modern History*, vol. 12, *The Era of Violence, 1898-1945* (Cambridge: Cambridge University Press, 1960), p. 312.

10. G. P. Gooch and H. Temperley, eds., *British Documents on the Origins of the [First World] War, 1898-1914*, 11 vols. in 13 (His Britannic Majesty's Stationery Office, London: 1926-1938), vol. 3, app. A, p. 419.

11. Blanche E. C. Dugdale, *Arthur James Balfour* (New York: Putnam, 1937), p. 286. Prince Bernhard von Bülow, in his *Memoirs*, 4 vols. (Boston: Little, Brown, 1931), vol. 2; 1903-1909, p. 148, confirms that Russian feeling was running high.

12. For text of the Convention, see Frederick H. Hartmann, ed., *Basic Documents of International Relations* (New York: McGraw-Hill, 1951), pp. 22-42. Italics added.

13. Otto, Prince von Bismarck, *Bismarck, The Man and the Statesman: Reflections and Reminiscences* (New York: Harper, 1899), vol. 2, p. 50.

14. Ibid., pp. 276-77.

15. Ibid., p. 282.

16. Gooch and Temperley, *British Documents on the War*, vol. 7, pp. 487-88. Italics added.

17. Ibid.

18. Harold Nicolson, *National Character and National Policy*, Montague Burton Lecture, 1938, University College, Nottingham. Reprinted in Frederick H. Hartmann, ed., *Readings in International Relations* (New York: McGraw-Hill, 1952), p. 48.

19. Cited in A. J. Grant and Harold W. Temperley, *Europe in the Nineteenth and Twentieth Centuries, 1789-1939* (London: Longmans, 1940), p. 459.

20. Ibid., p. 446.

21. Bernhard von Bülow, *Memoirs*, pp. 143-44.

22. Early versions of the plan reversed the sequence. For the documents, see Gerhard Ritter, *The Schlieffen Plan* (New York: Praeger, 1958).

Part II

FACTORS AFFECTING POLICY DECISIONS

5

DECISION MAKING: THE POLICY ROLE

The decisions and actions of government are . . . resultants in the sense that what happens is not chosen as a solution to a problem but rather results from compromise, conflict and confusion of officials with diverse interests and unequal influence. . . .

Graham T. Allison[1]

[I]n foreign policy formulation (the act of making a choice) how much does the pulling, hauling, and bargaining below the President affect presidential choice?

Robert J. Art[2]

We have established so far that there is no normal amount of enmity but that there is some minimum amount, which can be increased if care is not taken. Every factor examined in Chapter 3 added to the sense of the varia tions that are possible. True, certain locations bring about higher likelihoods of involvement in war, of armed embroilment with opponents. At times certain areas become highly tense, as significant increases in arms spending show. Some frontiers, because of their contours or their uncertainties, invite trouble. But when all this is considered, there is an enormous variation in how much enmity nations encounter. Chapter 4 has shown how a significant part of that variation is directly traceable to the policies nations adopt toward one another. It suggests that acquiring enemies in undesirable proportions or quantities is importantly an act of will. It indicates that the end product, the list of enemies to be faced, is heavily influenced by the degree of good or bad judgment each nation shows in its policy formulation and revision. And it warns that the roster of enemies to be faced is in significant ways a *matter of choice*.

The argument is not a flat proposition that all enmity is a matter of will; rather, the argument is made in proportional terms: that the length of the list and the numbers it includes (past some minimum) are a matter of will. It is in this sense that policy is the throttle, encouraging a range of responses from hostility to friendship.

While there can be many arguments over just how much enmity is controllable, *any* emphasis on this point is at variance with the notion that a nation takes potluck, accepts the hand of fate—whatever figure of speech best conveys the image of helplessness—that nations confront whatever assortment of enemies assemble to be confronted. The system as it presently functions determines that some minimal enmity will exist, but its amount is determined through individual state behavior.

The case study in Chapter 4 shows that there is clear empirical evidence that a roster of enemies can be altered by specific nations through specific acts of policy. What the case study does not tell us is *how much* the list can be altered. The chapter recounts what the British and Germans *did*, but does not inquire whether more could have been done, that is, whether either nation could have been even more or even less successful with additional policy change. That is another way of saying that we have not looked in depth at the phenomena that impose limits on the process of altering an enemy list.

These phenomena are of two kinds, those that are national in origin and those originating from the system of nation-states, from the external environment. To understand just how much choice exists, therefore, it is necessary not only to look at individual national policy decisions and the national context in which those decisions are made, but also to see the multilateral interactions among all the states involved, as they react to one another. Ultimately we must see these two sets of phenomena, not only in relation to each other, but as part of an ongoing dynamic process.

To do so requires a distinct effort, since scholars so frequently have emphasized one or the other of the two perspectives without making much effort to relate them. As Stanley H. Hoffmann once said,

recent theories of international politics seem to divide into opposite extremes. Some focus on the international system; they tend to describe it as a compelling, even tyrannical, sociological divinity. Others scrutinize national decision-making; they patiently list all the organs that take part in it and all the "inputs" that go into decisions.[3]

The first emphasis overplays the "weight" of the system, while the second tends "to be casual about the environment."

This dichotomy of emphasis is not surprising; it is merely the political reflection of the age-old tendency noted by Erich Fromm to emphasize either free will or determinism in human affairs. Relating national decision making and the international system together effectively is exceedingly difficult because each easily appears to be self-sufficient in point of view. One who looks at the system and the recurrence of certain kinds of decisions easily underrates free will on the part of the decision maker, since one "knows" what that decision maker will decide. As Robert J. Lieber says, "Freely made choices can still exhibit statistical regularities."[4] But one who looks at any single national actor making decisions immediately loses this sense of inevitability.

To achieve a balanced view is very difficult, but it must be attempted. This chapter concentrates on the national phenomena, on foreign policy decision making, leaving the international environment for Chapter 6.

"Policy" is defined in the dictionary as "a definite course of action adopted for the sake of expediency, facility, etc." or as an "action or procedure conforming to or considered with reference to prudence or expediency." It is further defined as "prudence, practical wisdom or expediency" and again as "sagacity" and "shrewdness." That leaves rather little room for the notion that policy can be wise or unwise, depending on its results. But perhaps the definitions intend this to be understood; policy is designed to be good and effective, hopefully demonstrating "practical wisdom" by the results it brings. To start out to be prudent or wise in no way guarantees a wise or prudent result, however. Kaiser Wilhelm did not think he was planning disaster for Germany. Much depends upon how correctly the nation assesses the total situation and perceives how each party to it is affected.

For reasons to be developed in Chapter 7, perception of a situation by states that are parties to a potential enmity resulting from it will not readily or often be identical or uniform. Furthermore, it may be much more vital to one party than to another to prevail. As Baltasar Gracián advised in 1647 in his book, *A Handy Oracle and Art of Worldly Wisdom*, "Never battle with a man who has nothing to lose, for then the conflict is unequal."[5] The Vietnam War is a relevant case illustration. For one party the war was total and the stakes maximum; for the other party the war remained limited and so did the stakes.

In any case, the astuteness with which the parties appraise the total circumstances surrounding the policy alternatives they confront will directly affect what they choose to do and how they fare. If they are not coldly realistic in *foreseeing the interaction that will occur*, they will probably fail — or at least fall short of achieving maximum results. Wisdom in foreign policy making then depends upon the sureness with which decisions makers analyze the total circumstances affecting the choice and the clarity with which they foresee the future outcome of their decision. Decisions and their presumed consequences must therefore be seen as a package. The most significant aspects of a policy will be determined by the *concept* (intellectual framework) that in turn governs the choice of the *content* to be *implemented*.

Policy studies can usefully be made of any part of this three-phase progression. Studies in bureaucracy can show how a policy is altered or even subverted in its implementation phase, at the hands of a hostile or indifferent officialdom. Studies in content can examine the alternatives from which the choice was made. Studies in concept can show why the problem was visualized in the terms it was. But these three phases or stages of the foreign policy are not really equally critical. What is most critical is the conceptual phase, because everything that is done or attempted through the policy reflects assumptions about how to deal with other states within a system that is presumed to operate in a certain way. Such assumptions about the negative or positive consequences of the choices made dictate the inclusion or rejection of particular national interests as the content of the policy.

In an idealized form the conceptual process can be visualized as responses to three questions asked sequentially for any (every) scenario consistent with what the concept assumes about the rules of the system. These three questions are (1) What is sought? (What would the world be like if it happened?) (2) Who would help and who would hinder? (3) What additional resources would have to be used? (What must the nation itself contribute if it seeks a certain set of results?) From such scenario analyses, each with a likely cost-benefit ratio, it becomes fairly obvious which policy content (which choice of national interests) ought to be pursued.

If we think of the conceptual phase of policy in this way, what we are really doing is visualizing which set of national interests will likely be selected by other nations (from their alternatives), when and if the first policy makers select a particular set themselves. This way of thinking about the policy process can be criticized from three points of view: that this method is seldom actually followed; that decisions are influenced by irrational factors; and that it is not always clear what a nation's interests are.

Decision makers, say the first set of critics, do not in fact make careful analyses of a range of "options," weighing their advantages and disadvantages. They resort to intellectual shortcuts. Morton H. Halperin, for example, makes exactly this point. He first sketches out the main steps of a "rational" approach much like the one just given.[6] But, says Halperin, seldom does a participant do that, because "problems are too difficult, and time is short." Instead he will "focus . . . on a few variables and develop a set of programmed responses. . . ." He mentions John Steinbruner's findings about the use of pat images, arguments by analogy, inferences of transformation ("wishful thinking"), ideological thinking, and so on.[7] Halperin says of ideological thinking that it is an intellectual time saver: it permits *the selective perception of information.*[8] As a consequence, when "participants share a set of global images, these will decisively shape stands taken. . . ." He cites American officials and the cold war.[9]

Halperin's argument that most participants in the decision-making process have not time to do the analysis and will focus instead on a few variables and "programmed responses" is probably correct in terms of the actual process, as opposed to the ideal. Nevertheless, whether the full range of "options" is considered or not, some planning function (however truncated), based on some set of ideas (however vague or stereotyped), is still the inevitable first phase of policy making. Some planning function must precede the choice of particular objectives, through whatever means are available. To the extent that national planning is done with stereotypes, indeed the whole conceptual phase hustled through, it demonstrates that the concept guiding the policy, rightly or wrongly, is no longer considered in dispute. The intellectual process has become ritualized.

The ideal model, say a second set of critics, does not take sufficient account of irrational and contradictory factors complicating the decision. The more complex the governmental apparatus for decision making, the more it may be necessary to look beyond the ultimate decision maker to the lesser bureaucratic and organizational levels for an explanation of what really happened.

To explain such inconsistencies, Graham T. Allison, in an already classic study, examines American decision making in the Cuban missile crisis by considering three models, each yielding a different perspective on the same set of choices: the rational actor, the organizational process, and governmental politics.[10]

By "rational actor" Allison means "happenings in foreign affairs" seen "as the more or less purposive acts of unified national governments" in which the nations or governments act as they do because of the strategic problems they face.[11] He argues that the rational actor view "must be balanced by the appreciation that [decisions can] result from innumerable and often conflicting smaller actions by individuals at various levels of bureaucratic organizations in the service of a variety of only partially compatible conceptions of national goals, organizational goals, and political objectives."[12]

For this reason Allison calls attention to a second decision-making "model" in which large organizations are seen as "functioning according to regular patterns of behavior."[13] He then adds a third "model" that assumes "a number of distinct players, with distinct objectives but shared power," whose moves can be visualized "as the resultant of collegial bargaining."[14] In describing bureaucratic politics, Allison quotes the axiom, "Where you stand depends on where you sit!"[15]

Obviously these are useful insights. The most obvious difference between Allison's argument and the viewpoint of this book is that his second and third models are substantially concerned with implementation rather than policy concept. We have argued that *important* foreign policy decisions are best understood in the light of the particular perception of the problem predominating at the top level of the foreign policy elite. Our argument is that the way one acts is determined above all by *how one thinks* about the problem. Allison does not give major attention to this point. This is one reason why Allison's models, hailed with enthusiasm by many, have also encountered severe criticism.[16]

Moving beyond what Allison calls the "rational model" aim of showing "how the nation or government could have chosen to act as it did, given the strategic problems it faced," our explanations have been intended to show that the answers cannot be found merely by looking at the problem faced or at a nation's bureaucracy or organization. It is also necessary to consider which particular nation is facing that problem and what problem its policy makers think they face.

Anyone with significant government experience with the policy-making process of the United States will have some clues as to why the academic arguments persist. The government is vast, and any one person within it, no matter how highly placed, only sees part of what happens. In general, paper does not flow across major units, so major units are frequently quite ignorant of what is occurring elsewhere in the government. If the paper moves "upward," its supporting parts are frequently deleted. Even when the paper crosses unit boundary lines for "coordination," the arguments over it within the unit usually stay in the unit. My own experience is that it is easy to reach quite wrong conclusions as to what actually happened at each stage or level. Written records and minutes can also frequently be misleading although not necessarily deliberately so. To the extent that academic investigation tends to focus more on disagreements among major units (the air force versus the army, for example) and less on variations in handling and style at the different levels, it leads to too much confidence in the axiom that where you stand depends on where you sit. Level has a good deal to do with the *way* a stand is taken, regardless of where the ones who are responsible sit.

Any bureaucracy has to work in an orderly way. At every level or stage, as an issue works its way through the bureaucracy, some one person within each unit must make a decision. That decision is taken after "staffing" and perhaps after some lateral, formal or informal "coordination" with other units or with other levels, to test which way "parallel" staffing is proceeding or to test the possible reception "upstairs" if the proposal should clear that person's unit and level.

Most importantly, the decision maker at a given unit and level has to decide whether to forward the position recommended by his or her staff. Once the paper clears that particular decision maker, it is "staffed" at the next level until a more senior single decision maker decides again whether to forward it. Consequently, what happens at each level is much like what happens at every other level, but the level makes for significant differences in style.

Suppose that an issue is within the Navy Department. At that level it will be argued within accepted, or at least acceptable, navy patterns of thinking, simply because that is the natural language of the group. When and if the issue reaches a Department of Defense (DOD) level, however, the very way of arguing it may have to change. And when the issue is coordinated with the State Department, more change, both in style and in approach, will probably be required. Such coordination conferences have to remain within the guidelines provided by the heads of departments.

During this whole process — and this is the important point — at any given level and within any given unit, the process can be deemed "rational" (appropriate in view of institutional attitudes, prejudices, and interests within that unit and level). The *whole* process, on the other hand, may appear "irrational."

Robert Jervis, taking a somewhat different approach, argues that "what seems to be a clash of bureaucratic interests and stands can often be more fruitfully viewed as a *clash among values* that are widely held in both the society and the decision-makers' own minds."[17]

At this point three separate although overlapping explanations have been given of bureaucratic behavior. Allison's models suggest how parochial interest or standard organizational and operational patterns of behavior can affect decisions. Allison focuses on the Cuban missile crisis, in which the top group convened (the "Excomm") included individuals who did not currently hold office, like Dean Acheson, and Robert Kennedy, the president's brother, who hardly confined himself to a bureaucratic role as attorney general. It operated far more like a committee to explore all the options than as a group representing agreed divisions of bureaucratic responsibility. Dean Rusk refused to "represent" the State Department, acting as "devil's advocate" instead. Robert McNamara strayed far from defense issues as such. The accounts of their deliberations leave a distinct impression that the group members disagreed very little if at all on "bureaucratic" grounds and that they also really disagreed very little over the values at stake. They tended to focus on ways of producing a particular result — removal of the Soviet missiles from Cuba — at an acceptable cost, that is, without starting a major war. They do not appear to have behaved very differently from what the ideal process might prescribe, and they do not really seem to have resorted much to Halperin's shortcuts.

My own explanation of bureaucratic behavior, above, stresses the effects of handling decision papers at successive levels of parallel units, as these papers rise to some top-level committee or to some ultimate single decision maker. My explanation draws a distinction, then, between the top level and lower levels. At the top level, which is where the rational actor model is most useful, my argument is that the perceptions held by the senior decision makers are the most critical and decisive factor. Below the top level, some of the more confusing twists and turns become easier to understand in light of the separateness of the parallel units and the carefully compartmentalized nature of much of the proceedings at any given level of handling. Much in Allison's models applies here.

Jervis offers yet a third explanation, pointing to what he calls "a clash among values." There are two contrasting ways in which Jervis's point can be taken. If we are looking at top-level problems, we can take him to be referring to cases either where a clear sense of priorities is not agreed to or where there is disagreement over which outcomes or results are most likely to ensue from the decisions taken. The disagreement may really be over goals, or it may really be over consequences.

Part of Jervis's thought fits not uncomfortably with what in Chapter 6 we shall call "counterbalancing national interests," where typically there is something quite positive that may be gained from pursuing *either* alternative of any pair. Where each alternative represents some desirable value, the decision will turn (bureaucratic power apart) on which value seems superior or on what result from the two contrasting or opposing choices is deemed most likely. Both values and expectations are pertinent at any level of the decision process, but they are especially pertinent at senior levels and in regard to "big picture" issues involving national security. Senior decision makers in the series of hierarchical decision makers will normally believe they are proceeding "rationally" when handling such issues, so it is really the question of conflicting values and divergent expectations that is the critical set of variables at this level.

Perhaps the best way to focus the present discussion is to note Warner R. Schilling's careful distinction on this point. Schilling contends first that many bureaucratic conflicts simply reflect a "diversity of opinion . . . re-garding the state of the world and what America should do in it."[18] These arguments "cut across formal institutional and organizational lines." They will occur over what my formulation calls top-level issues. But in contrast, says Schilling, many bureaucratic arguments reflect an "allocation of responsibility":

Not sharing the same responsibilities (or, put the other way, not charged with the same values or skills), government organizations will necessarily bring divergent interests and approaches to common problems. When conflicts of this order occur, the lines of battle are more likely to conform to the boundaries of the organizations involved. [Such] divergent responsibilities are built into the structure of govern-ment. The allocation of responsibility may be changed, but the effect is usually to shift the location of battle rather than to bring it to an end.[19]

Allison's bureaucratic model and his organizational process model are most helpful with Schilling's second group, which in my formulation tends to reflect lower-level (staffing and implementation) issues. It is apparent how my own remarks on bureaucratic decisions, earlier in this chapter, parallel Schilling's point.

Henry Kissinger's memoirs provide some recent and detailed comments on the whole bureaucratic process in the United States, looked at from the White House. He points out many times how the bureaucracy performed with a will of its own: "Day after day that spring the bureaucracy chipped away at the President's declared policy, feeding expectations of arms talks."[20] Again: "No sooner were these instructions issued than the departments began to nibble away at them. Departments accept decisions which go against them only if vigilantly supervised. Otherwise the lower-level exegesis can be breathtaking in its effrontery."[21] Or, finally: "The ABM directive went the way of many other Presidential instructions to the Defense Department. Opposition was simply too powerful."[22] But, to balance the picture, much of the rest of the book is a series of illustrations of how Nixon and Kissinger, using "back-channels" of communications, kept most of the bureaucracy isolated from the real decision process. Nixon at one point, at the Moscow summit, enlists Brezhnev's aid to surface some already agreed-upon "principles" whose existence had been carefully hidden from the U.S. secretary of state!

Kissinger lends little support to those who make much of the where-you-sit-determines-where-you-stand school. For example, he portrays Secretary of Defense Melvin R. Laird taking a point of view his general and flag officers consistently opposed: "Laird, as always, favored the maximum withdrawal. . . ." Laird argued this course each time troops were to be rotated out of Vietnam "as the best means of tranquilizing public opinion."[23] Although Kissinger makes the conventional assertion that presidents find it difficult, because of the "system," to make "new departures," he offers a somewhat different reason:

The departments and agencies prefer to operate by consensus. They like to make policy through a pattern of clearances that obscures who has prevailed — and also any clear-cut direction. They tend to be attracted to the fashionable. They shun confrontation with one another, the media, or the Congress. When thwarted they do not shrink, however, from political warfare against the President by leaks, and, in extreme cases, by the encouragement of Congressional pressures.[24]

Kissinger substantiates the view that it is difficult to impose a sense of objective on a large bureaucracy, and that this is unlikely to occur at all unless the top leadership has a clear policy concept it wishes to implement. Of course, Kissinger's tenure in office represented one of those periods when Americans had great differences of opinion over the proper policy path to choose. Such differences can come about when the president is too far "ahead" of his people or too far "behind." Most frequently, however, the people are prepared, at least initially, to follow strong leadership. Even so, Franklin D. Roosevelt had problems convincing his people that it was necessary to take stronger action in confronting the Germans and Japanese in the 1930s.

In Harry S. Truman's time it was sometimes argued that he was deliberately trying to overstate the Russian threat, to rally the American people behind him. But that was in a time of transition in American thinking about what actions would produce what results. Ernest R. May relates how Truman, appointing Clark Clifford to the position of White House counsel, asked Clifford to prepare a full briefing on U.S.-Soviet relations:

After talking with almost every knowledgeable person in the administration, Clifford delivered a report nearly a hundred thousand words in length. It confirmed everything that Truman had been told earlier. Describing the Soviet Union as bent on aggressive expansion, the report declared, "The language of military power is the only language which disciples of power politics understand."[25]

And, says May, when Truman began to speak in such language, he found somewhat to his own surprise that his popularity increased.

When President Johnson in 1965 decided to send combat troops to Vietnam, he did not doubt that the American people generally shared his views. Even his phrasing suggests that. At one press conference he said that defeat in South Vietnam "would encourage and spur on those who seek to conquer all free nations within their reach. . . . This is the clearest lesson of our time. From Munich until today we have learned that to yield to aggression brings only greater threats and brings even more destructive war."[26]

Much evidence suggests that once a president takes decisive action with an acceptable rationale there is a strong tendency to arrive at a consensus, just as during the Vietnam War those who had doubts tended to be squeezed out or leave. Much evidence also suggests that elite views begin to change only when the actual outcomes diverge significantly and for a long enough period from anticipated outcomes. When that happens, an argument over alternative values tends to take shape.

Once Vietnam became such an endless killing ground that "defending freedom" and "repelling aggression" began to seem hollow, "ending useless bloodshed" seemed more worthwhile. President Nixon, wanting "peace with honor," found himself caught between those at home who wanted peace and those who wanted to avoid humiliation. A bureaucracy will be very restive under such conditions, because both of Schilling's points come to bear: there will be clashes over values and arguments over allocated responsibilities; for instance, the armed forces may argue that they "can't win because their hands are tied." Either that kind of situation changes or a government falls apart.

The third criticism of the ideal process centers on the notion of national interests. Critics have argued that the term is vague or meaningless, although they admit that governments around the world use it every day to justify or explain policy. It is true, as Fred Sondermann points out, that "any . . . user of the concept must face perplexing questions. Whose interests? How determined? By whom?"[27] Bernard Brodie raises a similar point when he writes:

The phrase *vital interests* rolls portentiously and somewhat granitically off the tongue, pregnant with meaning but nevertheless obscure. What do we mean when we call interests "vital," as distinct, say, from merely important? Who determines at any one time what those interests are for our country, and by what criteria and processes do they do so?[28]

Both Sondermann and Brodie know that there is a clear and simple answer to this, however: the decision makers believe they know; they are the ones who are in power and they decide. Whether history will agree with their judgment or, for that matter, their own people, is quite another thing. Put the point in reverse: What government ever sets out to act *contrary* to the national interest?

What Sondermann and Brodie really want to highlight is the question of whether the decision making is wise. Since arguments over policy almost always compare different alternatives, each of which is justified and sponsored as in the national interest, the claim itself proves nothing.

Many of the criticisms levied at the term "national interests" really reflect adverse reactions to the implication that there is a single (and obvious?) national interest to be followed, rather than a choice to be made. Hans J. Morgenthau may have created such an impression by closing his book, *In Defense of the National Interest*, with a ringing declaration "that it is not only a political necessity but also a moral duty for a nation to follow . . . but one guiding star, one standard for thought, one rule for action: the national interest."[29] Or one can cite Charles O. Lerche, Jr., defining foreign policy as "the courses of action and the decisions relating to them that a state undertakes in its relations with other states in order to attain national objectives and to advance the national interest."[30]

Either following Morgenthau's "guiding star" or attempting with Lerche to "advance" the national interest presupposes not only knowing what ought to be sought in policy, assuming acceptable costs, but also what ought *not* to be sought, for whatever reason, cost included. Such judgments implicitly assume *some preceding analysis* as to which alternative sets of interests should be bundled together into a policy. If the term "interests" is not used to label these opposing views, it will be necessary to use some other labels, so it seems more useful to simply follow ordinary state practice.

Defined as Lerche defines it, foreign policy is encountered rather late, as the last steps in carrying out conclusions reached earlier in some undisclosed rational process. That rational process must presumably have evaluated the world scene, looked at possible alternative postures toward it, considered the likelihood of success or failure for each alternative, and considered, above all, the likely costs. It must have followed either my ideal model or Halperin's truncated version. Only after this procedure can a state follow "courses of action" and make "the decisions relating to them." In short, a plan of some sort must precede any program of actions to be implemented.

The value seen in choosing or rejecting a course of action (a set of national interests) is subject to change over time. For example, those who in 1979 greeted President Carter's establishment of diplomatic relations with the People's Republic of China were just as sure it was a national interest of the United States as those who for years earlier had argued vehemently that establishing diplomatic relations with the People's Republic would be contrary to the national interests of the United States. The latter group typically contended that it was a national interest only to back Taiwan.

As the example shows, any alternative to the interest chosen for implementation is also considered by its advocates to have a positive national value, and often the alternative will have its day as policy at a later time. This situation argues against restricting the term national interest only to content items chosen at a given time to be included in policy, and in favor of using the term quite broadly to refer to any item that is a candidate for inclusion, which is what I shall do.

Turning now to the systems effect of such national interest choices, what the planning process estimates will happen, and what the implementation of a policy causes to happen, is the creation of a pattern of reactions by other states. Some will like some parts of the content and dislike others. Some will like most parts. Some will dislike most parts. There will be a great range of interactions, which could be graphed in a progressive series from essentially negative to essentially positive. If Nation A and Nation B, each with a twenty-part content, found eighteen parts acceptable in each direction, a very "friendly" relationship could be anticipated. If the reaction was eighteen parts negative, a very "hostile" relationship could be anticipated. Largely common interests exist in the first case, and largely opposed interests in the second case.

The example just given is of a bilateral relationship (between A and B), at a time when, for the sake of convenience, the whole process is being held still. In real life, of course, the reaction of A to B cannot be determined so simply because the world is not bilateral but multilateral, and the process also will not hold still. One of the most dangerous possible ways for a nation to conduct foreign policy, as was pointed out in Chapter 2, would be to forget that multilateral feature. When the British were under pressure to take active military measures in the 1930s to thwart Italy's attempt to conquer Ethiopia in defiance of the League of Nations, the British leaders in fact did not forget that a real Anglo-Italian conflict would permit Nazi Germany complete freedom elsewhere. Again, as an illustration, one quite unsought and serious result of the U.S. involvement in the Vietnam War was the strategic freedom the Soviet Union enjoyed for some years because of the immobility of the Chinese, who were caught between the hammer and the anvil.

Because the world does not hold still, that is, because nations will alter policies they find unrewarding, in this specific instance both China and the United States had a very great incentive to reduce their mutual antagonism. Expressing the same point another way, nations are not passive vehicles registering antagonism on some kind of scoreboard, with some finding higher totals than others and wishing it were not so. Rather, they ordinarily are willing to accept only a certain total amount of antagonism. When the total "collected" from all sources begins to exceed "safe" levels, most nations feel a strong incentive to revise the policy and reduce the hostility. It is here that their perception of the motives and interests of others and their conception of how the system operates become crucial.

NOTES

1. Graham T. Allison, *Essence of Decision: Explaining the Cuban Missile Crisis* (Boston: Little, Brown, 1971), p. 162.

2. Robert J. Art, "Bureaucratic Politics and American Foreign Policy: A Critique," in John E. Endicott and Roy W. Stafford, Jr., eds., *American Defense Policy*, 4th ed. (Baltimore: Johns Hopkins University Press, 1977), p. 244.

3. Stanley H. Hoffmann, "Restraints and Choices in American Foreign Policy," *Daedalus* (Fall 1962): 668.

4. Robert J. Lieber, *Theory and World Politics* (London: George Allen & Unwin, 1973), p. 7.

5. Baltasar Gracián, *A Handy Oracle and Art of Worldly Wisdom*, 1647, was a much quoted work in its time.

6. Morton H. Halperin, *Bureaucratic Politics and Foreign Policy* (Washington, D.C.: Brookings Institution, 1974), p. 21.

7. Ibid., pp. 21-22. Halperin cites John Steinbruner, *Decisions under Complexity*, chap. 4, as forthcoming from Princeton University Press.

8. Halperin, *Bureaucratic Politics*, p. 23. Italics added.

9. Ibid., p. 11.

10. Allison, *Essence of Decision*.

11. Ibid., pp. 4-5.

12. Ibid., pp. 5-6.

13. Ibid., p. 6.

14. Ibid., p. 7.

15. Ibid., p. 176. Allison attributes this to Don K. Price.

16. See, for example, Art, "Bureaucratic Politics," p. 251.

17. Robert Jervis, *Perception and Misperception in International Politics* (Princeton, N.J.: Princeton University Press, 1976), p. 28. Italics added.

18. Warner R. Schilling, "The Politics of National Defense: Fiscal 1950" in Warner R. Schilling, Paul T. Hammond, and Glenn H. Snyder, *Strategy, Politics, and Defense Budgets* (New York: Columbia University Press, 1962), p. 21.

19. Ibid., pp. 21-22.

20. Henry Kissinger, *White House Years* (Boston: Little, Brown, 1979), p. 137.

21. Ibid., p. 154.

22. Ibid., p. 1129.

23. Ibid., p. 1166.

24. Ibid., pp. 840-41.

25. Ernest R. May, *"Lessons of the Past:" The Use and Misuse of History in American Foreign Policy* (New York: Oxford University Press, 1973), p. 41. Italics added.

26. *Public Papers of the Presidents: Lyndon B. Johnson, 1965* (Washington, D.C.: Government Printing Office, 1966), vol. I, p. 449.

27. Fred A. Sondermann, "The Concept of the National Interest," *Orbis* (Spring 1977): 129. The whole article is pp. 121-38.

28. Bernard Brodie, *War and Politics* (New York: Macmillan, 1973), pp. 341-42.

29. Hans J. Morganthau, *In Defense of the National Interest* (New York: Knopf, 1951), p. 242.

30. Charles O. Lerche, Jr., *Foreign Policy of the American People* (Englewood Cliffs, N.J.: Prentice-Hall, 1961), p. 4.

6

THE INTERNATIONAL SYSTEM

"Ah." Poirot looked again at the snapshot. "Yes—it is as you say
—quite obvious when you have been told what it is!"
"So much depends on how you look at a thing," laughed
Warburton.
"That is a very profound truth."

Agatha Christie[1]

Decisions by states will be wise if they reflect a determination to control or
contour enmity, but how far that goal can be achieved also depends upon
the nature of the state system. Decisions on the part of nations will be made
with some assumptions as to the kind of behavior that system seems to
tolerate or punish. In this chapter the direct question will be asked: How
indeed does the system function?

To answer that question requires the development of an initial point of
view, subject to elaboration and correction in the course of discussion. For,
as Karl von Clausewitz insisted, "Nothing is more important in life than
finding the right standpoint for seeing and judging events [and] only by
holding to that point of view can one avoid inconsistency."[2] Albert Einstein,
in a parallel thought, emphasized the importance of having some initial
conception of what one is observing: "A theory can be tested by experience,
but there is no way from experience to the setting up of a theory."[3]

To provide such an initial view of the system, in this chapter we shall first
examine how the assumptions one makes shape any model and, with that as
background, sketch out the essentials of our first formal model, the cardinal
principles. Later, in Part III, we shall elaborate each of the four principles of
that model. Then, in Part IV, we shall offer three alternative formal models
of the system for comparison. As will be seen, each of the four models
reflects a particular point of view as to how the system operates.

The question examined in Chapters 1 and 2, of whether enmity is a
"natural" part of the system or not, is a first and basic question about how

the system works. Richard A. Falk is not the first reformer to seek a formula for ridding the system of its enmities. Utopians have looked for such a formula through the ages. Like the medieval alchemists who sought to turn stones into gold, these contemporary optimists seek to transmute hate into friendship and fear into love through such devices as redistribution of resources or mechanical constitutional reform for the UN.

Such suggestions are not new. In the 1930s a widely used textbook[4] in international relations argued with great confidence that enmity arises from maldistribution of economic resources between the "haves" and the "have-nots." The "have-nots" named in this book were Germany, Italy, and Japan!

Machiavelli, like Thucydides before him and many another after him, believed that no policy, no matter how adroit, could eliminate enmity altogether or permanently, so long as a multilateral state system persisted. We saw Emery Reves following in this long tradition when he argued that the system itself produced some minimum tension that, unless carefully managed, could bring about war. Reves pointed to the supreme irony represented by the superpower confrontation, where the stakes are literally life and death. Yet the decision to permit Americans to continue living or, contrariwise, be destroyed by nuclear weapons, is one that can be made only in Moscow — and vice-versa. So long as paradoxical situations like this persist, some enmity among nations is unavoidable.

If this is true and the logic of the situation suggests that nations concentrate on redistributing rather than eliminating enmity, the case study in Chapter 4 still raises a disturbing question: how practical is redistributing enmity as a way of avoiding periodic war? The redistribution of enmity examined in Chapter 4 was accompanied by an obvious and steady increase in system *tension* (expectation of violence), culminating in war. England, for one, may have profited by the redistribution, in that England subsequently confronted fewer enemies when war came. But it would be hard to say that the system as a whole profited; it had to endure the war. Could a more adroit redistribution of enmity by particular states have saved *the system* from that war?

It is not difficult to think of alternative decisions to those actually made by Kaiser Wilhelm that the Germans or Austrians could have made that would have reduced the tension (expectation of violence). Enmity and tension in the system, while closely related, do not necessarily vary directly with one another as cause and effect. If that were not so, it would not be justifiable to treat enmity as a constant that can be redistributed, and tension as a variable increasing or decreasing in level.

To stress that enmity is normal and natural to the system in the sense that Reves asserts, that it cannot be eliminated short of eliminating the multilateral state system itself, is therefore a first assumption about the system. We make a second assumption when we next point to the tendency of most states to revamp policy to reduce marginal enmities when confronted with more centrally important (or threatening) enmities. Some states do this inefficiently. If the states are too inefficient, they disappear. Short of that, they are defeated, and short of being inefficient enough for defeat, they waste resources for little gain. But most nations most of the time can be counted on to play the game with tolerable efficiency. This efficiency is a third assumption. It means that an increase in enmity or threat very likely will trigger policy changes in the system designed by states to keep the threat to tolerable limits. A limited expansion may produce only a limited response, but sooner or later an expansion seen as unlimited tends to generate a general alarm response in most policy makers. This is seen in the histories of Louis XIV, of Napoleon, of Wilhelm, of Hitler. It is here that the expression "My neighbor's neighbor is my friend" tends to take on its concrete meaning. For the most effective counteraction a threatened state can mount may not be to forge a common front in the path of anticipated expansion but to produce or increase the threat to the prospective enemy's flank or rear.

Such reactions took place when Egypt drew nearer the United States and away from the Soviet Union after Russia became a sort of feudal lord to a neighboring and client Marxist Ethiopia. Again, although it is "natural" for Western Europe to want U.S. support against an "unnaturally" extended Russia, it is not at all "natural" for Eastern Europe to align as a bloc against the West. Left to their "natural" tendencies, the Eastern European nations might quarrel among themselves. Or, because fairly uniformly threatened, they might try to concert a policy (presently open to only one or two) of balancing Soviet influence with West German influence. For them to align as a group solely against the Western bloc at the price of being subordinate to the Soviet Union is contrary to the "tendency" of the system and explains in part the Hungarian revolt of 1956, the Czech "spring" of 1968, the Polish turbulence of 1980-1981, and the recurrent Rumanian flirtation with China.

If these assumptions about the system are correct, expansion by any one nation tends to bring about counterpressures designed to limit that expansion. Such a proposition should not be taken too literally or too mechanically to imply that *equal* counterpressures inevitably arise that ultimately "compress" the expansion back to its original limits. Nor are any reactions fully automatic and completely predictable, since individual policy decisions are required. But the process tends to work this way.

We are now ready to describe in connected fashion the features of the system the model will have to take into account, beginning with the proposition that nations fear any other nations they believe might, given sufficient temptation, assault them. In a rare case it is possible to imagine a nation with no active fear of being attacked, but in practice there is always someone. This focusing of concern on particular potential enemies is a first characteristic of the system and of the international environment to which states must relate. Such behavior is "natural" to the system, then, although each nation's list of enemies varies, as found in Chapter 3. By such a list, a nation defines its *power problem:* those foreign nations considered a source of potential attack.*

Efforts to resolve the power problem, which, whatever its specific nature from case to case, always confronts each nation, produce a second distinguishing mark of national behavior within this international environment. Nations with power problems that are identical or nearly so have the strongest possible incentive for pooling their strength, in view of the threat. Such a pooling of strength is known technically, of course, as an alliance.

There are considerable advantages in seeing alliances in this light. Much useless discussion can otherwise go into inconclusive argument over whether an alliance is "strong" or "weak" and whether it is likely to endure. Arguing such points in the abstract is quite unavailing, since it tends to focus attention on national "will" and domestic events instead of on the prime reason for the existence of the alliance and for its strength or weakness. So long as common perceptions of common sources of danger to two or more states persist, so will their alliance. Change the common nature of that perception and you change the basis for the alliance, or "weaken" it.

Alliances reflect one response to the power problem; armaments are another, furnishing a third fundamental characteristic of behavior in the system. Nations accumulate or increase arms as the direct result of their perception of the threats they face. Armaments increase national power, while alliances pool that power with foreign power.

States face enmity as an unavoidable feature of the system, and they respond to it by forming alliances and maintaining or increasing armaments. To say it another way, they perceive a threat and try to respond by adjusting upward the power they can amass or produce as a counterweight.

There is a fourth fundamental characteristic of behavior in this system or environment — the one stressed at greatest length so far in this book. Perceiving a threat, nations may attempt to decrease the enmity they confront by altering the foreign policies they follow. As a result of their choices, tension fluctuates.

These are four relatively simple main features of the system; the following pages will describe some more subtle and complex features.

---

*This concept or definition is roughly the same as what military strategists mean by "the threat." *Power problem* is a term I have used since 1957 in the various editions of my textbook, *The Relations of Nations* (New York: Macmillan).

We can begin with the fact that the present nation-state system consists of over 150 separate, sovereign units and ask whether these 150 all approach the world with the same assumptions, define problems in identical terms, and approach their resolution with identical expectations? If not, the meaning of the phrase "present nation-state system" is more restricted than one would normally think to stipulate.

All these units are physically present in the world at the same time; for example, their representatives to the UN can all gather for a meeting of the General Assembly. But in a subjective sense they are *not* all in the same "present" moment. Stated differently, the same present moment, identical to all by the clock or calendar, is otherwise not identical. Nations younger or older, richer or poorer, with a colonial or noncolonial past, having been in many wars or no wars, are in the same present only in a restricted or incomplete sense, as are a grandfather, an adult parent, a teenager, and a baby, whose lives intersect in a given moment stipulated by watch and calendar, but for whom that moment comes at quite different "times" in terms of the tempo of their lives. Normally it serves the purpose to describe what is common at a given moment, and that is true enough so far as it goes. But what is not common is equally true, and perhaps more important.

Which of the following alternative descriptions of a great power conference is more correct? (1) Three states, meeting in Geneva on Monday, October 12, with a printed agenda of three items, are by virtue of those facts dealing with the same problems. (2) Three states, meeting in Geneva on Monday, October 12, despite a printed agenda of three items, are probably addressing quite different problems.

If you choose Version 1 you attach greater importance to the "photographic" reality of the situation. If you choose Version 2 you would probably also agree that the meaning of the agenda items will vary from state to state, depending on the historical experience of each and its varying expectations of the future. You would be prepared to accept reality as having dimensions beyond what you could photograph.

In one sense, since the states in a conference are only there in the same "present" in a physical sense, it is the divergent expectations of the decision makers that is the most real and pertinent feature. Consequently, a diplomatic conference may be said to have a true meaning in both a physical, photographable sense and a nonphotographable, more-than-physical — literally, a *meta*physical — sense.

Such observations do not fit in congenial fashion into the storehouses of our minds, for we are a generation that tends not to believe in ghosts. If we can't see something, it doesn't exist. Yet we are also a generation that believes the whopper that the wooden desk on which we write is really neutrons and protons in motion. So perhaps it is ultimately a question of finding appropriate vocabulary to express the notion.

If the foregoing makes any sense, it follows that much of the vocabulary already in use in discussing hostility and violence ought to be reexamined. Take a notion like deterrence. Does one apply it to some objective reality that can be photographed? Some certain pile of weapons, perhaps? In equal piles, perhaps? How much is deterrence a subjective notion? But if it is essentially a subjective notion, can it be perceived as uniform in content from subject to subject, from actor to actor? Is deterrence something that, if it were one of the three items at the hypothetical Geneva conference of October 12 stipulated above, would somehow have the same meaning to each participant and evoke the same expectations? (Much of the literature would convey that impression.)

There is a further subtle feature of the environment that must be taken into account. Unfortunately, it too is of a disturbing sort, although perhaps slightly easier to accept. In the form of a riddle, if two states are negotiating on arms agreement, how many states are in effect present at the negotiations? I would argue that the correct answer is: those two and anyone else feared by either state.

Here again our common-sense vocabulary is inadequate to describe the environment. The most meaningful "participant" in a two-party conference may be a third state that is not physically represented, but whose armaments dominate the discussions and their outcome. If the Soviet Union and the United States negotiate, China is present in every sense but the physical. China may be the most important party "present" even though China is "absent." A photograph would show part but not all of the reality. To show the whole reality means to go beyond photographs.

Curiously enough, although some novels and plays, attempting to overcome this problem, have used the device of repeating scenes from the viewpoint of various participants, modern art and science have not shown an equal concern with this problem of showing a more rounded reality than is otherwise displayable.[5]

Ultimately, such problems force us to consider the nature of knowledge and the nature of reality. In this sense Plato was the first of a long line of philosophers to grapple with the definition of the real. As was implied above, metaphysics, that branch of philosophy that treats of first principles and of the relation of universals to particulars, bears most directly on the problem outlined here. Metaphysics has always received a great deal of attention from the theologians, because they, above all, have the problem of explaining what cannot be seen or grasped in the ordinary way by the senses. But the study of metaphysics, in its fatal fascination with the teleological doctrine of causation, became hopelessly entangled with religious controversies and thus lost its usefulness. As Baron Bowen of Colwood is reputed to have said in the last century, "A metaphysician is a man who goes into a dark cellar at midnight without a light looking for a black cat that is not there." It is hard for metaphysics to recover from *that* indictment; besides, *my* black cats *are* there. It is just that they do not show up in the photographs. What do I call my nonphotographable black cats in a world not much disposed to think in metaphysical terms? We are just not used to thinking in the terms I want us to. The mind-set of our age makes us see other shapes and forms.

Consider the most traditional symbol of international relations, the one artists frequently use for dust jackets and "brochures": the chessboard. The image is one of chessmen arrayed in opposition, with some pieces, like the knights, capable of intricate moves and some pieces, like the queen, able to bring paralyzing power to bear. This image is highly useful and relevant to a description of important truths about international relations, including how shrewd planning can pay off, how brutal power can win the day, and so on. It also is very good for showing the adversarial nature of a two-power confrontation. But to satisfy my needs as I have described them, I must be able to have a large number of players in a chess game simultaneously, some lending each other pieces, while other players influence the game drastically by making no moves at all, or no moves until the others are exhausted. Perhaps the game play will be heavily influenced by some new pieces called technological advances, inserted at random intervals, whose properties are uncertain.

Where the standard chess game is a stylized confrontation, with each antagonist responding to the other in abstract, uniform moves set according to rules each player must concur in and which neither can alter, my nonconventional chess game would have comparatively odd rules. The rules would have to provide for some players who are in the game from the start and others who enter at various times and depart before the game is played out. There would be pieces and rules that would vary in time and with the perceptions of the players, and objectives that would not always be clearly defined. (In this game a stalemate might be preferred to a checkmate.) Even the list of opponents would not always be clearly known. At times, before the game could begin, the players would have to decide who they were really playing against—who their enemies were.

To find ways to describe a reality as complex as this one, the discussion has to range quite widely. On the one hand it must include some odd-sounding questions, simple to phrase if not to answer: Who decides who should be enemies? Must every nation select some enemies? Is this done by mutual agreement, on a bilateral basis? (What would that mean in a multilateral world, such as actually exists?) Do some nations "naturally" acquire more enemies than others? How do they manage this feat?

On the other hand, the discussion has to dwell on some very complicated issues, difficult even to phrase clearly, plus others easier to express but constantly in dispute from ancient times — whether human beings are aggressive by nature, for example, and whether free will exists in any meaningful sense.

Apart from what may remain in controversy from lack of convincing evidence, this problem involves both mind-set and vocabulary. Consider a large number of nation-states, each existing in a "present" (as certified by clock and calendar), with certain prevailing intellectual styles of comprehension, but also each living by the truths of its own past and in the fear and hope of a future with contours or makeup that are largely or importantly unique to itself. In a multilateral state system such as we have, any conference these states hold or any communication they make with each other has dimensions that a photograph of the conference or a transcript of their communication will not reveal. Each lives in its own "universe of discourse" and is always preoccupied with a nation-particular view of reality. Each perceives its neighbors within a total system with all its parts, as neighbors in an infinite regression: once removed, twice removed, thrice removed. In such an environment, enmity becomes a highly relational quality, with dimensions reaching forward and backward in time (but not necessarily on a common time scale for all participants), and with dimensions reaching sideways and backwards rather than merely oriented frontally as the conventional chess figure or symbol suggests.

The image used of the present that can be photographed, as contrasted with the multidimensional (metaphysical) aspects of reality, is a fair indication of the range of problems that must be confronted here. A "photograph" of a crisis or war situation, like a chess game, shows two opponents already in an antagonistic relationship. To understand how that antagonism comes to be, it is necessary to probe more deeply.

We come at this point to the four cardinal principles model, as a first cut at trying to provide a description of the international environment and the parameters of national choice. Of the four principles of the model, two have to do with the perception of a situation and two have to do with its operational handling. The perceptual principles, which are an attempt to post a graphic warning about the need to remain aware that we cannot "photograph" the full dimensions of reality, are called *third-party influences* and *past-future linkages*. Third-party influences as principle warns us that in a multilateral system no relationship can be truly or solely bilateral. Past-future linkages as principle reminds us that every nation confronts the "same" problem from a different background and experience. As to the two operational principles, *counterbalancing national interests* refers to sets (usually pairs) of alternatives decision makers choose between, and the *conservation of enemies* describes the principle that guides a prudent nation in making its choices.

The principle of counterbalancing national interests incorporates a number of assumptions. It assumes at the outset that there *is* some alternative to every important national interest included as an element in any nation's foreign policy. According to this hypothesis, a "reserve team" of interests has been rejected, put on the shelf for some shorter or longer time period. We can think of every nation having such a shelf of interests it is not pursuing, but could pursue if its decision makers changed their minds, provided they changed their perception of the problem they confront.

The reason for the name "counterbalancing interests" is that the interest choices that heavily influence the enmity-friendship relationship with other nations are often in fairly even counterbalance, with a plus and a minus on either side of the equation. The alternatives that comprise each pair of counterbalancing interests usually reflect or imply opposite courses of action, however, so the concept of counterbalancing interests, while incorporating some of the features economists include in the idea of "opportunity costs," is a somewhat broader proposition.

Rarely is one counterbalancing interest worth trading in for its alternative (or opposite) when looked at in merely bilateral terms. What strikes the eye then is the status quo: the inertia that makes the balance of pluses and minuses seem fixed. It is only in a multilateral context that momentum is really imparted to the system. To refer to our case illustration, Britain saw no real need to adjust its enmities with either France or Russia until Germany's policies put those relations with France or Russia into a different context. Altered perception played a key role.

This is a highly important point that will be met again and again. The most important effect of third-party influences is that they induce a reappraisal of bilateral enmities, the configuration of which can be altered through a shift in the counterbalancing interests of one party or the other, thereby reducing or changing or conserving enemies, as the British did in the decade ending in 1907.

The very fact that one set of alternative or counterbalancing interests has been rejected at any one time tells us that at the moment of decision they were considered of lesser utility than the ones actually chosen for implementation. Such choices for and against the alternatives were made initially through some analysis (either sober or cliché-ridden) that assumed that other nations would make specific choices among their own counterbalancing interests. Suppose that preliminary judgment proved false? Or suppose it proved true at the time but was no longer true? In principle, the "swap," or substitution, of a counterbalancing interest by any significant player must call forth a reexamination of counterbalancing interest options on the part of all the players. When the United States in the 1970s began to alter its policy toward China, Japan at first complained of inadequate prior consultation, of the "shock" stemming from the U.S. action. Nevertheless,

Japan soon outstripped the United States in its rapprochement with China, a development that in turn helped put pressure on the United States to move further in the same direction so as to prevent divergent policies between America and its Japanese ally.

Any alternative chosen for implementation has advantages and disadvantages. So does the alternative that for the time being is rejected. The advantages of the chosen alternative and the disadvantages of the rejected alternative are not, of course, the same; so four distinct values are therefore involved in each choice or pair of counterbalancing interests.

The primary disadvantage of the 1950s-1960s policy of active opposition by the United States toward the People's Republic was that it freed the Soviet Union from substantial worry about China. Once attitudes changed and the United States moved to formal recognition of China, the primary disadvantage was the problem of maintaining sufficient disassociation from China's obvious wish to enlist the United States in its anti-"polar bear" (anti-Soviet) club. In other words, the disadvantages of the alternatives were not mirror images. These remarks are made, of course, from the vantage point of a single nation looking out at the system.

This point can be clarified more fully by examining a problem area from a systems point of view, using a larger matrix. Consider Iran in this fashion. What is the value, plus or minus, to the United States if Iran is an ally? What is the value to the Soviet Union? What is the value to the United States if Iran is an enemy? To the Soviet Union? What is the value to the United States if Iran is neutral? To the Soviet Union? All these values are different. To sketch in the total system would increase such a value matrix to very much greater proportions. China could be added, for instance. What is the value to China if Iran is an enemy or ally or neutral vis-à-vis the United States? And so on.

This, then, abstractly considered, is how assessments and reassessments of alternatives can and frequently do take place. Whether the process operates effectively and what value nations will assign to their choices is another question. There, a great deal must be known before anything is known at all. The individual variations among nations "playing" this "game" are substantial. Each one views the problem through its own set of lenses, each with its own distortions, as was brought out in the discussion of past-future linkages. If one nation's past differs significantly from another's, its interpretation of the present, as it prepares for the future, will be different, too. So it is necessary to keep in mind, constantly, that the game rules and the individual player peculiarities are two different things.

Nowhere are these differences more marked and their effects more fateful than when it comes to the collecting of enemies, the phenomenon highlighted by the fourth cardinal principle, the conservation of enemies.

Just as there is no built-in compulsion that makes every nation automatically reassess its counterbalancing interests when some other nation makes a
shift, neither is there some fail-safe system that shorts out the action if an im-
prudently large number of enemies is being collected. What can be said,
generalizing about the game rather than particularizing about individual
players, is that the unwritten and implied rules of the game center on the
question of contouring the enmity encountered. If the players are equally
skilled, the tension level should remain steady.

Unlike some phenomena in international relations, this redistribution of
enmity can be visualized most effectively as a zero-sum game. What seems
to cause a nation to change its policies toward one set of states is that it
already has run into significant opposition in its policies toward other
states. To persist in policies that cause unfriendly relations with a large
number of other states is highly dangerous, so each player feels compelled
to decrease its "share" of the total enmity. The normal logic of such situations is to single out states that are only partly disposed to be enemies and
make enough adjustments to make them friends: say 60-40, converted to
40-60. Less frequently a nation will do what the British did before World
War I: come to terms with old enemies because of the appearance of new
enemies.

To illustrate this way of visualizing the relationships, consider Figures 3
and 4. They show, for crucial stages of the case study of Chapter 4, how we
could try to explain with this model what happened following 1901 and
1907. Figures 3 and 4, in contrast with the conventional forms used in
Figures 1 and 2, attempt to illustrate a zero-sum system of enmity
redistributed through policy actions.

The cardinal principles model sketched out above represents only one
theory about the international system and environment. By providing an
explicit model (what Erich Fromm calls a "frame of orientation"), the principles are intended to illuminate some essential features of a very complex
chess game. They attempt to explain some of the fundamental behavior
observable in the system and in the foreign policy decisions made in the
various capitals. These four principles are not intended to tell us everything
of value about international behavior, but they do point to its most important parts. An operational principle such as counterbalancing national interests accommodates a good deal of data and illustrates a complex process
quite vividly. Similarly, the assumption behind the principle of conservation of enemies, that a more or less "fixed" amount of hostility is
redistributed through substitutions by players of alternative (and hitherto
reserved) national interests, accommodates much of the data and helps us
visualize relationships. Whether the model is "true" is ultimately a question
that turns on whether it accommodates more of the data than some alter-

Figure 3. European Alliances and Alignments, 1901
(pentagonal format).

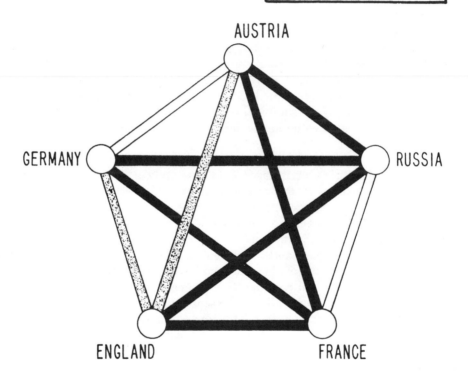

RUSSIA, LIKE FRANCE, IS
"MORE BURDENED";
ENGLAND IS NEXT WITH
NO FRIENDS AND TWO
ENEMIES

AUSTRIA

GERMANY

RUSSIA

ENGLAND

FRANCE

■ Predominantly opposed ("bad" relations).
□ Predominantly common ("good" relations).
▓ Mixed ("fair" relations).

Figure 4. European Alliances and Alignments, 1907
(pentagonal format).

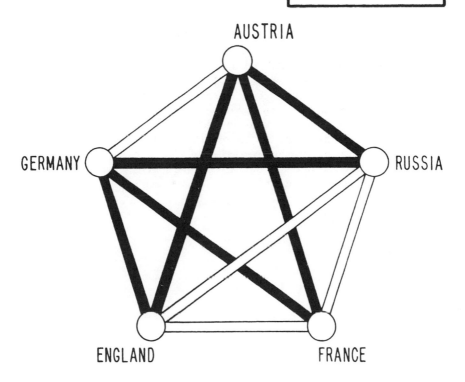

ENGLAND UTILIZES
COUNTERBALANCING
INTERESTS OF
FRANCE AND RUSSIA
TO CHANGE THE
BALANCE OF HOSTILITY

AUSTRIA

GERMANY

RUSSIA

ENGLAND

FRANCE

■ Predominantly opposed ("bad" relations).
□ Predominantly common ("good" relations).

native model. It is presented here to provide a "first cut," a point of view for clarifying ideas about how decisions are made and how the state system operates. If these principles are used consistently, it ought to be possible to comprehend much of what is done by the players and the general aim in the game they play.

This chapter, like Chapter 5, raises questions about the perception of relationships, of cause and effect, and of what is real; because of this, Chapter 7 will deal with the problems involved in the perception of reality. Once that is accomplished, each of the four cardinal principles can be examined at greater length.

NOTES

1. Agatha Christie, *Dead Man's Folly* (New York: Pocket Books, 1961), p. 40.
2. Karl von Clausewitz, *On War*, ed. and trans. Michael Howard and Peter Paret (Princeton, N.J.: Princeton University Press, 1976), p. 606.
3. Einstein quoted by Robert Jervis, *Perception and Misperception in International Politics* (Princeton, N.J.: Princeton University Press, 1976), p. 166, from Errol Harris, *Hypothesis and Perception* (London: Allen and Unwin, 1970), p. 121.
4. Frank H. Simonds and Brooks Emeny, *The Great Powers in World Politics* (New York: American Book Company, 1935).
5. Ryûnosuke Akutagawa's *Rashômon*, one of the most famous of Japanese short stories (and films), is a notable exception.

7

PERCEPTION
AND REALITY

We begin with the observation that if [elementary] particles didn't interact with each other, things would be incredibly simple. Physicists would like such a world because then they could calculate the behavior of all particles easily (if physicists in such a world existed, which is a doubtful proposition). Particles without interactions are called *bare particles*, and they are purely hypothetical creations; they don't exist.

Douglas R. Hofstadter[1]

Two points raised earlier are fundamental to any inquiries about enmity. Enmity as a phenomenon is real; even if its causes are not entirely clear, it is an objective fact. Yet, part of the enmity policy makers encounter may be simply the product of their own thoughts. Such thoughts, leading to policy actions, can produce enmity where it did not truly exist before. Germany's high seas fleet, which in British eyes had been built to challenge the Pax Britannica, was really the product of a virile and unrestrained national pride. Any other two nations might have acted and reacted differently, and in the process kept the tension level lower.

So there is reality: the state system as it in fact exists, regardless of whether decision makers in individual nations understand its workings and regardless of the fashion of an age in describing those workings. There is also perception.

Three levels of perception bear on the problem. The first level is intellectual-professional, where viewpoints distinguishing different major professional groups from one another prevail, shown in Chapter 2, where the biologists, the psychologists, and the psychoanalysts address questions of free will and discuss whether or not there are instincts. The second level is national, where viewpoints on problems are heavily influenced by national cultures and diverse national experiences. The third level is universal or quasi-universal, where viewpoints are distinguished by the "spirit of the age."

Starting with the intellectual-professional level makes it possible to approach Graham T. Allison's observations about decision making from a different angle. One of Allison's models implies that individuals advocate the departmental or career interests they need to protect. Warner R. Schilling, however, argues that "divergent responsibilities are built into the structure of government."

There is a subtle difference in emphasis here, and it concerns a critical point. Allison directs attention toward selfish interests; Schilling directs it toward collegial duty. If a military officer of the United States works relentlessly for larger military appropriations, what description should be given of that officer's actions? If a U.S. Air Force officer urges a B-1 bomber system, how should *that* be described? Are these officers motivated by selfish interest or collegial duty? Perhaps even these terms are not quite right; it may be appropriate to ask how such individuals perceive and conceptualize the issues.

For example, if one starts with the typical intellectual approach of the military to U.S. national security problems and then compares it with the typical approach of State Department officials, significant differences emerge. These differences center on capability analysis, with the military, in estimating the "threat," stressing much more order-of-battle data, while the diplomats tend to a more rounded and complete assessment going well beyond the merely military aspect of the problem. (This point is treated at length in Chapter 17.) Since the military, though, is charged with preparing adequate forces to cope with enemy forces, it is not at all surprising that it takes a hardware-oriented view, since that is the military "allocation of responsibility." Military people are supposed to worry about that particular part of the national security problem, and they do. They may do so to the point of exaggerating the effects of the enemy's hardware, because by focusing on order-of-battle data they tend to ignore or pass lightly over some factors that must go into a full assessment of the situation. A military officer's preoccupation about the enemy can easily sound like "If he can, he will." Is this behavior self-serving, or is it the natural result of having an institutionally oriented point of view? It is more instructive to see it as an illustration of the effects of perspective.

We saw earlier that Karl von Clausewitz insisted on the need for a point of view. But there are also penalties attached. To emphasize one part of a problem tends to involve ignoring other parts. As Thomas S. Kuhn observes in his highly provocative book *The Structure of Scientific Revolutions*,

one of the things a scientific community acquires with a paradigm [an overall conceptualization or generalization about facts and relationships that achieves currency] is a criterion for choosing problems. . . . A paradigm can . . . even insulate the community from those socially important problems that are not reducible to the puzzle form, because they cannot be stated in terms of the conceptual and instrumental tools the paradigm supplies. . . .[2]

Illustrating Kuhn's point, a couple of decades ago or so, when American political scientists began to take being "scientific" seriously, certain problems fairly predictably began to be ignored or downgraded. At the height of the popularity of the new approach, which coincided with the maximum involvement of the United States in the Vietnam War, the American Political Science Association's annual meeting in Chicago contained over a hundred panels on professional topics. But not a single regular panel was actually devoted to the "soft" policy issues raised by that war!

This is not to suggest that the "scientific" approaches are devoid of useful or significant insights but that, in ignoring certain kinds of emphases, they also revealed strong cultural biases. Consider, in view of the American fondness for mechanical flow diagrams and "input-output" comparisons, how well the following contemporary approaches in the United States fit American biases: game theory, integration theory, cybernetics and communications theory, and international power and conflict systems theory.[3]

The same phenomena occur at the second, or national, level, where background differences of culture, geographical location, and historical experience often produce significant differences in appreciation of events beyond national frontiers.

In the conceptual phase of a foreign policy, as the three questions are asked, the answers to which determine the choice of content, this distinction becomes of critical importance. Recall that these questions sequentially ask (1) what "we" want the world to look like at the end of the period contemplated, (2) who can be expected to help or hinder if that particular scenario future situation is sought, and (3) what will be the expected net national cost of achieving the envisaged result. The answers given to each of these questions vary depending on how the policy makers visualize the world, and the whole analysis by which the policy is chosen is influenced decisively by the degree to which the national perception is realistic.

The most fundamental mistake at this level of perception would be to assume that identical situations normally look identical to decision makers from various national backgrounds. A number of readers of Morton H. Halperin's manuscript on *Bureaucratic Politics and Foreign Policy*[4] (see Chapter 5) remarked that its observations about bureaucratic politics and foreign policy could readily have been made about the in-fighting in most large American corporations. In their opinion Halperin was describing *American* behavior in structured group situations as much as, or more than, he was describing foreign policy.

It is not accidental that Richard A. Falk[5] and Emery Reves[6] are American authors, since a great deal of the "formula-to-save-the-world" literature is produced in the United States and read primarily by Americans, for reasons worth thinking about. When Harold Nicolson, quoted in Chapter 4, compared the Germans with the English, he said, "I know we [British] think it funny, frightfully funny, that the German should be so sensitive, but we must remember that the Americans are also sensitive; they are very much closer to the Germans than we are."[7] Since most Americans think themselves much closer to the English ("two peoples separated by a common language"), this thought may come as a shock.

Cultural differences are reflected in many ways. In his book *How Real Is Real?*, Paul Watzlawick remarks:

In every culture, there is a very specific distance that two strangers will maintain between each other in a face-to-face encounter. In Central and Western Europe and in North America, this is the proverbial arm's length. . . . In Mediterranean countries and in Latin America, the distance is considerably shorter. Thus, in an encounter between a North American and a South American, both try to take up what they consider the right distance. The Latin moves up; the Northerner backs away to what he unconsciously feels is the proper distance; the Latin, feeling uncomfortably distant, moves closer, etc. Both feel that the other is somehow behaving wrongly. . . .[8]

Otto Klineberg, a social psychologist, gives a second illustration of the effects of culture and national perception, from another part of the world:

A Japanese will smile when he is amused, but he will also smile on certain other occasions: for example, it is customary for a servant to smile when he is scolded by his master. A smile is the appropriate response under those conditions, and serves the purpose of smoothing over an otherwise unpleasant situation. To a Westerner who employs a Japanese, such a response may be infuriating; he interprets it to mean that the servant is making fun of him. . . . Among the Chinese, it is customary to open the eyes wide as a sign of anger, and to stick out the tongue in surprise.[9]

Edwin Reischauer, in his book *The Japanese*, describes the distinctive fashion in which the Japanese conduct labor relations and the way they reach foreign policy decisions. The emphasis is on reaching consensus, avoiding confrontation, and saving face. Much discussion occurs through intermediaries. This is in marked contrast with practice in the United States, where the "action" is essentially around a conference table, even though informal contacts do occur.[10]

Language is a primary expression of culture in more than one sense. The structure of our language not only reflects our sense of values but indeed structures our thinking.

We are most of us aware that certain expressions do not really translate. Less well understood, however, are the important constraints the diverse structures of languages place on understanding of relationships and on patterns of thought. Linguists are quite aware that languages represent and project philosophical outlooks. H. A. Gleason, Jr., points out that

English speakers can never make a statement without saying something about the number of every object mentioned. This is compulsory, whether it is relevant or not. In Chinese, objects are noted as singular or plural only when the speaker judges the information to be relevant. . . . You may [in some cases] have to learn to think of every action as either completed or incomplete, and to disregard the time of the action unless it has special relevance. . . . In some languages, situations are not analyzed, as they are in English, in terms of an actor and an action. Instead the fundamental cleavage runs in a different direction and cannot be easily stated in English.[11]

Gleason mentions Benjamin L. Whorf's research. Whorf's own study of verbs used in the Hopi Indian language led him to write:

All this . . . is an illustration of how language produces an organization of experience. We are inclined to think of language simply as a technique of expression, and not to realize that language first of all is a classification and arrangement of the stream of sensory experience which results in a certain world-order, a certain segment of the world that is easily expressible by the type of symbolic means that language employs.[12]

Robert A. Hall, Jr., also a linguistics specialist, referring to overinflations of the "Whorfian hypothesis," writes that Whorf is only arguing "that a naive person's attempts at philosophizing and categorizing his experience are likely, if he is not careful, to be mere reflections of the structure of his language."[13] But Georges Mounin goes further. "Every language," he wrote, "has its latent ideology. Each one chooses different aspects of reality, and we see in the universe only what our language points out." The French philologist, Joseph Vendryes, argued that "the habit of always putting the verb in a certain place makes for a certain way of thinking . . . ."[14]

The national differences that language and culture vividly reflect are part of the larger reality of international relations. In considering phenomena from a systems viewpoint, it is important to keep individual national cultural differences in mind. The converse is also true: it is very useful to remember that these cultural differences fundamentally affect how the system is perceived. Either end of the intellectual telescope provides useful perspectives. From a systems viewpoint, the ubiquity of these differences throughout the system is most apparent, rather than specific differences between one national perception and another. In describing the operation of any part of the total system, however, an appropriate stress must be laid on these individual national variations in perception.

We turn now to the third, and perhaps most difficult, level of perception. This level involves very delicate phenomena: the "spirit of an age" and what it calls true or meaningful. These are inherent in the very way people conceptualize and address problems. It will help to start with historical variations in perceptions of the truth.

We have already quoted from Kuhn's widely read book, where he wrote that a paradigm directs thinking and research into certain areas while ruling out others. Robert Jervis remarks on this general point that

the paradigm leads scientists to reject flatly evidence that is fundamentally out of line with the expectations that it generates. An experiment that produces such evidence will be ignored by the scientist who carries it out. If he submits it to a journal the editors will reject it. Even if it is printed, most of his colleagues will pay no heed even if they cannot find any flaws in it.[15]

Kuhn gives a very telling illustration of this tunnel vision effect when he discusses Copernicus and Galileo. The Aristotelian-Ptolemaic explanation of the universe was a highly elaborate and comprehensive theory that prevailed over a long period of time, eventually to be challenged by Nicolas Copernicus (1473-1543) and, more effectively, by Galileo Galilei (1564-1642). Copernicus argued that the earth was one of six (then known) planets that revolved around the sun. Galileo, sometime in the 1590s, accepted the Copernican view. Primarily because of a publication by Galileo in 1613 on sunspots, the Catholic Church issued a decree in 1616 that the Copernican doctrine was "false and absurd" and could not be advocated.

The Church rejected the notion that the earth moved around the sun as only one of several planets[16] because this challenged orthodox religious beliefs. Nonetheless, Galileo persevered. In 1632 he published his *Dialogo . . . sopra i due massimi sistemi* (Dialogue on the Two Chief Systems of the World). Galileo, called before the Roman Inquisition, was forced to plead guilty and deny his findings.[17] Legend has it that, after denying out loud that the earth moved, he added in a whisper as he got up off his knees, *"E pur si muove"* (Nevertheless it does move).

Kuhn, however, relates the "other half" of the story, not about orthodox religious opposition but about pre-Copernican scientific tunnel vision:

Can it conceivably be an accident . . . that Western astronomers first saw change in the previously immutable heavens during the half-century after Copernicus' new paradigm was first proposed? The Chinese, whose cosmological beliefs did not preclude celestial change, had recorded the appearance of many new stars in the heavens at a much earlier date. . . . Nor were sunspots and a new star the only examples of celestial change to emerge in the heavens of Western astronomy immediately after Copernicus. Using traditional instruments, some as simple as a piece of thread, late sixteenth-century astronomers repeatedly discovered that comets wandered at will through the space previously reserved for the immutable planets and stars. The very ease and rapidity with which astronomers saw new things when looking at old objects with old instruments may make us wish to say that, after Copernicus, astronomers lived in a different world. In any case, their research responded as though that were the case.[18]

The nature of an age, then, and its spirit, directly affect perception. The times influence the way people think and what seems real or true or obvious or self-apparent. The mind, if it moves logically and in orderly fashion, cannot by definition leap about intuitively, but if it has been disciplined to think (perform) in patterns, then it must conform to its own system, to its own habits. So it is not just that what we think of as "knowledge" in any one age changes, but also that certain "truths," obvious enough in one age (to one system of thinking), are extinct to another age, which possesses no way of comprehending them.[19]

C. S. Lewis, in a book about medieval modes of thought, wrote:

We are all, very properly, familiar with the idea that in every age the human mind is deeply influenced by the accepted Model of the universe. But there is a two-way traffic; the Model is also influenced by the prevailing temper of mind. We must recognize that what has been called "a taste in universes" is not only pardonable but inevitable. We can no longer dismiss the change of Models as a simple progress from error to truth. No Model is a catalogue of ultimate realities, and none is a mere fantasy. Each is a serious attempt to get in all the phenomena known at a given period and each succeeds in getting in a great many. But also, no less surely, each reflects the prevalent psychology of an age almost as much as it reflects the state of that age's knowledge.[20]

And Einstein, after writing that "physical concepts are free creations of the human mind" rather than "uniquely determined by the external world," went on as follows:

In our endeavor to understand reality we are somewhat like a man trying to understand the mechanism of a closed watch. He sees the face and the moving hands, even hears its ticking, but he has no way of opening the case. If he is ingenious he may form some picture of a mechanism which could be responsible for all the things he observes, but he may never be quite sure his picture is the only one which could explain his observations.[21]

In the same vein Jervis quotes Norwood Hanson, who agrees with Einstein and Clausewitz that "theories . . . constitute a 'conceptual Gestalt.'

A theory is not pieced together from observed phenomena; it is rather what makes it possible to observe phenomena as being of a certain sort."²²

In any given age, some ways of visualizing relationships seem more "natural" than others. It should not be surprising, therefore, unless some fundamental intellectual revolution intervenes, to find building-block approaches to knowledge, where the later theorist builds on the basis of what is already "known." Karl Marx, for example, not only thought in Darwinian terms but was understood in Darwinian terms, in a century accustomed to look at things that way.

This tendency is marked in those extraordinary works of intellectual synthesis that, appearing from time to time, have diverted the world of action from its accustomed orbit by changing perceptions of reality and truth. Immanuel Velikovsky brings out this point as follows:

The theory of evolution dates back to the age of classic Greece. . . . What was new in Darwin's teaching was not the principle of evolution in general but the explanation of its mechanism by natural selection. This was an adaptation to biology of the Malthusian theory about population growing more quickly than the means of existence. Darwin acknowledged his debt to Malthus, whose book he read in 1838. Herbert Spencer and Alfred R. Wallace independently came to the same views as Darwin, and the expression "survival of the fittest" was Spencer's.²³

Charles Darwin himself substantiates Velikovsky's point, calling Spencer's expression more accurate. From there Darwin goes on to discuss what he calls "the struggle for existence."²⁴ Yet if Darwin had not been thinking in Malthusian terms, he might, for instance, have chosen words that would have emphasized how many living things of different species coexist within the same area. He might have called his book The Harmony of Species — leaving an entirely different impression.

The intellectual trail of Karl Marx (1818-1883) and Friedrich Engels (1820-1895) is even more intriguing. The Communist Manifesto's principal axiom, much like Darwin's, is "that the history of all hitherto existing society is the history of class struggles." Dialectical materialism, Marx's method of analyzing phenomena, came from the work of Georg Hegel (1770-1831), with its thesis, antithesis, synthesis. Hegel, in turn, was building on Immanuel Kant (1724-1804). So when Marx took Hegel's dialectic and applied it to what he called the "class struggle," many earlier ideas were his building blocks. It is curious that the nineteenth century became so preoccupied with the idea of struggle, since internationally speaking, it was a relatively peaceful period.

In light of such intellectual developments, it is impossible to avoid a fundamental skepticism about humanity's ability to keep an open mind. Far from being open to ideas of all kinds, at any one moment in its history the human race seems prepared to accept only certain ideas as "self-evident." These ideas directly affect the way relations in the international system are conceptualized and conducted.

As generalizations achieve or lose popularity, the vocabularies in use alter. The very styles of expression change considerably over time. For instance, descriptions of the balance of power that date from the eighteenth century, with its fascination with Newtonian physics and its joy in all things mechanical, were couched in clock or machine terms. Calling it a "balance" is itself a sign of the imagery of early modern times.* In a monarchical age, when rulers were so frequently blood relations, it did not seem strange when Talleyrand spoke of the balance as "a combination of the rights, interests, and the relations of the powers among themselves, *by which Europe seeks to obtain*" a situation in which "a rupture of the established order and of the tranquility of Europe [will be] difficult or impossible."[25] Despite national rivalries Europe could be perceived, whether accurately or not, as united on certain principles.

Any discussion of the nature of reality has to take such changes in style and habits of perceiving relationships into account, not only because of the obvious problem of "translation" of the real meaning, but because what is considered obvious in one age or culture can go unnoticed in another that has a different mind-set.

It is extremely difficult today to grasp why the early Christians were rent by schisms over the "pre-existence" of Jesus. The fiercest politico-religious issues of the third and fourth centuries, which flamed up at the Council of Nicaea and were resolved again in part at the Council of Chalcedon in 451, concerned the nature of the Trinity, which today stirs little attention or controversy in any church councils. On another point, John A. T. Robinson, in his *The Human Face of God*, quotes Neill Hamilton: "There is no way for the convictional structure in which we are working now to *conceive* of a way or a place for Jesus to continue to live literally after having died."[26] This may overstate the point, although it illustrates the problem. Just as it is inconceivable for a contemporary Western person to quarrel about how many angels can dance on the head of a pin, so too it would have been inconceivable to a medieval person that seemingly solid matter is mostly empty space.

A modern reader of Francis Bacon's 1605 remarks about Machiavelli can too casually allow their real meaning to slip by, because they were addressed to a different age. Bacon wrote, "We are much beholden to Machiavelli and others, that write what men do, and not what they ought to do."[27]

---

*The idea of the balance of power can be traced back to at least the fourth century B.C., but the modern term for it is no older than the sixteenth century.

Bacon was referring to the general literary trend of the day, which was filled with homilies on the community of mankind and the universal nature of values, but he was praising as realistic a point of view that in many respects must seem extremely cynical or coldblooded or inadequate to the modern reader, who knows where the advice Machiavelli offered can easily lead. Machiavelli wrote that a prince "ought to have no other aim or thought, nor select anything else for his study, than war and its rules and discipline; for this is the sole art that belongs to him who rules."[28]

As early as 1580 Montaigne, in his essay "Of What Is True and What Is False," wrote, "Our minds become accustomed to things from the familiarity of our eyes with them, and feel no wonder, and ask no questions about the causes of things which they continually behold."[29] Montaigne did not go far enough; it is not just that we become accustomed to what we see but that we grow used to thinking about some things in particular ways. Some things we do not see at all.

August Comte (1798-1857), who is not read much nowadays but who even a few decades ago retained much impact, argued that knowledge developed in Western civilization through three (presumably irreversible) stages: theological (fictitious), metaphysical (abstract), and scientific (positive). Of course it was the last stage, the scientific, that Comte considered both permanent and "best," and this stage is still so considered. Today it reaches what many regard as its highest expression when its precepts can be expressed in completely dispassionate, push-pull, input-output computer language. At that point the scientific is joined to the mathematical, which are then "programmed" into a "system." Try bucking that!

And yet the "scientific" way of thinking, like any connected set of thoughts, is restrictive and constrictive, and represents the mind fashions of a particular day just as surely as clothes reflect the latest fashions in dress. Contemporary fashions of thought cannot be more "real" than other systems unless they take "everything" that is true and relevant into account. As we have tried to show, however, any system of ideas almost by definition leaves something out, and each system makes use of some mental shorthand constructs. Consider John A. T. Robinson's quotation of Van Peursen:

Van Peursen neatly illustrates the difference [in thinking] by comparing the way in which medieval man viewed the soul and modern man thinks of the intelligence quotient: "An I.Q. is nothing in itself; it is not a hidden entity in our heads; it is merely the result of certain tests." Yet the reality it refers to is no less real for that.[30]

Intelligence quotients and neutrons and atoms seem much more real to modern people than ghosts and souls. Numbers now seem more exact (and therefore much more true), even if the properties of numbers are merely features given to them by the consent and design of the human mind—which is, after all, what also creates art. Like the broom of the Sorcerer's Apprentice, numbers take on a life of their own.

In our age numbers also seem more real than the story Charles Dickens tells in *The Christmas Carol* of Ebenezer Scrooge and the three ghosts: Christmas Past, Christmas Present, Christmas Yet to Come. Yet Dickens's point is quite fundamental in probing the full dimensions of reality. He tells us that the "present" is bordered by the past and the future. In every present moment the person sees that present through his or her past experience and communicates about it in the accepted thought "language" of the time (in terms of souls or in terms of IQs), judging the present finally in the light of what he or she thinks will follow if a given decision is made. As I argued in Chapter 6, only the fleeting present can be photographed, but all three dimensions are part of the total reality.

How much should we believe in "ghosts," and how much only in what can be photographed? Most of us in this age are more ready to believe in contemporary mysteries and miracles than in the mysteries and miracles of other times, because of our conditioning. If we find it relatively easy to believe that a solid piece of wood is really energy in motion, since science assures us that this is correct, we are children of our age.

The observation most fundamental to this chapter is that, while we are ingenious in thinking up propositions and theories about the world as we see it, what we see is much more conditioned than we tend to believe. Not conditioned by the actual circumstances or environment, as Skinner would have it, but by the way we view reality.

Our views are conditioned by the groups we associate with. They are strongly conditioned by our national experiences. Because the people who come to Einstein's watch and listen to its ticking and see its hands move come from different national backgrounds and cultural settings, they still often come to diverse conclusions about it. This is the critical variable that determines which one of the universal national security models, whether the cardinal principles or the other models elaborated in Part Four, seems most realistic. Each such model provides a plausible way of explaining the clock, but at any one time the explanations will not seem of equal merit to any two different nations. Finally, our views are significantly shaped by what "everyone knows" in a given age: by Darwinism, Marxism, and so on. These social paradigms have a great hold on us, more than we might think.

For these and more reasons, people do not keep open minds in any literal sense. Whether the evidence is there or not, they do not avoid judgments on major problems in their environment—judgments intended to predict the future consequences of present actions. Judgments are made, all the time and by everyone, because without such judgments no actions can be taken.

Erich Fromm explains the point from a rich psychoanalytic experience:

The impressive fact is that we do not find any culture in which there does not exist such a frame of orientation. Or any individual either. Often an individual may disclaim having any such overall picture and believe that he responds to the various phenomena and incidents of life from case to case, as his judgment guides him. But it can easily be demonstrated that he takes his own philosophy for granted, because to him it is only common sense, and he is unaware that all his concepts rest upon a commonly accepted frame of reference.[31]

In yet another place, Fromm states quite directly: "Man has a vital interest in retaining his frame of orientation. His capacity to act depends on it, and in the last analysis, his sense of identity."[32]

It is for these reasons that we have argued that, to understand policy questions, it is not enough to study bureaucratic interests and procedures and compile facts such as voting records and patterns or to survey events data in the media. All of these activities can contribute to what we "know," but they are not sufficient. We must also ask what a particular people expect the future to be like and why, especially the decision makers. We must study their view of reality and how closely it conforms to the nature of the international system.

With these thoughts in mind, we shall turn to an elaboration of the cardinal principles as a prelude to assessing other ways of viewing the universe.

NOTES

1. Douglas R. Hofstadter, *Gödel, Escher, Bach: An Eternal Golden Braid* (New York: Basic Books, 1979), p. 142.

2. Thomas S. Kuhn, *The Structure of Scientific Revolutions*, 2d ed. (Chicago: University of Chicago Press, 1970), p. 37.

3. The listing is the table of contents, less the introduction and conclusion, of Robert J. Lieber's lucid survey of the newer emphases in his *Theory and World Politics* (London: George Allen & Unwin, 1973).

4. Morton H. Halperin, *Bureaucratic Politics and Foreign Policy* (Washington, D.C.: Brookings Institution, 1974).

5. Richard A. Falk, *A Study of Future Worlds* (New York: Free Press, 1975).

6. Emery Reves, *The Anatomy of Peace* (New York: Harper, 1945).

7. Harold Nicholson, *National Character and National Policy*, Montague Burton Lecture, 1938, University College, Nottingham. Reprinted in Frederick H. Hartmann, ed., *Readings in International Relations* (New York: McGraw-Hill, 1952), p. 48.

8. Paul Watzlawick, *How Real Is Real? Confusion, Disinformation, Communication* (New York: Vintage Books, 1976), p. 7.

9. Otto Klineberg, *The Human Dimension in International Relations* (New York: Holt, Rinehart, Winston, 1964), p. 136.

10. Edwin Reischauer, *The Japanese* (Cambridge, Mass.: Harvard University Press, 1977).

11. H. A. Gleason, Jr., *An Introduction to Descriptive Linguistics*, rev. ed. (New York: Holt, Rinehart, Winston, 1961), pp. 7-8.

12. Quoted by Robert A. Hall, Jr., *Introductory Linguistics* (Philadelphia: Chilton Books, 1964), p. 402.

13. Ibid., pp. 402-3.

14. Richard Mayne, *The Europeans* (New York: Library Press, 1972), pp. 61-62.

15. Robert Jervis, *Perception and Misperception in International Politics* (Princeton, N.J.: Princeton University Press, 1976), p. 156. Jervis cites Michael Polanyi, "Commentary," in A. C. Crombie, ed., *Scientific Change* (New York: Basic Books, 1963), p. 376.

16. For an excellent account of the history of the progress in medieval thinking about astronomy, see George Abell, *Exploration of the Universe*, 2d ed. (New York: Holt, Rinehart, Winston, 1969), chaps. 2 and 3.

17. Galileo's *Dialogue*, as well as Copernicus's *De Revolutionibus* and Johann Kepler's *Epitome*, remained on the Index of Prohibited Books until 1835.

18. Kuhn, *Structure of Scientific Revolutions*, pp. 116-17.

19. Any modern reader, doubting this, should read James G. Frazer, *The Golden Bough* (New York: Macmillian, 1922).

20. C. S. Lewis, *The Discarded Image* (London: Cambridge University Press, 1967), p. 222.

21. Albert Einstein and Leopold Infeld, *The Evolution of Physics* (New York: Simon & Schuster, 1950), p. 33.

22. Jervis, *Perception and Misperception*, p. 170, from Norwood Hanson, *Patterns of Discovery* (London: Cambridge University Press, 1965), p. 90.

23. Immanuel Velikovsky, *Earth in Upheaval* (New York: Pocket Books, 1955), pp. 212-13. Velikovsky, incidentally, takes great issue with Darwin's assumption that evolution occurred in very small steps over eons of time.

24. Charles Darwin, *The Origin of Species* (New York: Mentor Books, New American Library, 1958), p. 74. The sixth-edition text apparently used in this version appeared in January 1872. (The first edition was published in November 1859.)

25. G. Pallain, ed., *The Correspondence of Prince Talleyrand and King Louis XVIII during the Congress of Vienna* (New York: Plenum, 1881), pp. xv-xvi. Italics added.

26. John A. T. Robinson, *The Human Face of God* (London: SCM Press, 1973), p. 23, quoting Neill Hamilton, *Jesus for a No-God World* (Philadelphia: Westminster Press, 1969), p. 182.

27. Francis Bacon, *Advancement in Learning*, Second book, pp. xxi, 9.

28. Nicolo Machiavelli, *The Prince*, trans. W. K. Marriott (New York: Dutton, Everyman's Library, 1940), p. 111.

29. *The Essays of Montaigne*, trans. George B. Ives, 3 vols. (New York: Heritage Press, 1946), vol. 1, p. 241.

30. Robinson, *The Human Face of God*, p. 184, from John Bowden and James Richmond, *A Reader in Contemporary Theology*, p. 121.

31. Erich Fromm, *The Anatomy of Human Destructiveness* (New York: Fawcett Crest, 1973), p. 259.

32. Ibid., p. 223.

Part III

CONTOURING ENMITY:
THE CARDINAL
PRINCIPLES MODEL

8

THIRD-PARTY INFLUENCES

A superpower like the United States does have unique, though far from unlimited, capacities to influence events throughout the world. . . . [That] world extends beyond [our] shores, and Americans and America itself live in that world. We have nevertheless been made abundantly aware of the tendency of our national leaders to slip into expansive habits of interpretation concerning the real meaning to ourselves of threats that are quite remote in space. . . .

Bernard Brodie, *War and Politics*[1]

We have seen that once it has formed a theory the tidy mind rejects what is "irrelevant" and arranges the rest to buttress the argument; but we have also seen that we cannot do without theory. Facts and figures mean nothing until assembled in some combination. True scientists always have to bear in mind that they may be wrong. Any theory is therefore by definition tentative, but there must be one if an analysis is to get anywhere at all. In Chapters 1 through 7, and especially in Chapters 5 and 6, we have been steadily developing such a theory. Now its assumptions should be summarized, and then elaborated upon.

Our theory assumes that change does take place in international relations and that the spirit and concern, and even the way of visualizing relationships, in one age is not merely a reiteration of what has gone before. The Greek city-states have indeed passed away as a system; their characteristics will not likely be repeated again in exactly the same form. Our contemporary system has similarities, but it *is* different. So change can occur and does occur, even radically and quickly, as with the change in the law of the sea in modern times, with its drastic shift away from narrow-width sea frontiers. In parallel, it is conceivable that today's critical issues, such as energy, pollution, and nuclear weapons, which transcend national frontiers and the starkest implications of which may pose the choice between life and extinction, will some day induce humanity to unite and solve its problems in peace and concord on a universal basis. It is possible that conflict will be drastically reduced by cooperation and good will and that world enmity will decrease steadily until it vanishes.

The thesis of this book is not that such developments are impossible, but only that they are unlikely from the evidence so far. Never has the political organization of the world been so fragmented. Even colonial imperialism, detested by its victims, imposed far more unity on the world of states. Looked at in economic terms, more and more of the peoples of the earth are less and less impressed with the general rise in well-being that unhampered international trade is supposed to bring in its train for everyone. Instead, among the poorer nations, there is shriller emphasis on husbanding scarce natural resources, to prevent their waste and consumption in the factories and furnaces of the rich nations. The demand is more strident from the poorer nations to divide up the resources of the sea among a steadily increasing world population. But while scientists warn of the potential effects of the accelerating use of fossil fuels on the polar ice cap, burgeoning populations clamoring for industrialization may be the prelude to even more of the same.

Cooperation is possible to solve all of these problems, but cooperation does not seem to be the primary or sole human reaction. Whatever humanity's hopes, the steadily mounting supply of armaments around the world is an accurate clue to its fears. People believe in the reality of enmity.

Our theory says that, whatever the nature of a human being may truly be, the separation of people from one another into groups that today are called nation-states represents preferred or customary behavior. The political organization of humankind into larger numbers of ever smaller units shows few signs of reversal. Each such state remains, as a first order of importance, self-centered and concerned for its own rights and advantages, its interests. It negotiates with other nations not for the universal interest (if one can be defined) but for its own interests. Suspicious of others, it cooperates basically for two reasons: (1) because it must, if it wishes reciprocal treatment, or (2) because it fears one group and therefore needs the support of others. Neither of these two reasons implies altruistic love.

The cardinal principles model, to which we now turn, accepts the reality of enmity. It focuses in its four principles on how states control (or fail to control) the amount of enmity faced. Where the first two principles focus on the differences among states that account so largely for the variety in perceptions of the power problem, the second two concentrate on the operational reactions of states in their decisions affecting policy, especially those contouring enmity. In this chapter we shall explore *third-party influences*, and in the next, *past-future linkages*. The third and fourth principles will be the subjects of Chapters 10 and 11.

Third-party influences have to do with the effects of location. Location defines one's neighbors. It defines a whole set of primary spatial relationships, for it establishes which third parties are seen as important as one contemplates dealing with a particular neighbor. If that neighbor is at the "front," other neighbors constitute the flanks and rear (and a change of "front" is also a change in flanks and rear). A study of third-party influences looks at these circumstances and at how states address these circumstances. In a world of sovereign states, most states are aware that if they deal with a neighbor (or set policy) as though neither had flanks or a rear, or as though "fronts" never change, they may be committing suicide.

It follows that some amount of 360-degree awareness is a first condition for success, even for survival, in a multilateral world: by definition, every state is " surrounded." With some states the surrounding is more immediate and obvious from the point of view of enmity. Large oceans in place of land frontiers can cultivate an illusion that this is not so, especially for states that have abundant sea power. At the reverse extreme, as we pointed out in Chapter 3, few states have land frontiers with other states on a 360-degree periphery. The fact that there are few land-locked states in existence probably illustrates its dangers.

A study of third-party influences is most of all a warning that the world is round, that a bilateral focus and preoccupation is in principle wrong for any state and potentially dangerous as well. In the nuclear age the tendency to ignore this point is pronounced; contemporary theory is much too mechanical and slighting of geography.* No purely bilateral relations can exist in a multilateral world, although bilateral preoccupation comes quite naturally. Americans, for example, typically think of the Soviets as *the* problem. But this tendency should be resisted, because a nation's enemies, as well as its friends, always have neighbors, and these neighbors at their flanks and rear have influence on their policy.

So a study of third-party influences is a study in how states conduct themselves in spatial terms, and particularly how they respond to neighbors (and at what distance). There is nothing foreordained about these reactions; that is, the location does not dictate the policy response. Yet certain tendencies exist. For example, one of the prime operational differences between small powers and great powers is that great powers act in a wider sphere, while small powers are primarily concerned with their own frontiers.

Some small states are especially interesting in that they have survived in highly dangerous locations. States such as Switzerland and Afghanistan, while also possessed of significantly defensive mountain terrain, have survived more by their peoples' wits and determination to remain free than by the security of geography or by power. As Machiavelli once put it, they

---

*For discussion, see Chapter 17. Conversely, from the standpoint of my theory, the difficulty with traditional geopolitics is that it assumed that geography gave more direct clues to policy than I would feel is warranted.

have imitated the fox to cope with the lion. The determined (and adroit) resistance of the Afghans to the Soviet invasion of December 1979 is a case in point. In the terminology of general balance of power theory, such units are called "buffer states." Taking the term literally, they mark the intersection of distinct cultural groups, which indeed is true. Also, their territories are difficult for one neighbor to absorb because other powerful neighbors do not agree to it. So these units remain largely at peace, although rimmed completely by land neighbors.

By contrast, Korea and Belgium, sometimes linked in this category, and each with some sea and some land frontiers, have had far less stable histories; long-suffering Korea has not always kept such strong naval forces as defeated the Japanese invasion off Pusan in 1592. Belgium has the misfortune to be situated on the easily transited north European plain and cannot be protected sufficiently even by a powerful navy. Each has been far from immune to the invasions of neighbors.

Thailand, with mixed sea and land borders, has a history nearer to that of Switzerland or Afghanistan than to that of Korea or Belgium, but Thailand has the great advantage that it has no immediate powerful neighbors.

The modest power of such small states will at least assure an easy answer to one set of decisions that often is the most difficult for great powers and superpowers to make. That set of decisions begins with the question: How wide a sphere should the nation be active in? Bernard Brodie puts the point in the headnote to this chapter: If a nation has the power to pursue policies further afield, at what distance from the home territory should an active concern with events stop? If the world is round, and events anywhere are connected to events everywhere, where should a security-defense line be drawn? How far distant from one's own terrain should troops be deployed? On what grounds and by what rules should such issues be decided?

While such decisions trouble only nations secure enough and powerful enough to extend their commitments significantly beyond their own frontiers, it is those nations that above all the rest cause tensions to develop into wars with serious implications for the rest. So it is worth stressing their problems and behavior.

Such a study quickly reveals quite varied great-power behavior. A great power may be much more ambitious and aggressive or expansive in one period than in another. Great powers also vary in their readiness to send troops into combat far from their national frontiers. It is not clear why these variations exist, but it is clear that possession of great power does not necessarily lead to a vigorous or extreme role. It only permits a greater role.

Some years ago a somewhat cynical analyst pointed out that the Italians, dominated into the nineteenth century by Austria-Hungary, spoke movingly of national freedom. And then, with that achieved, they turned to conquests in Africa! Is the answer that simple? Does a great power, once sufficiently secure at home, go in fairly automatically for adventures abroad? Or does it take the power of some great idea (like "the white man's burden," or the spread of communism, or the defense of freedom) to provide the motive? Why are not all the great powers simultaneously expansive?

What leads a nation in its time to think that an era or century belongs to it and that it must dominate its time? What leads a nation to be willing to pour out its blood and treasure in far-distant places for little tangible reward? How does its perceived opportunity for this kind of domination, and its success or failure, link to its assessment of third-party influences?

An interesting tale is told of Phyrrus in *Plutarch's Lives*. Phyrrus is at leisure when Cineas asks what he plans to do next. The general responds by sketching in a series of proposed conquests, one leading to the next. When all the Mediterranean has in effect been listed, the questioner asks, "And then what, Phyrrus?" And Phyrrus answers, smiling, that he would take his ease. Cineas asks, why then go through such risk and bloodshed to do what they are doing right at the moment?[2] Phyrrus, of course, by such intemperate ambitions, eventually gave his name to history in the expression "Phyrric victory," meaning one too costly to be considered worth winning. Compare this with the early eighteenth-century French general's report to his king after Marlborough's fourth victory: "If God gives us another defeat like this, your Majesty's enemies will be destroyed."

It is often more obvious what causes states who have been cleaving to a neutral or modest role to reverse themselves. Franklin D. Roosevelt made an eloquent and dramatic speech on June 10, 1940; the *New York Times* front pages for that week, with a daily map of the front line in Europe, could hardly keep pace, so rapid was the German advance, so rapid the Anglo-French retreat. The disaster was overwhelming, and Mussolini's intervention completed it. In FDR's words, "The hand that held the dagger has struck it into the back of its neighbor." Seeing these events, FDR denounced any thought that, in a world so dominated by brute force, the United States could exist as a lone island of isolated peace and security. This, he said, would be living out "the nightmare of a people lodged in prison, handcuffed, hungry, and fed through the bars from day to day by the contemptuous, unpitying masters of other continents."

Roosevelt made clear his intention to furnish material aid to friendly European nations. Brodie writes that FDR's actions became "a fatefully important expansion of the concept of American security, one that considerably enlarges the domain over which we will insist that conditions be tolerable in our eyes."[3] A consensus so formed about an area of involvement may endure a long time.

From the standpoint of the cardinal principle of third-party influences, there are really, then, two sets of states: those that, being able, decide to play such a larger role and those that, being either unable or unwilling, do not. To restate the point in terms of the principle, those who play the larger role are necessarily forced, if they are prudent, to consider a much more complete and complex set of third-party relationships. And, since they have the power to deploy at a distance, they have the special problem of deciding when to do so.

To examine third-party influences in action, we shall use four examples: first, Switzerland, a small power literally surrounded by great powers but one which has escaped most threatened disasters; second, France, a great nation with a role that has varied from very large to very modest; third, Russia, a nation that, while suffering much tragedy, can still be said to have benefited enormously from good fortune; fourth, Japan, at a critical moment, debating whether or not to go to war with the United States. With these examples in hand, we shall end the chapter with a look at U.S. threat analysis compared to the assessments by Sweden and Finland, as each copes (or, in the case of the United States, really fails to cope) with the implications of third-party influences.

After German unification in 1871, the Swiss found themselves wedged between four great-power neighbors: France, Italy, Germany, and Austria-Hungary. Since the Austrian frontier is small and truly difficult and Austria's energies were directed elsewhere, that frontier posed very little problem. The Italian frontier was quite literally and drastically downhill — a considerable safety factor. Add to that the essential disinclination of the modern Italians for martial activities. France, preoccupied with a strong Germany after the Franco-Prussian War, was never a threat. But Germany, with easy access across Lake Constance, which forms a significant part of the frontier, was a problem. Since the population of Switzerland is five-sevenths German speaking, the Swiss position after Hitler came to power in 1933 was precarious. The Alps lie across the middle of Switzerland, extending to the south, but the northern rim is as easy to transit as much of Germany. It was no natural barrier.

As Hitler's ambitions began to be fulfilled, and especially after World War II began in 1939, the Swiss felt the full fury of Hitler's anger. Their free press, published in German, was widely read in Germany and blatantly contradicted Hitler's controlled press. When France fell in 1940, the entire 360 degrees of the Swiss border became controlled either directly by Nazi troops (about two-thirds of the total) or by Mussolini's allied troops. The danger had become acute.

Since the Swiss are permanently neutral, by international decree and by their own wish, they could not call upon allies of their own. Their resources for dealing with the threat were limited, but those resources, besides a highly trained armed force, included (1) a long experience with surviving under difficult conditions, (2) a compact and well-integrated elite group, and (3) a bit of blackmail to use against Benito Mussolini.

Items 2 and 3 were the most critical. The elite group, confronted with the dilemma of either publicly controlling the free press, which their own people resisted and which would have simply led to more demands from Hitler, or defying Hitler, which would certainly have led to invasion, found a middle way. They nominally kept the press completely free, and in fact kept it substantially free, through discreet but firm instructions promulgated by the reserve colonels of the Press and Information Office, who were sometimes themselves editors or members of the Swiss parliament, which ultimately supervised the operation. In a compact nation like Switzerland, guidance could be given and implemented with very few violations, avoiding provocations to Hitler when Swiss tempers might be high. Relatively little needed to be put on paper.

At the same time, the Swiss maintained one of the largest merchant marine fleets in the world, based in Genoa—a gaping hole in Hitler's siege position around most of the circumference of Switzerland, through which were imported the necessities for a continued independent existence. I do not know whether Adolf Hitler ever knew why Benito Mussolini would not cooperate against the Swiss, but the true story is this: Mussolini, as a leftist troublemaker, had been forced to leave Italy and went to Switzerland. There, in Zurich, he stole a watch! Fingerprinted and mug shots taken, he was expelled to Italy again, where as a *rightist* he led the march on Rome and became Il Duce—the most vain and egotistical dictator of the period before World War II. The Swiss never revealed the secret while Mussolini lived, and a grateful Il Duce did what was necessary for the Swiss.[4] When he fell, the Swiss danger became acute. Luckily, for no special reason, Hitler never found time to punish the Swiss.

Switzerland's danger in World War II was extreme because its neighbors had usually had opposed policies or been historic enemies (France and Germany, Italy and Austria). But Switzerland's history includes a long experience with foreign tyrants, as its legend of Wilhelm Tell indicates, and the Swiss have cultivated 360-degree vision to a remarkable extent. They have learned to integrate their policy in a realistic way with the terrain they occupy and the neighbors who surround them. In one sense, however, since Switzerland makes no alliances, its foreign affairs problems have a certain simplicity. In older days the Swiss were often involved in a mercenary role abroad (*pas d'argent, pas de Suisse*—no money, no Swiss, as the homily summed it up), but since then they have not had to relate much to problems generated far away. Today Castro's Cubans fill this mercenary role.

A great power or a superpower, as we have seen, is by definition at the other extreme: it is involved with faraway problems as well as those nearer home. To say it another way, its frame of reference for enmity is necessarily wider. It still must deal with the 360-degree problem, but its field of activity is more extensive geographically. No great power or superpower, interestingly enough, has ever had 360-degree land frontiers. The nearest to it was Austria-Hungary.

The histories of France and the Soviet Union provide contrasting illustrations of how more powerful nations attempt to decide on limits for involvement in faraway problems. In different periods, these two nations have gone through a somewhat parallel process of expansion of their frames of reference, with resultant serious problems.

In Louis XIV's day, French policy was still largely confined to European affairs. Although colonial ventures were in the making, these were essentially side actions. The significant rivals of France were England on the one hand, especially for the contests abroad, and Austria on the other, for the mastery of Europe at home. The prime rationale of French policy was the drive for "natural" frontiers, such as the Rhine. French policy was quite coherent, although France's ready resort to war was extravagant. Indeed, in his long wars Louis XIV undermined French finances. As his successor so aptly put it, "*Apres moi le déluge*," which happened in Louis XVI's reign, exactly as predicted.

Napoleon played his role on a wider stage, dabbling with adventures abroad, including an expedition to Egypt and one to Haiti. But he ultimately settled for liquidation of the colonial empire, selling the Louisiana Territory to the United States and concentrating on conquering Russia and Spain. That sounds prudent, but Napoleon's one great policy defect was that he could not stop. With more power at his disposal than Louis XIV had commanded, he dissipated his resources in a larger field. He crossed the Pyrenees when he did not really need to, and he crossed the Niemen into Russia with little provocation.

In the nineteenth century, France acquired Algeria (1830). Under the romantic, or quixotic, Napoleon III, France sent troops to Mexico and then had to withdraw them; fought the Crimean War, rather inconclusively and to little point; and lost the Franco-Prussian War. This last was a serious calamity, costing Louis Napoleon his throne. The whole policy lacked focus or a serious sense of priorities, especially the indulgence in faraway adventures and neglect of adequate preparations to deal with a threat at home. There was no real sense of third-party influences at all.

In the 1860s, the French had already begun taking over Indochina. After the Third Republic came into existence, France sought additional glory overseas in Africa and Asia, enjoying peace at home, especially because during Bismarck's tenure Germany wanted stability in Europe.

Because of this colonial expansion, France emerged from World War II with serious problems. Weak and divided against itself at home, France wished to keep Germany powerless in Europe (posing the riddle of how Europe then would be strengthened against Russia). Simultaneously, in an age when colonialism was dying, France could not reconcile itself to decisive action in Indo-China or Algeria but pursued a policy in these areas that made victory and defeat almost equally unattainable, thereby prolonging the problems. One group insisted on putting down the rebellions; its opponents, on freedom for the rebels. Neither could prevail at home, and so the bloodshed went on abroad.

Ironically, the growth in French security in Europe contributed to the indecision. With the signing of the North Atlantic Pact in 1949 and the establishment of NATO in 1950, United States troops stood more or less permanently between the French and the Russian threat. For all these reasons, the Algerian War was allowed to drag on until it produced a crisis. When Charles de Gaulle took the leadership of the Fifth Republic, he settled the issue with a referendum, which he honored though his opponents sought to assassinate him.

With French attention no longer diverted far afield, French security policy took on more coherence at home. De Gaulle, favoring a full nuclear response to a full and deliberate Soviet aggression – before the Soviets should reach France – took France in 1966 out of the organized features of NATO, while still retaining membership in the alliance itself. This move forced foreign troops from French soil, compressed the rear logistical area into the crowded Lowlands, and made a mockery of the U.S. doctrine of flexible (staged) response. Space was now lacking for the leisurely upward climb the United States wished to maintain on the so-called ladder of escalation; the projected Russian advance had to be stopped sooner because there was less space available to do the stopping. This was exactly the result De Gaulle had intended to produce.

How well have the French acted in terms of third-party influences? Louis XIV spent most of his efforts on "natural" frontiers; his fault was that he spent his resources too lavishly. But French colonial efforts had marginal utility. To be active abroad in establishing an empire or in conducting a war is only practical if one enjoys relative security on one's own frontiers. The early French hold on Canada and India fell victim because France could not defend itself simultaneously on so many fronts, while its prime opponent, England, could afford and needed control of the seas but could make do with fewer land forces. Napoleon's record, as we saw, is mixed: cutting losses overseas to deal with higher-priority problems at home, but carrying his wars to the geographical extremes of Spain and Russia. Thus he progressively created more extended borders, more exposed flanks, and a more vulnerable rear regardless of which way he faced.

His nephew, Louis Napoleon, was a greater blunderer. His Mexican adventure could only continue so long as the British consented and the United States was deep in civil war. Louis saw no danger in allowing Bismarck to defeat Austria and in continuing to alienate the Italians through French occupation of Rome. In the end such policies isolated France and brought about its defeat by Prussia in 1871.

In the decades that followed, tranquillity in Europe made French expansion overseas possible. But the events of World War II and its aftermath created new conditions, to which France, until De Gaulle, only sluggishly responded.

Third-party influences in particular shaped Franco-Russian relations from 1890 on. Until Germany was unified, France's major enemy (as seen in Chapter 4), was England. Once Germany was united, the French, who had once invaded Russia, actively sought a Russian alliance. They made one in 1894, and again in 1935, and again in 1944: my neighbor's neighbor is my friend. The alliances did not always serve the purpose: that of 1894 did, in World War I; that of 1935 was vitiated by the events of the Munich crisis of 1938 and Czechoslovakia's dismemberment by the Nazis in 1939; that of 1944 became a dead letter when Germany's weakness and division after World War II, and Stalin's aggressive behavior, made the Soviets a greater threat to the French than Germany was. To the extent that the great bitterness stemming from the bloodletting of two world wars between the French and the Germans is now past, it is entirely due to their common perception that the Russians are a greater danger to them both. A common enemy is the handmaiden of reconciliation.

Now consider the Soviet Union, a second land power, a great power now somewhat loosely called a superpower, a nation with both land and sea frontiers, and a nation with frontiers that border territories in three of the world's major geopolitical subdivisions (Europe, the Middle East, and Asia).

Many years ago Robert Kerner, a University of California historian, wrote a book on Russia's drive to the sea — its efforts to acquire shores with access to warm waters. This drive has been a recurring theme in Russia's history. Concomitant has been the experience of recurrent invasion of Russia by other peoples. In some ways the drive to the sea was an attempt to end these invasions.

Sometimes "Russia" has barely survived, all but the Moscow area and the Kremlin fortress passing into the hands of the Mongols and other invaders. Sometimes overrun by Mongols and Tartars, who even reached into Poland, at other times Russia has been overrun from the opposite direction, by Poland.

Initially Russia's territorial expansion in Europe was painfully slow. The small "Russian States" shown on the map in 1360 were little changed by

1560. It was only the partitions of Poland that by 1795 finally advanced Russian frontiers westward to Brest-Litovsk, after earlier slices had been obtained in 1772 and 1793.

Contemporary observers in the early nineteenth century regarded the expansion of Russia as painfully (threateningly) rapid. Sir Edward S. Creasy quotes, and concurs with, the (unnamed) author of *Progress of Russia in the East*, which appeared in 1839, that

the acquisitions which Russia has made within the [then] last sixty-four years, are equal in extent and importance to the whole empire she had in Europe before that time.... In sixty-four years she has advanced her frontier eight hundred and fifty miles towards Vienna, Berlin, Dresden, Munich, and Paris; she has approached four hundred and fifty miles nearer to Constantinople; she has possessed herself of the capital of Poland, and she has advanced to within a few miles of the capital of Sweden, from which, when Peter the Great mounted the throne, her frontier was distant three hundred miles. Since that time she has stretched herself forward about one thousand miles towards India, and the same distance towards the capital of Persia.[5]

A series of maps showing Russian expansion in Asia illustrates the same point: slow beginnings in expansion; rapid follow-through at the end. The Russian eastern frontier in 1533 was perhaps 300 miles or a bit less east of Moscow, but up to about 800 miles east of Moscow to the northeast. By 1598 the area north of the Caspian Sea and north and east around Tobolsk had been incorporated. By 1689 Russia had pushed to the Pacific and held Lake Baikal and the whole area above Outer Mongolia. All the rest came later: Baku in 1806, Turkestan in 1864, the areas north of Afghanistan in 1869 and 1881-1885. The whole of the area north of Manchuria was taken from China only a relatively short time ago, between 1858 and 1860. It comprises a vast area above the Amur and Ussuri rivers.

A list of some modern-day invasions of Russia illustrates quite clearly its long-continued vulnerability. Between 1700 and 1941, European Russia was invaded by the Swedes (1700-1709), the French (1812), the British and French (1854-1856), the Germans (1914-1918), the Poles (1920), the Allies (during the Russian Revolution), and the Germans (1941-1944). And we have not mentioned the many wars with the Turks.

Looking at the connections between geography and policy, we could hardly find a great power with more — and more dangerous — neighbors. In early modern times Russia had survived assault, war, and invasion from the north, east, and west, and at times its survival was a near thing. Luck played a role, as well as shrewd policy. In part the Swedes, the Mongols, and the French were defeated by the great distances they came from: their centers of power were far away. It is the Poles (and Lithuanians) and the Germans, as well as the Turks, who have been the serious, persistent enemies. China and Japan might have played much more significant roles but for rather unusual accidents of history, although their hostility could only be fully meaningful after Russia had acquired Asian territories, gaining China and Japan as neighbors.

The Poles were removed for a long time as a coherent threat by the Polish partitions, the forerunner of the German partition of 1945. By these acts Prussia and Austria made Russia a neighbor and a part of Europe, and the Russians acquired a role in the European balance of power and new advantages and disadvantages as a consequence of altered frontiers. The net gain for the Russians was substantial, even though a frontier with Germany (Prussia) was created.

An immense boon for the Russians was the defeat of Napoleon and the unusual hundred years that followed — unique in modern times in that, between 1815 and 1914, or for a whole century, there was no general war. Long before the decade beginning in the 1870s when England and France turned to Africa and Asia for empire, Russia was accumulating territory along its southern and eastern flanks against relatively small opposition and with its western frontier generally as secure as it has ever been in modern times. How did this fortunate state of affairs come about?

In Chapter 4 we saw Bismarck determined to maintain firm links with Russia — and that for a very good reason. If France was the enemy, or at his front, Russia was at his rear. Thus Germany under Bismarck would not permit Austria to move aggressively against Russia. Germany's need contributed to Russia's welfare. When Wilhelm discarded the ingenious Treaty of Reinsurance of 1887, Russia responded with the French alliance. This move continued to tranquilize Russia's European frontier through a different, though less satisfactory, approach. These links facilitated Russia's expansion in Asia because they kept the peace in Europe, even if at the price of rising tension.

In the east, China's weakness contributed at least as much to Russian security, especially coupled with Japan's isolationism.

Until Japan was "opened" by Commodore Perry in 1854, Japan remained aloof from the modern age. In the last quarter of the nineteenth century, Japan hurriedly modernized and armed itself with modern weapons. But Japan was not ready for war until 1894, and then fought China over Korea. The Treaty of Shimonoseki in 1895 gave Japan Formosa and the Liaotung peninsula, while recognizing Korea as an independent state. Europe's great powers forced some alteration in these arrangements, whereby Russia ended up with a "lease" on the Liaotung peninsula. Perhaps most important, though, the war further weakened China. In 1898 Britain, Germany, and France joined Russia in extorting leases of Chinese territories. Although the Liaotung lease was to run for only twenty-five years, the other leases were for ninety-nine years. The Boxer Rebellion of 1900 was an early sign of Chinese resentment. When this resentment blossomed into actual revolution in October 1911, China began a period of turmoil that lasted until the Chinese Communist victory in the civil war in 1949.

These events conferred comparative immunity on Russia along the Asian frontier, although it is true that Japan's ambitions on the Asian mainland were at times a danger. There was the Russo-Japanese War in 1904, and again, during the Russian Revolution, Japanese troops occupied Russian Far Eastern territories for a time. Then in May 1939, just before World War II, Japan and Russia fought one another in an undeclared war along the Mongolian frontier. This clash, which ended in a draw, was nominally between Manchukuan and Mongolian forces (that is, Japanese and Russian forces). These tensions simply highlight what was missing in the equation: on the one hand, the difficulty of small Japan subduing the Russian giant; on the other hand, the lack of a vital, organized China, able to assert itself along the Soviet border.

The logic of Russia's expansion into Asia was that Russia, seeking security or satisfaction through that process, would nonetheless and sooner or later achieve common frontiers with significant powers able to set limits to Russian ambitions. That this result was postponed during the period just considered was one of those flukes of history. It was an unearned security increment, and it was inevitably to be limited in duration. Once Japan either finished absorbing China (in the campaign begun in the 1930s) or was defeated and withdrew, as happened at the hands of the United States in 1945, China would sooner or later be a source of concern to a Russia which had exploited Chinese weakness.

That the inevitable was postponed a second time, after 1949, as it had been the first time through Japan's ambitions, was a second piece of luck for Russia. It came about because the Korean War shelved U.S. plans to remain neutral in the last stage of the Chinese civil war, a stage that would have seen Peking's occupation of Taiwan. After the Korean involvement of American and Chinese troops against one another began in 1950, the United States concluded a defense treaty with Taiwan and conducted an essentially anti-Chinese foreign policy. Eventually the United States, pursuing this policy, rounded it out by putting a half-million U.S. troops ashore in Vietnam, on China's southwestern flank, beginning in 1965. This forced China to move troops protectively into that area, making it essential for China to restrain friction with Russia. So Russia's Asian security was extended one more time by the actions of its worldwide enemy, the United States, until U.S. troops were withdrawn from Indo-China. Finally, after these long delays, the Soviets began to experience once again the geopolitical problems their frontiers imply.

The Soviet Union is hardly likely to benefit again from such an extraordinary interplay of events, which came about not so much from Russian wisdom in creating policy as from the errors and preoccupations of others. With a dozen nations as neighbors, Russia has a really extraordinary problem in handling third-party influences.

Japan has been mentioned in reference to China and Russia. But consider, from the viewpoint of third-party influences, the events that led up to the Pearl Harbor attack.

After 1937, with Japan heavily involved south of the Great Wall of China, as well as in Manchuria, the Japanese had to worry about both Soviet and American reactions. Relations with the United States continued to deteriorate. Secretary of State Cordell Hull began to speak with righteous indignation about nations that bombed women and children from the air (Japan over China). Finally, the United States cut off shipments of steel and oil. In the meantime, in the shadow of World War II, Japan and Russia, as detailed above, tested one another on the Mongolian frontier.

Consider Japan's circumstance. Either a war with Russia or a war with the United States was a possibility for Japan. The idea of fighting both was unattractive. Japan did not move decisively so long as this situation persisted, but in June 1941, Hitler invaded Russia. Hitler's action effectively sealed the Russian threat to Japan until one or the other should win the savage contest in Europe. Should Japan now join in the attack on Russia, or seize the opportunity to fight the United States? Either alternative had advantages and disadvantages. Russia would presumably be weakened severely whether Japan attacked Russia or not, however, while this opportunity to engage the United States with Japan's back secure from *both* China and Russia was unprecedented. The rare chance thus offered induced the Japanese to choose to attack the United States.

Although most of the examples in this chapter have been the concerns of large powers, this is partly because their history is better known and the illustrations have more impact and value. The principle of third-party influences applies to all: the difference in *situation* is only that some nations have enjoyed more freedom of choice than others, because of location, historical accident, nature of the frontiers, or policies of third states. To such variables they have had to react with what wisdom they could muster.

As already discussed, nations like Switzerland or Korea, although their affairs have important implications for other nations, normally concentrate their attention on their own frontiers. At the widest, their concern about third-party influences extends to their neighbors' immediate neighbors. On the other hand, nations like the United States or Russia or France or Japan have, or have had, to concern themselves with third-party influences in a more extended sense. As a rule of thumb, such nations, each capable of deployments overseas in some significant fashion, have had to balance worldwide third-party influences, even to the neighbors of the neighbors of their neighbors. Their policy, if it is to be wise and effective, necessarily has to take more complex possibilities into account.

In surveying the examples in this chapter, one is struck by their diversity. For instance, there is the variation in power, which significantly affects the range of policy actions. Moreover, great variations have been shown in the behavior of single nations over periods of several centuries. Only some of these variations are due to changing internal consensus over what ought to be done; some significant part derives also from the actions of the other states in providing or closing off initiatives for action. Great variations have also been shown in the results of policies chosen to deal with third-party influences.

Nations, if they would pursue optimal policies, must take third-party influences into account, but nations are under no effective compulsion to prosper. Indeed, a nation may use an analytical process for resolving national security issues that, in its very composition, falls short of promising effective results. (In Allison's terms, the "rational actor" is not necessarily going to be sufficiently rational!)

Consider U.S. "threat analysis" from this point of view. It contains no noticeable emphasis on third-party influences, as a glance at the official Department of Defense definitions will show. "Threat" is not listed as such. Instead, "capability" is cross-referenced to "intentions," and vice versa.[6] But how much does such a two-part concept look at third-party influences or make a 360-degree analysis inescapable? Such factors will not be incorporated in a look at enemy capabilities versus one's own (known as "net assessment"). If it occurs at all, that analysis will come in the other part on "intentions."

But intentions, military people often believe, can change overnight as policy changes. Is it therefore surprising or unwise that military planners look lightly and skeptically at the intentions of possible or probable enemies but take their arrays of weapons very seriously indeed? A two-sided threat analysis shrinks at this point to a compulsive concentration on enemy arms. The next step is known as "worst-case analysis." The assumption is made that the enemy is able to initiate the attack under ideal conditions of its own choosing.

By now the thought process, although perfectly reasonable by its own standards, has drifted rather far afield from third-party influences, the 360-degree frame of reference. By its very structural form, this two-sided threat analysis diverts attention from the ultimately more substantial question of what circumstances permit nations to shift policy and, especially, embark upon military adventures. The argument in this chapter is that such decisions are normally made with third-party influences very much in mind, that most states estimating the danger of attack will consider *three* factors; capability (what he can oppose me with), intentions (whether he would like to), and circumstances (whether the situation at his back and flanks gives him freedom to act).

The American approach naturally reflects the American perception. Finland's approach makes an interesting comparison. The Finns have published in English a *Report of the Second Parliamentary Defense Committee*, in 1976.[7] The report is a clear and relatively candid appraisal by a neutral located in a position of considerable danger. Its emphasis and flavor are well represented by the following:

Geomilitarily Finland lies between the leading military alliances and close to the common land boundary of these alliances. It is neighboring state of one of the two leading great powers and of two small states. Our position is affected, moreover, by the fundamental factors of our location close to the Norwegian Sea-Barents Sea area and the fact that we are off the probable routes of attack by forces.[8]

And again:

Finland has no targets whose occupation would significantly further anyone's strategic objectives in the present situation. The position of Lapland is delicate in a potential war situation between the East and West [but] Arctic conditions do not favor major land operations in the north-tier of Europe.[9]

It is only after an extended analysis of Finnish defense circumstances and some discussion of East and West intentions (discreetly noted as a "situation") that the Finns discuss capability.

The Swedish approach contains a quite distinct emphasis on third-party influences. Swedish Prime Minister Thorbjörn Fälldin, in a speech on February 6, 1978, said:

Sweden's security policy is supported by an overwhelming majority of the Swedish people. To most people, the policy of neutrality is self-evident. . . . Swedish strategy has been designed in the form of what the experts call the marginal strategy. This strategy is based on the assumption that . . . most of the forces of the two blocs will always be committed against each other, just as they are in Central Europe today. A superpower contemplating an attack on Sweden must therefore accept two limitations: it can only detail a minor portion of its military strength for this assignment and, secondly, it must be prepared for possible countermeasures by the other superpower.[10]

Perhaps what the contrast of the American approach with the Swedish and Finnish approaches tells us most particularly is that nations with armed forces that stand little chance of victory against large neighbors will be more inclined to see capability as the last part of the analysis. If it comes down to war, the most they can hope for is to survive until their great-power neighbors run into trouble at their flanks and rear. When a nation's historical experience has been gained in the shadow of strong and immediate neighbors, the tendency is for that nation to think much about third-party influences. Conversely, a nation dominant along the circumference of its own frontiers runs into the constant intellectual temptation to downplay a 360-degree look at circumstances, precisely because its own circumstances need less appraisal.

NOTES

1. Bernard Brodie, *War and Politics* (New York: Macmillan, 1973), p. 350.

2. Robert Maynard Hutchins, ed., *Great Books of the Western World: Plutarch* (Chicago: Encyclopaedia Britannica, 1952), pp. 320-21.

3. Brodie, *War and Politics*, p. 347.

4. See Frederick H. Hartmann, *The Swiss Press and Foreign Affairs in World War II*, University of Florida Monographs, Social Sciences no. 5 (Gainesville, Fla., Winter 1960).

5. Edward Creasy, *The Fifteen Decisive Battles of the World* (New York: Heritage, 1969, original published in 1851), p. 149; quoted from *Progress of Russia in the East*.

6. U.S. Department of Defense, Joint Chiefs of Staff, *Dictionary of Military and Associated Terms*, JCS Publication 1, September 3, 1974. Rev. ed., June 1, 1979.

7. *Report of the Second Parliamentary Defense Committee* (of Finland), Committee Report 1976:37, Helsinki, 1976.

8. Ibid., p. 25.

9. Ibid., pp. 25-26.

10. "Swedish Security Policy," Speech by Prime Minister Thorbjörn Fälldin, February 6, 1978. (Stockholm: Ministry for Foreign Affairs, Press and Information Department, 1978), pp. 1, 5. See also "Swedish Security Policy and Total Defence," (Stockholm: Ministry of Defence, 1977), p. 1.

9

PAST-FUTURE LINKAGES

For centuries, Europeans dominated the African continent. The white man arrogated to himself the right to rule and to be obeyed by the nonwhite. . . . Under this cloak, the Europeans robbed the continent of vast riches and inflicted unimaginable suffering on the African people.

Kwame Nkrumah[1]

The second cardinal principle, past-future linkages, underlines the fact that every nation's view of its present and future is heavily influenced by its past, that the differences in the historical experiences of the nations affect their comprehension of present reality as well as shape their future expectations.

National characteristics and attitudes are, of course, not a constant. What is true of the "political culture" of a people in one period may be vastly untrue of the political culture of the same nationality in another. If a people's situation remains relatively constant, however, its reactions to it are likely to remain consistent.

Such national differences are a fertile field for humor. Josh Billings once said, "Put an Englishman into the Garden of Eden, and he would find fault with the whole blarsted concern; put a Yankee in, and he would see where he could alter it to advantage; put an Irishman in, and he would want to boss the thing; put a Dutchman in, and he would proceed to plant it."[2] Again, many of us know the old tale about the scientists and the elephant. Scientists of different nationalities studied the elephant and then went off to write their books. The Englishman wrote *The Elephant: His Natural Habitat*. The Frenchman wrote *The Love Life of the Elephant*. The German wrote a twelve-volume work entitled *An Introduction to the Study of the Elephant*. And the American wrote a 100-page paperback with the title *All You Ever Wanted to Know about the Elephant in a Nutshell*.

National characteristics need not be considered eternal or permanent to be taken seriously as an element of study. While the national outlook will change often over time, differences between national outlooks can be expected to persist. These differences are the natural fruit of great variations in the historical experiences of nations. Kwame Nkrumah's way of looking at African history may not be shared by a majority of Europeans, but few Africans would repudiate his views. To expect Russians and Americans, with such divergent histories, to have a common viewpoint on most issues is to expect far too much.

Chapter 8 gives a second reason why these national differences in character and outlook occur and persist, since the problems faced by different nations are so different — perhaps not always in kind, but certainly always in detail. Every nation may worry about defense, but each worries about different enemies who may attack, because their circumstances are various.

Reformers and idealists like Emery Reves[3] and Richard A. Falk,[4] so conscious of the world's pressing problems, of the need for universal solutions, tend to jump to the conclusion either that national differences in attitude are irrelevant or that they will become unimportant as the problem needing solution becomes increasingly and obviously urgent. There are no good grounds for believing this is so. Even within nations, consensus is extremely difficult to maintain. Civil wars and coups are the outward sign of this inward ferment, and when the violence becomes overt, it does not stop because there is a rational need for it to stop. It is easier to list countries — and it makes a short list — that have *not* had civil war or overt and continuing civic violence, that have *not* had military coups, than to list those that have had such experiences. It is quite a bit to expect that nations collectively so troubled with the internal problems of governing themselves will resolve world problems in a peaceful and timely manner. It is already too much to assume that they define the "same" problem in the same way. It is more realistic to start with a sharp appreciation for national differences and to realize that these differences are not easily bridged over. These differences significantly affect the way nations perceive the future consequences of present-day decisions. In that sense it means that when nations approach a "common" problem, they in fact may each perceive a different problem.

Salvador de Madariaga wrote an extremely original and interesting study on national character, published in 1928. It is the sort of insightful book, written by a sensitive observer, that is rarely published in our scientific-computer age. In *Englishmen, Frenchmen, Spaniards*, he argues that each of his three peoples has "a distinctive attitude which determines their natural and spontaneous reactions towards life."[5] As key to these reactions, he gives three words, each of which, as he says, is untranslatable: "In the Englishman: *fair play*. In the Frenchman: *le droit*. In the Spaniard: *el honor*."[6] A little later on he connects these words to an emphasis, respectively, on group action, intellect, and passion. As the psychological center of gravity of these peoples, he gives body-will (Englishman), intellect (Frenchman), soul (Spaniard). Then, to complete his trinitarian framework, he describes "the natural reaction towards life" of an Englishman as *action*, of a Frenchman as *thought*, of a Spaniard as *passion*.[7]

One of Madariaga's three nations, England, has accumulated many foreign assessments in its long history. Thomas Jefferson once characterized England as "a pirate spreading misery and ruin over the face of the ocean";[8] an English patriot would have said, "bringing the rule of law and the healing benefits of good trade to all the world." Napoleon I called England "a nation of shopkeepers," borrowing a phrase from Adam Smith, but Nietzsche got nearer the point: "They are not a philosophical race, the English."[9] Add to Nietzsche's thought the saying first heard around 1885: "The English always manage to muddle through."

Harold Nicolson said that

the most marked characteristic of the inhabitants of these Islands is mental indolence and . . . I think mental indolence does produce a distaste for extreme courses. Extreme courses require thinking out, and one thing that no Englishman would ever do is think anything out. He always stops before he gets to the extreme. That is called British commonsense.[10]

Nicolson has his tongue in cheek, but not very far. When he turned to how England took over Egypt, he said:

A foreigner would say that it was the most brilliant bit of carefully planned imperialism . . . executed with diabolical cunning. . . . But it was not that. We did not know what was happening. We thought it was a noble mission of civilisation. We really did not mean to go in; we did really mean to come out. We gradually slipped into occupying Egypt and then began to search for moral motives.[11]

Those who observed this England at work gave it the title "perfidious Albion," but Madariaga simply points to the English proverb: "You must not cross the bridge before you come to it." He translates that as "We should not seek to solve our problems until actually before us."[12]

A letter by Foreign Secretary Palmerston to the British ambassador in Russia confirms Madariaga's point: "It is not usual for England to enter into engagements with reference to cases which have not actually arisen, or which are not immediately in prospect."[13] While Palmerston ascribes the English habit to constitutional reasons, in that "Parliament might probably not approve of an engagement which should bind England prospectively to take up arms in a contingency which could not as yet be foreseen,"[14] it is clear that the Parliament looked at the problem that way because it was English and shared English attitudes.

To continue with what Madariaga says:

Now, the Englishman avoids abstract and intellectual operations and thinks only in connection with action. What is meant, more or less obscurely, by "practical sense" is precisely this attitude of the bee that goes straight to the flower which is the attitude of the Englishman when, on his way to action, he comes up against ideas or sentiments across his path. He brushes them aside, surmounts all obstacles without hesitation and goes straight towards his goal without worrying about preconceived plans.[15]

Nicolson, Madariaga, and Nietzsche are closest to the mark, although now that Britain is so much less prominent in world affairs, it may not be very obvious to the present generation. England is a nation that has been much concerned with control of the seas, trade, and empire, and little concerned with philosophical principles. The English are the most pragmatic people to play a first-class role on the world stage. The whole British Empire was a conglomeration of crown colonies, dominions, protectorates, private business preserves such as the East India Company exercised over India, and so on. There was little natural administrative tidiness to it, and perhaps that was a major reason for its success. After all, George III, who dealt so stubbornly and uncompromisingly with the American colonies, was quite untypical of the English style, and he was, of course, really a German. The English, historically, have been the great compromisers. The English common law grew by accretion, by custom, in direct contrast with the logically complete and orderly Code Napoléon or the Latin civil law on which that code is based.

These are not the traits of a philosophical people but of pragmatists brought into intimate contact with a hundred civilizations, all different. The old cliché about the Englishman dressing for dinner in the jungle misses half the point: that he was there. It is true that the English kept their national qualities wherever they went, building Hotel Britannicas and Hotel Reginas in scores of cities as fit places for English people to stay. But they also learned not to try to force other nations to accept British values as substitutes for their own. It is this quality, added to their excellent geographic location, that gave the British world predominance in their time—that and an instinctive reluctance to rely on violence more than was strictly necessary.

Hitler, having defeated these English in 1940, assumed quite logically that they could be induced to make peace. But the British, who are a sporting nation even if not heavily inclined toward abstract thought, did not consider that the match was over. As Winston Churchill broadcast to the French people on October 21, 1940: "We are waiting for the long-promised invasion. So are the fishes." This is the authentic British spirit, however much the road since has been downhill from glory.

Let us shift our attention to the Germans, who contrast with the British in so many ways. We can begin with some fairly obvious observations, because they can lead us to deeper manifestations of character and attitude.

German love for uniforms has been much remarked, as well as the German tendency to string titles together. In Germany a professor who is a Ph.D. is "Herr Professor Doktor." If he is also a military man, as was Karl Haushofer, the geopolitician, he becomes "Herr Professor General." The learned title comes first, despite the love of uniforms. Philosophy comes first.

It is also said, with some reason, that Germans are not a humorous people — although whoever said that was never in the Rhineland in *Karneval* season. The story is told about the revolution that did not occur because the revolutionists missed their train: no one was there to punch their platform tickets! We laugh at this tale but behind it is the German slogan, "*Ordnung muss sein!*" What is easy to confuse here is the desire with the fact. Having lived in Germany, I would say that the natural lack of order with which Germans do many things has forced them to adopt orderly methods in many outward things. They do not naturally stand in line for a bus, as the English do — or did.

Of the German commitment to learning and philosophy, Richard Porson (1759-1808) once wrote: "German scholars dive deeper and come up muddier than any others." Of the German search for orderliness, Nicolson said,

the dominant feature in the German character is spiritual uncertainty. The main cause of this German uncertainty, diffidence and hesitancy is, to my mind, Germany's perpetual lack of outline. By that I mean not geographical outline only, although being on the edge of other countries does seem to have given the Germans no sharp sense of geographical frontiers. It is also a lack of cultural outline, by which I mean a blurred cultural tradition.[16]

Nicolson says it is also a lack of historical outline because of what happened to the German lands after Augustus withdrew the Roman legions from the Elbe, and a lack of racial outline because of Slav "infiltrations" and "dilutions" of the "pure German blood." Nicolson ends this part by saying: "We who have somewhere at the back of our minds the consciousness that our shores are washed by the silver sea, should try to understand this almost passionate longing of the German to find an outline."[17] We might rephrase Nicolson and say the passionate longing of Germans to achieve a sense of stability.

These lines of Nicolson's were written at the very time, in Germany, when massed thousands of Nazis, assembled at Nuremberg, with the great swastika banners flying in the light of torches, chanted, "Sieg heil! Sieg heil! Seig heil!" Nicolson paraphrases Frederick Sieburg to the effect that "every

German is like a grain of sand, but that in every grain there is a passionate desire to coalesce with others and become one rock."[18]

Adolf Hitler's movement was not an inevitable outgrowth of German traits, but it spoke to a number of German needs: to be organized, to have a sense of mission and direction (of outline), to work together toward some end. These needs may explain in part the extraordinary interest of Germans in philosophy.

It is probably no accident that Germany, which in the cultural sense includes Austria, gave birth to so many philosophers, for this German interest in first principles and in the meaning of things has always been very pronounced, whether for the reasons Nicolson gives or some other reasons. Hegel, Schopenhauer, Nietzsche, Freud, Engels, and Karl Marx are only a few from a long list.

Heinrich von Treitschke, their great nineteenth-century historian, described a philosophy of the state that gained much recognition from Germans. In his book *Politics* (1897), he argued that if the state "neglects its strength in order to promote the idealistic inspirations of man, it repudiates its own nature and perishes. This is in truth for the State equivalent to the sin against the Holy Ghost. . . ."[19]

Philosophy, which has brought mankind many benefits, has two features with negative potentialities. One is its thirst for logical consistency (by definition, inhuman). The other is its tendency toward the ideal – or extreme (by implication, given the circumstances, inhumane). If Germany needed living space, the obvious thing might then be to exterminate millions of "inferior" peoples; but that is a notion of the intellect, disconnected from the emotions.

A philosophical people capable of extremes, the Germans became also a military people in order to survive. Located on the North European plain and bereft of natural frontiers, the Germans had to learn to react quickly in a military sense. The Schlieffen Plan, with its railroad deployments during a mobilization, was merely an industrial-age application of behavior learned ages ago.

The German combination of difficulty in finding a psychological center of gravity, coupled with a tendency toward philosophical first principles, is not a fortunate combination. It may account for a trait popularly attributed to Germans that certainly has some historic substance: the tendency to extort concessions from a position of strength and to show rather marked self-pity in conditions of weakness. The former is perhaps best illustrated in the famous exchange between the English and the Germans in 1911, already quoted. Chapter 4 mentions the *Panther* incident and the German argument "that the dispatch of a ship to Agadir . . . was really meant *to make it easier* for the French Government to defend any compensation they might be ready to give. . . ."[20] Nicolson caught part of the picture when he said, "The German heroic conception of life leads to what I may call a warrior conception of policy and diplomacy."[21] After World War II this quality was far less pronounced. Germany instead sought constant reassurances of support. "Poor, weak Germany" was a phrase often heard in the 1950s* before it began to be elbowed out by pride in the "German miracle" of economic leadership of Europe. Having said all of that, one should add in justice that the stable and prosperous postwar conditions in Germany in the 1960s and 1970s have brought about much less tendency to oscillation between extremes.

It is not difficult, when one compares the traits of the English and the Germans, to understand how they could talk past one another. Their history and experiences have also been very different.

It must be particularly difficult for the present generation to understand either of these peoples, for the days of British hegemony are long gone, and London's streets filled with garbage while the economy drifted aimlessly in 1980. The British people were still not prepared to make the extra effort that is needed to replace the largesse of empire.

The Germans apparently accept the continued division of their country with hardly a murmur. How much "the Germans have changed" continues to furnish ammunition for heated arguments. One school of thought contends that the new German forbearance is the fragile product of economic prosperity.

The Russians are quite convinced, for their part, that the sleeping German lion still has his teeth. They share with the Germans a long experience in war, as we brought out earlier. They are a people who have never known freedom in a Western sense. Germany may have known tyranny under Hitler, and England under Cromwell, but Russia has always lived under tyranny. The common people, the serfs, were bound to the land like slaves until the time of the U.S. Civil War. They needed the lord's permission to marry, and he was their judge and jury. The whole system of society was one that a sensitive man like Leo Tolstoy found morally repugnant. Although serfdom has been abolished, the arbitrariness of Russian life remains a leading feature.

The authoritarianism of Russian society, both historically and today, is hard to grasp. A stamp on a card or a particular kind of a pass will perform wonders in such a society. I know an American tourist who, while I was in

---

*In private conversation with the author in Bonn in 1959, during the Soviet "six-months ultimatum," the head of the American Affairs Section in the German Foreign Office said several times that he feared the United States would desert Germany under pressure. Poor Germany!

Moscow, got to the head of the mile-long line at Lenin's Tomb by flashing his U.S. Naval Reserve Retired card! With its very impressive set of seals and its black and white set of colors, it has a very "official" visual impact. Stories of this sort abound.

Hedrick Smith, in his absorbing book *The Russians*, tells of a conversation he had in Moscow with an experienced American diplomat, who said,

You . . . can live right here among them and not really know how they live. The controls are so tight they shut you out. One night, one evening you can talk and drink with them — especially if they can explain it away later as an accidental encounter. But the next morning, they think it over and decide it's too risky to go on.[22]

These words were not written about Stalin's Russia, at the height of the terror, but contemporary Russia. Of course, little has changed in this respect from what Neil S. Brown, the U.S. minister to Russia, wrote Secretary of State Daniel Webster in 1853: "One of the most disagreeable features . . . is the secrecy with which everything is done. . . . Nothing is made public that is worth knowing."[23]

The secrecy in Russia is almost unbelievable. It is perfectly possible to stand on a Moscow street corner and see an event of significance take place that is neither announced in the press beforehand or reported afterward. By American standards, Russian newspapers have virtually no content. I have a very vivid personal memory of Czechs in 1968 rushing for newspapers, which had suddenly been allowed to publish news. They were the only such newspapers to be found at the time, anywhere in Eastern Europe.

Not only is the society starved for news and not only are events of general interest shrouded under an all-embracing security blanket, but Russia's rulers have historically had very little contact with cultures outside Russia. The great exception came with and after Peter the Great, who himself went abroad to learn Western ways. After that time the Russian ruling elite became quite aware of Western ideas and cultures, even to the extent that polite conversation might be in French and the Russia state archives were maintained in French. But this was the interlude between the terror of Czar Ivan and the terror of Lenin and Stalin.

Stalin himself knew virtually nothing of the West from personal observation. Nikita Khrushchev, in later years, in his memoirs, dictated an arresting passage. It is at the time of his invitation to Camp David, during the crisis in 1959 over Berlin.

[I]nformed by our embassy in Washington that a certain number of days in our schedule had been set aside for meetings with the President [Eisenhower] at Camp David, I couldn't for the life of me find out what this Camp David was. . . . One reason I was suspicious was that I remembered in the early years . . . when contacts were first being established with the bourgeois world, a Soviet delegation was invited to a meeting held someplace called the Prince's islands. It came out in the newspapers that it was to these islands that stray dogs were sent to die. . . . In those days the capitalists never missed a chance to embarrass or offend the Soviet Union. I was afraid maybe this Camp David was the same sort of place, where people who were mistrusted could be kept in quarantine.[24]

Khrushchev goes on to say that even the Russian embassy could not tell him "for certain what Camp David was." The very thought that Eisenhower might be planning to quarantine Khrushchev is astounding to most Americans, but here is the Soviet leader soberly recording his fear—and ignorance.

It is fairly well known that public telephones in Moscow are not equipped with telephone books, nor will one find out much by dialing information. The idea is that you will know the number you want if you have a good reason to call it. Otherwise, no.

There can be little doubt that the Russian character includes suspicion of foreigners to an advanced degree. The whole history of Russia has served to confirm the thought that foreigners are trouble. Stalin, who was not a moderate when it came to having people shot as enemies of the state, piled up a particularly impressive score after he suspected the army leadership of conspiring with the Germans in the 1930s. He destroyed a significant proportion of the senior officer corps. Writing of these events, Khrushchev says of one case in particular, in which he knew the individual well, that "when we opened the archives and looked into the files of all the people who had been declared enemies of the people and shot or strangled—I found out that [the] testimony was all a lie."[25]

Only in such a nation, where autocratic rule, suspicion of foreigners, and secrecy exist in such advanced degree, could these events have occurred.

The Russians have always lived on Europe's fringe, and their culture has large admixtures of non-European influences. The contrast between Moscow and Leningrad (the "window on the West") is marked; so is the comparison of Moscow with any of the great capitals of Europe—and nowhere more meaningfully than in the capitals of Europe behind the Iron Curtain. Compared to Prague or Budapest or Warsaw, Moscow has little of cultural significance to recommend it. The Russian realization that this is so is a continuing source of chagrin and unease for the Soviets.

Both suspicion of foreigners (even Communist foreigners) and a deepseated sense of cultural inferiority are behind the Soviet behavior, even in areas of Europe they control with bayonets. In 1959, Soviet headquarters in East Berlin was a cordoned-off area, heavily and closely guarded from everyone outside, even the fellow-Communists of the German Democratic Republic. Perhaps it still is.

The Russian approach to life has a great vigor and coarseness to it. A German I knew well who had been a prisoner of war in Russia once told me the Russians had allowed the Germans to organize a symphony orchestra in the camp. On the night of the first concert, the Soviet commandant sat in the front row center, flanked by his officers as the orchestra played its first selection. Behind sat the German prisoners, who applauded wildly as the orchestra finished. But the Russians sat unmoved, and the orchestra rather shakily began its second number. When it came slightly discordantly to the end, nobody at all applauded this time. In the tension, the camp commandant bawled out an order for the orchestra to line up in front of the stage. He snapped out a second order and three Russian machine gunners lined up facing the orchestra. The lieutenant in charge looked at his colonel, who nodded decisively, and the lieutenant ordered "Ready." "Aim." Then the colonel burst out laughing and began to applaud. He called out again and other Russians carried in tables of vodka and food and the colonel invited the orchestra to eat. "What's the matter," he finally asked. "You have no appetite?"

In the Soviet army in World War II, detailed personnel records were not kept below the rank of major. Even today, when soldiers or sailors go sightseeing, they are not permitted to go off alone.

These are elements in a very different way of life from English life or American life. If Madariaga were to apply one word to the Russians, what would it be? Suspiciousness? Xenophobia? Toughness?

The Chinese, neighbors to the Russians, offer some marked contrasts in behavior and outlook. Francis Watson, in *The Frontiers of China*, remarks that "the simplest fact of Chinese frontier-attitudes in ancient tradition is illustrated by the location of the Great Wall. The long sea-frontier presented no danger until comparatively recent times, nor was the danger understood when it appeared." In the south "the lie of range and river favoured infiltration towards the south rather than invasion from it." To the west there were formidable mountains and, further along northward, deserts. The "Great Wall completed the definition of monsoon-China . . . as distinct from the outer wilderness. . . ."[26] Nevertheless, China was invaded and partially conquered from the north in the fourth and twelfth centuries A.D., and in the thirteenth century the Mongols entirely overran China and annexed it to their own empire. But in the end, as C. P. Fitzgerald says of the whole growth of the Chinese empire, over more than three thousand years, "the barbarians were conquered, then absorbed and turned into Chinese by slow assimilation and cultural influence. To deny this process, to claim that it had, or should, come to an end, was to Chinese thought a denial of the right, a recognition of failure."[27] That is why, Fitzgerald argues earlier, the Chinese view was that "territory which was once Chinese must forever remain so, and if lost, must be recovered at the first opportunity. Such loss cannot be legal or valid; it is at best a recognition of passing weakness."[28]

This attitude did not feature resort to violence but rather the inevitable and expected reward of virtue (a superior culture). As the Chinese proverb says, "Good iron is not beaten into nails, and a good man does not become a soldier."

This attitude became stronger even as China became militarily weaker. When King George III of England in 1793 sent a delegation to China, bearing written greetings couched in the usual flowery language, but designed with a more practical motive in mind, he was greeted in his turn by Emperor Ch'ien Lung as follows:

Swaying the wide world, I have but one aim in view; namely to maintain a perfect governance and to fulfill the duties of the state: strange and costly objects do not interest me. . . . As your ambassador can see for himself, we possess all things. I set no value on objects strange or ingenious, and have no use for your country's manufactures. This then is my answer to your request . . . It behooves you, O King, to respect my sentiments and to display even greater devotion and loyalty in the future, so that, by perpetual submission to our throne, you may secure peace and prosperity for your country hereafter.

. . . Tremblingly obey and show no negligence.[29]

The old Confucian doctrines governed Chinese attitudes for two thousand years. Claude Buss says that "if the facts fell out of line with the theory, the Chinese procedure was to change the facts to fit the theory."[30]

Order was maintained, not by force or tyranny, but by an enlightened and correct moral attitude. The essential task of government was to provide leadership. Confucius, asked about government, gave a threefold answer: sufficient food, sufficient weapons, and the confidence of the common people.

Tzu-kung said, Suppose you had no choice but to dispense with one of these three, which would you forego? The Master said, Weapons. Tzu-kung said, Suppose you were forced to dispense with one of the two that were left, which would you forego? The Master said, Food. Danger of enemies, danger of starvation, such were recurrent perils . . . which could be overcome if confidence were unshaken. But once let confidence go, neither arms nor food can save the country.[31]

In Chinese terminology, if it came to this point, the government would lose the "Mandate of Heaven"—as pragmatic an attitude toward government as one can find anywhere.

An account of Chinese life and manners written in the nineteenth century by Arthur H. Smith is very informative about other Chinese behavior. Smith, who was an American missionary for twenty-two years in China, and whose book went through many editions in the late 1800s, began by commenting on "face":

A Chinese thinks in theatrical terms. When roused in self-defense he addresses two or three persons as if they were a multitude. [His actions have] nothing to do with realities. The question is never of facts, but always of form. If a fine speech has been delivered at the proper time and in the proper way, the requirement of the play is met. . . . Properly to execute acts like these in all the complex relations of life, is to have "face."[32]

Smith contrasts Chinese and Western politeness. Where the Westerner may think of politeness as the surface expression of an inwardly felt kindness (a reflection of a civilization that at least theoretically regards the welfare of one as the welfare of all), "in China politeness is nothing of this sort. It is a ritual of technicalities which, like all technicalities, are important, not as indices of a state of mind or of heart, but as individual parts of a complex whole." The whole system of honorific terms was designed simply "to keep in view those fixed relations of graduated superiority which are regarded as essential to the conservation of society" and "as lubricating fluids to smooth human intercourse." Smith compares it to a game of chess "in which the first player observes, 'I move my insignificant King's pawn two squares.' To which his companion responds, 'I move my humble King's pawn in the same manner.'"[33]

Smith's whole book is fascinating. He discusses the Chinese concept of distances as it then prevailed, pointing out that distances uphill were considered longer than distances downhill. He tells of a river which was only ninety *li* downstream, whereas upstream (which is harder) it was 120 *li*. Everyone agreed this was so.

One final quote from Smith. Speaking of anxieties, he says that the Chinese are far more burdened than most, "there is a large proportion who are always on the ragged edge of ruin." Starvation or floods or lawsuits threaten.

Many of these disasters are not only seen, but their stealthy and steady approach is perceived, like the gradual shrinking of the iron shroud. . . . The Chinese face these things, perhaps because they seem to be inevitable, with a "clear-eyed endurance," which is one of the most remarkable phenomena of the race.[34]

Kenneth Scott Latourette sums up Chinese attitudes by saying that

the primary emphasis in Chinese culture has been upon the materialistic. The Chinese have been primarily interested in this life, in making it happy and comfortable. . . . They measure the success of any government by the material well-being of the nation. Continued hard times are sufficient to cause unrest and even revolution. Their ethics emphasize man's duty to man rather than man's duty to God. . . . To the Chinese this life is not, as to the Indian, a passing shadow, but a reality. They have not willingly indulged in transcendental speculation.[35]

Sun-Tzu, writing circa 500 B.C., laid down rules for conducting offensives that illustrate the practical nature of Chinese thinking very well.

What is of extreme importance in war is to attack the enemy's strategy. . . . Next best is to disrupt his alliances. . . . The next best is to attack his army. . . . The worst policy is to attack cities. Attack cities only when there is no alternative. . . . Your aim must be to take all-under-Heaven intact.[36]

Mao Tse-tung, writing about protracted war twenty-five centuries later, reflected the same Chinese view when he emphasized tactics for "defeating the enemy by misleading him and catching him unawares. We are not Duke Hsiang of Sung and have no use for his asinine ethics." (Duke Hsiang of Sung in 638 B.C. caught the superior forces of Chu crossing a river. When his generals urged immediate attack, the Duke said: "No, a gentleman should never attack one who is unprepared." When the battle finally occurred, the Duke's troops were disastrously defeated and the Duke wounded.)[37]

Theodore H. White, in his autobiography, tells of General Patrick Hurley's attempt in the Chinese Communist capital in Yenan in World War II to compose the differences between the Communists and the Nationalists. Taking the Communist draft, Hurley rewrote it that night in the cave quarters at Yenan, to provide that the new coalition government to be formed would "establish justice, freedom of conscience, freedom of the press, freedom of speech, . . . the right of writ of *habeas corpus*, and the right of residence."[38] White remarks of these rewordings that they concerned meanings and idioms reflecting "the sorrow-burdened attempt of men of different cultures to understand each other's ideas in translation."[39] White goes on to illustrate:

Our most hallowed word is "liberty." But translated into Chinese, the concept requires the words *tsy-yu-chu-i*, whose written characters mean "the idea of self-will" and connote "selfishness," or every man for himself. "Democracy" in Chinese translation goes back to the original Greek, coming out in ideographs as *min-tsu-chi-i*, "the idea of the people" as governing imperative. In American idiom, democracy is a process; translated into Chinese, it becomes theology. Of these linguistic difficulties Hurley had no perception whatsoever. He was no intellectual; he was a cartoon character out of American folklore.[40]

But it is enough for the purposes of this book to stop here. We have not been engaged in an effort to describe a series of foreign cultures so much as in an effort to describe differences among peoples. No definitive portraits of national character have been intended, but an assertion that these characters are quite diverse. We have been arguing for diversity to establish the fact that differences in national backgrounds and experiences are enormous (and, in many cases, obvious). It would be farfetched to assume that the peoples who are the products of these diverse cultures perceive international relations in a uniform manner and react to them with uniform assumptions and common expectations. Whether the particular national characterizations in this chapter are accurate, or have remained constant over time, is of lesser significance except to the specialist in particular cultures (to whom should be accorded the last word).

NOTES

1. Kwame Nkrumah, *I Speak of Freedom* (New York: Praeger, 1961), p. ix.

2. H. W. Shaw (Josh Billings), *Josh Billings, His Sayings,* 1865.

3. Emery Reves, *The Anatomy of Peace* (New York: Harper, 1945).

4. Richard A. Falk, *A Study of Future Worlds* (New York: Free Press, 1975).

5. Salvador de Madariaga, *Englishmen, Frenchmen, Spaniards* (London: Oxford University Press, 1928), p. 3.

6. Ibid.

7. Ibid., p. 8.

8. Thomas Jefferson, Letter to Walter Jones, 1810.

9. Friedrich Wilhelm Nietzsche, *Beyond Good and Evil,* 1886.

10. Harold Nicolson, *National Character and National Policy,* Montague Burton International Relations Lecture, 1938, University College, Nottingham, England. Reprinted in Frederick H. Hartmann, ed., *Readings in International Relations* (New York: McGraw-Hill, 1952), pp. 44, 45.

11. Ibid. (Hartmann, p. 46).

12. Madariaga, *Englishmen, Frenchmen, Spaniards,* p. 30.

13. Harold Nicolson, *Diplomacy,* 2d ed. (London: Oxford University Press, 1960), p. 136.

14. Ibid.

15. Madariaga, *Englishmen, Frenchmen, Spaniards,* p. 18.

16. Nicolson, *National Character* (Hartmann, pp. 46, 47).

17. Ibid.

18. Ibid.

19. Reprinted in *Introduction to Contemporary Civilization in the West* (New York: Columbia University Press, 1946), vol. 2, pp. 768-69.

20. G. P. Gooch and H. Temperley, eds., *British Documents on the Origins of the [First World] War, 1898-1914,* 11 vols. in 13 (His Britannic Majesty's Stationery Office, London: 1926-1938), vol. 7, p. 488. Italics added.

21. Nicolson, *National Character* (Hartmann, p. 48).

22. Hedrick Smith, *The Russians* (New York: Quadrangle, 1976), p. 6.

23. Neil S. Brown, Letter to Daniel Webster, 1853.

24. Nikita Khrushchev, *Khrushchev Remembers: The Last Testament* (Boston: Little, Brown, 1974), pp. 371-72.

25. Nikita Khrushchev, *Khrushchev Remembers* (Boston: Little, Brown, 1970), p. 88.

26. Francis Watson, *The Frontiers of China* (New York: Praeger, 1966), p. 17.

27. C. P. Fitzgerald, *The World Today* 19 (London: Royal Institute of International Affairs, 1963): 10-11, as quoted in Watson, *Frontiers*, pp. 18-19.

28. Ibid, p. 18.

29. From H. F. MacNair, *Modern Chinese History, Selected Readings* (Shanghai: Commercial Press, 1927), pp. 1-11, 25 quoted in Claude Buss, *The Far East* (New York: Macmillan, 1955), p. 40.

30. Buss, *The Far East*, p. 35.

31. Ibid., quoted from the Analects of Confucius in Maurice Collis, *The Great Within* (London: Faber and Faber, 1941), p. 140.

32. Arthur H. Smith, *Chinese Characteristics*, 13th ed. (New York: Fleming H. Revell, 1894), pp. 16-17.

33. Ibid., p. 36.

34. Ibid., p. 96.

35. Kenneth Scott Latourette, *The Development of China* (Boston: Houghton Mifflin, 1917), pp. 86-87.

36. Sun-Tzu, *The Art of War*, trans. Samuel B. Griffith, II (London: Oxford University Press, 1963), pp. 77-79. Each sentence is a lead-in to a paragraph.

37. *Selected Military Writings of Mao Tse-tung* (Peking: Foreign Languages Press, 1967), p. 240.

38. Theodore H. White, *In Search of History* (New York: Harper, 1978), p. 203. White is quoting Hurley here.

39. Ibid. White is commenting on Hurley.

40. Ibid.

10

COUNTERBALANCING NATIONAL INTERESTS

He who has a choice has trouble.

Dutch Proverb

There's small choice in rotten apples.
Shakespeare, *The Taming of the Shrew*, Act I, Scene 1

The third cardinal principle is counterbalancing national interests. It asserts that for everything of importance that might be included as content in foreign policy, an alternative is available that is usually its opposite. Like any hypothesis, it is only secondarily important whether this one can be proved to be true. What counts is whether it can accommodate the data adequately.

Counterbalancing national interests calls attention to the necessity of choice. It applies to both of the subdivisions of decision making explored in preliminary form in earlier chapters: (1) the nature of choice making as a bureaucratic process and (2) the kinds of choices and restrictions on choices imposed by the nature of the system.

To summarize, we argued that bureaucratic choice making reflects particular national values and attitudes. Regardless of strong resemblances from state to state, in the end there is always a unique national element in the way in which a problem is perceived and defined. By contrast, the nature of the choices to be made and the problems to be confronted has a strongly universal flavor, even though some nations are exempted by circumstances (including location) from some dilemmas. Thus the nature of choice making primarily reflects a particular culture, as we argued in Chapter 5, but the nature of the choices to be made primarily reflects the nature of the system, as we argued in Chapter 6.

Sometimes the distortions in the national perceptual lenses amount to a total reversal. President Nixon says in his memoirs that Henry Kissinger, returning in October 1972 from his unsuccessful trip to Vietnam to persuade

South Vietnamese President Thieu and his advisers to accept proposed peace terms, had found them with what Nixon calls "a surprising awe of Communist cunning and a disquieting lack of confidence in themselves." Then Nixon says an astounding thing: "As Kissinger saw the situation, we were up against a paradoxical situation in which North Vietnam, which had in effect lost the war, was acting as if it had won; while South Vietnam, which had effectively won the war, was acting as if it had lost."[1] In view of the real situation, which the South Vietnamese attitude much more realistically reflected, it is not easy to accept the idea that either Kissinger or Nixon could have believed this — but it certainly represents the perception of either one or both.

Any important decision ultimately involves weighing external against internal considerations, which is not to say that they are necessarily weighed thoroughly or well. At another point in his memoirs, Nixon is recounting his decision to intensify bombing and mine Haiphong — a decision likely to induce the Soviets to call off an impending summit conference. Just after putting this decision into effect, Nixon wrote a memorandum to Kissinger in which he expressed his dissatisfaction with the military's plan of allocating two hundred bombing sorties for the "dreary 'milk-runs'" that Johnson used from 1965 to 1968. Instead, Nixon wanted vigorous action.

What distinguishes me from Johnson is that I have the *will* in spades. If we now fail it will be because the bureaucrats and the bureaucracy and particularly those in the Defense Department, who will of course be vigorously assisted by their allies in State, will find ways to erode the strong, decisive action that I have indicated we are going to take. For once, I want the military and I want the NSC staff to come up with some ideas on their own which will recommend *action* which is very *strong, threatening,* and *effective.*[2]

Graham Allison says (with justice) that "making sure the government does what is decided [implementing the policy] is more difficult than selecting the preferred solution."[3] In this case, Nixon ideally had to weigh carefully not only the possible Soviet response but also (as he well understood) his own administration's probable degree of imagination, zeal, and loyalty in carrying it out. Nixon actually spent a fair amount of time on possible Soviet or Chinese reactions. He spent *least* time, in arriving at his decision, on the question of whether the results he anticipated would be achieved in Vietnam. That is, he reflected least on whether upping the pressure on the North Vietnamese would in fact incline them to bend to the American will — he simply assumed it would. He did not look at any detailed evidence about the results of bombing as they were known at the time. Nixon thought of it in simplified American conceptual terms as a contest between tough antagonists, in which victory would go to the tougher of the two.

The Nixon action in intensifying bombing and mining Haiphong helps to clarify a second point from the discussion in Chapter 5. The nature of choice making is such that decisions are not all of equal significance.

The choices made by a government vary in importance in the obvious sense that more significant issues are normally decided at the highest levels. But even top-level decisions vary significantly in their values and implications. A top-level choice to resume bombing in Vietnam would be, all other things being equal, a less significant choice than a top-level decision whether to bomb in the first place. That decision in turn would be less important than a decision whether to use force in Vietnam in the first place. And *that* decision is only understandable in the light of the even more significant question of how to take a stance vis-à-vis Communist China in particular and world communism in general.

This list shows that choices are of different degrees of importance, and also that they are connected by a certain implacable logic, once a turning point has been reached. The process is like that of a motorist who safely navigates the bleak world at the top of the Gotthard Pass in Switzerland, perhaps in the snows in July, eventually to emerge at the southern end. There the motorist gazes literally down, almost straight down, at sunny Italy. That is the moment of transition. Once the motorist begins to drive the car down the loops, one beneath the next, curve after curve, it will not be easy to stop until the first real plateau is reached. Decisions are like these loops, connected together and derivative from each other, but they lead somewhere rather than simply moving on. The motorist's first decision, of the greatest importance if the rest of the decisions are to be understood, is the most vital: the choice of the road. Those most fundamental decisions are the ones we shall examine closely under the heading of counterbalancing national interests. By their nature, we have argued in Chapter 5, such decisions are always "top-level" (i.e., have significant implications for the nation's future).

These top-level decisions often receive an astounding lack of attention. Germany's decision to commence building a high seas fleet, related in Chapter 4, was taken fairly casually, that is, without adequate consideration of the probable systems effects. So, essentially, was the German decision to refuse to renew the Reinsurance Treaty. Yet no decisions can compare in importance to those that bring on or avoid war and those that determine how much enmity must be successfully countered with how much support. Surely in both of these illustrations, the analysis of the external environment confronted and the probable effects of the decision were both skimpy and faulty.

One can make excuses for this sort of casualness about fundamental decisions. The easiest excuse of all to offer is that at the time the decision was not seen as being so vital as its results showed it was. Sir Harold Nicolson argues persuasively of the nature of choice making that

few indeed are the occasions on which any statesman sees his objective clearly before him and marches towards it with undeviating stride; numerous indeed are the occasions when a decision or event, which at the time seemed wholly unimportant, leads to another decision which is no less incidental, until, little link by link, the chain of circumstances is forged.[4]

To know all is to forgive all? But if that is all there is to decision making, the outlook is dim. As in George Orwell's *Animal Farm*, "All are equal, but some are more equal than others."

Certain forks in the road represent critical choices. President Johnson was at one, and knew he was, in March 1965 when he decided to send combat troops into Vietnam in an acknowledged combat role. The real question is whether all decisions that alter enmity (which by definition are critical choices) are recognizable at the time in their true nature to all actors in the system. Here the answer has to be a mixed one.

The answer is a clear "yes" when the decision involves declaring war or initiating or responding to an act of war. It is almost as clear a "yes" when the decision is whether to make a new alliance or equivalent commitment. It may be slightly less clear a "yes" when it involves a decision to deploy troops where they are not presently deployed, even if this is done as a "peaceful demonstration," and upon invitation. There are shades of difference here.

It is not likely that Nicolson is referring to such decisions. When that category of decisions that represent attitudinal shifts in policy is examined, however, Nicolson's point takes on added force. Such shifts may not appear as decisions at all, but instead as a more or less reluctant acceptance of an actual situation. At the time it may not be at all clear, even to the decision makers themselves, how far the new shift in policy should be taken. The decision makers may realize they have chosen a new road, but they may not have faced the question of exactly how far to travel on it.

The U.S. decision to pursue a containment strategy is a prime illustration. The "containment" thesis swept Washington at the end of World War II, and a version of it was subsequently embodied in President Truman's "doctrine." The U.S. government began on a course of action of which the direction was perfectly clear but the extent of future application still quite unclear.

The catalyst for the change was a telegram from George Kennan. Kennan's idea came at exactly the right time. As John Lewis Gaddis points out, Kennan's telegram arrived from Moscow "just as pressures were converging from several sources to 'get tough with Russia.' Truman himself had [as yet] done nothing to implement his resolution to 'stop babying the Soviets.' "[5]

As the draft of the doctrine began to be formulated, it took on the features of a compromise between two viewpoints. The final version included an aid program for Greece and Turkey. However, as Dean Acheson tells us in his memoirs, it also reflected Senator Arthur Vandenberg's insistence — and his Republican support was crucial — "that the problems of the two small countries be put in the setting of the larger confrontation between the Soviet Union and ourselves."[6]

When Kennan saw the final draft a few days before President Truman delivered the message to Congress on March 12, 1947, he was disturbed: "What I saw made me extremely unhappy. [It clothed] the President's decision in terms more grandiose and more sweeping than anything that I, at least, had ever envisaged."[7]

A section of the speech that Kennan took particular exception to "because of the sweeping nature of the commitments which it implied" was "the heart of the message and the passage that has subsequently been most frequently quoted. . . ."[8] Kennan refers to the passage that reads:

I believe that it must be the policy of the United States to support free peoples who are resisting subjugation by armed minorities or by outside pressures. I believe that we must assist free peoples to work out their own destinies [and] that our help should be primarily through economic and financial aid. . . .[9]

Interestingly, Dean Acheson's memoir account of the speech, while including this part, *omits* the section just in front of the above, a series of statements of a purple prose tone illustrated by the following: "At the present moment in world history nearly every nation must choose between alternative ways of life."[10] Acheson does not even quote or mention the even more far-reaching section just before *that* statement in the speech:

We shall not realize our objectives, however, unless we are willing to help free people to maintain their free institutions and their national integrity against aggressive movements that seek to impose upon them totalitarian regimes. This is no more than a frank recognition that totalitarian regimes imposed on free peoples, by direct or indirect aggression, undermine the foundations of international peace *and hence the security of the United States.*[11]

Kennan no doubt means all such statements in the Truman Doctrine when he says of the first passage quoted,

This passage, and others as well, placed our aid to Greece in the framework of a universal policy. . . . It implied that what we had decided to do in the case of Greece was something we would be prepared to do in the case of any other country, provided only that it was faced with the threat of "subjugation by armed minorities or by outside pressures."[12]

But how clear was this? Acheson's quotations from the speech are almost exclusively about Greece and Turkey. And when Acheson later testified on the Greek-Turkish aid bill in Congress, he reports that he was pressed by special advocates, such as Congressman Walter Judd on China, as to whether other nations threatened by communism would be aided. Acheson, on a spot, says that Senator Tom Connally, "a good friend in a free-for-all, summed up the position helpfully" and quotes the exchange:

Senator Connally: This is not a pattern out of a tailor's shop to fit every body in the world and every nation in the world, because the conditions in no two nations are identical. Is that not true?
Mr. Acheson: Yes sir, that is true, and whether there are requests, of course, will be left to the future, but whatever they are, they have to be judged, as you say, according to the circumstances of each specific case.[13]

Quite clearly Dean Acheson, a principal architect of the new policy, does not see it, at least primarily, as a global commitment, but rather as a resistance to specific Soviet pressures in a particular strategic area: Greece and Turkey. Yet from today's perspective, it is these general statements on containment that proved crucial, especially as these affected and directed United States policy in Asia. Kennan is right about how it turned out; he is also right that the doctrine implied a universal criterion for action. But it is true, even so, that those involved were not necessarily agreed as yet about what would come of the doctrine later.

When President Truman said to look at the map to see how the fall of Greece would be "of grave importance in a much wider situation" and described those dangerous effects, he was also saying that this had to be seen in context. Because the Russian Communists were aggressive and hostile, their challenge had to be met, or else. In short, he was perceiving the problem through an intellectual model and assuming, through his concept, that his actions would lead to certain results. To make that assumption, however, he necessarily had to assume that the system operated by certain rules. Otherwise he could not make predictions or specify current actions.

This is true throughout the system, although the concepts or models that appeal to one actor will not appeal to another. When national leaders choose among the critical alternatives (counterbalancing national interests) available to them, guided by their national perception of relationships in the exterior system, they reflect internal views of how that external system operates.

Nor are these views and preferences confined to the bureaucracy. They are widespread in the population, and choices reflecting alternatives that fairly equally touch the wellsprings of these emotional-intellectual predispositions are especially difficult to make for that reason. However, once the public debate is over and the issue resolved, the consensus formed is likely to endure a long time, until its inertia is counteracted by exterior events. Such a consensus typically extends far beyond the bureaucrats, then, and it does not come about simply because the people are "won over" by the executive. It happens primarily because "everyone" in the nation tends to come to look at the problem in much the same way.[14]

When President Truman stood up to announce the Truman Doctrine, he did not face a United States where the people rejected the notion that they stood to benefit if free peoples abroad remained free. Whether the idea that free peoples are friends of the United States and unfree peoples are enemies happened to be true from a systems point of view or not, Truman did not have to argue the point. He simply appealed to Americans on a basis they accepted to be true.

Between the Truman Doctrine of 1947 and President Johnson's commitment of U.S. combat troops in a combat role in Vietnam in 1965, the philosophical or attitudinal line of thinking and perceiving continued unbroken. In retrospect, we know that Truman's electoral victory of 1948 closed the issue for a very long time.

A consensus so reached will eventually erode if it conflicts with reality too obviously and persistently. When this happens, both popular opinion and bureaucratic alignments come to reflect that fact. President Nixon, quoted earlier, was dealing with this more unusual situation, where after enormous expenditures of blood and treasure, the elusive prize of peace seemed still to elude the United States. When such a lack of consensus exists, or when erosion ends a previously agreed consensus, people seek a new formulation.

Thus decision making on any critical national security issue is ultimately guided by such idea structures. In critical cases the decision makers resemble a group peering into the cages at the strange animals in the zoo. All the decision makers see the animals. Some may enjoy zoos more; some may like one animal more than another. Some may know more than others about the feeding habits of the animals. If the decision makers are then handcuffed together and required to decide which four out of six animal cages should be unlocked—and, if they cannot agree, all cages will be thrown open—there will be a lively debate. That debate will have very little to do with parochial bureaucratic interests, although it may be shaped in part by the standard organizational procedures available. What is certain is that the debate will end with a consensus of some sort, reflecting simultaneously the decision makers' experience and background and the prevailing view of what is most dangerous and least dangerous. It is quite instructive to read the accounts of the Cuban missile crisis from the viewpoint of this analogy.

Assuming the validity of this view of the formation of a consensus, we shall move on to the special or specific character and implications of choices between counterbalancing national interests, pointing out three things. First, we have asserted that every important potential content piece affecting outside danger has an alternative.* Second, these alternatives each have a plus and a minus value, four separate values in all. Third, such counterbalancing national interests acquire special significance in policy making because of their property of increasing or decreasing enmity. In considering choices between counterbalancing interests, it is important to know as much as possible about two things: whether the elite sees the choices clearly in this light, and whether the choices made do in fact produce what is envisaged (change enmity in the anticipated direction).

As we have argued throughout, the concept held by the decision makers will affect the content of the policy to be implemented, because that concept envisages alternative futures. It picks one counterbalancing interest over its alternative because that interest is believed to produce the most satisfactory results and keep costs to acceptable limits. When the thought process is explicit, it begins by posing a picture of an end result, then asks who outside would favor such a result and who oppose, and finally weighs the cost. This first scenario is then compared to all other scenarios until a balance is struck between the results to be achieved and the foreseeable costs of achieving them. As Morton H. Halperin quite correctly says, actual decision makers take shortcuts to arrive at choices.[15] Or, again, they may go through no explicit mental process at all—but what would be wrong to assume would be that they choose one interest over another by pure chance.

If every counterbalancing national interest has advantages and disadvantages, so does its alternative. If the United States decides on a negative stance toward Communist China, as it did in the 1950s and 1960s, it shows that it believes that the alternative has very little advantage and obvious disadvantages. The decision itself may or may not reflect the realities in the outside world; that is a separate issue. What is more important at the moment is to say that a reversal of the policy stance would not be a simple substitution of gains and losses.

Let us be as concrete as possible with our example. The great advantage of a stance against Communist China was that it permitted the United States

---

*Conceivably more than *one* alternative exists for a counterbalancing interest but it will serve the purpose in practice to consider most choices in pairs. Such choices are normally focused on having better or worse relations with particular third states.

to support free peoples (Chinese on Taiwan) against totalitarians (Chinese Communists). It permitted the United States to oppose a Chinese nation perceived to be an ally of Soviet Russia, itself an enemy or at least a threat to the United States. There were other perceived advantages. The disadvantages included arraying the United States against the most populous nation in the world and broadening the potential theater of conflict to Asia as well as Europe.

Reversing such a policy, as happened in the 1970s, did not simply change each plus to minus and each minus to plus. Where Communist China had been considered, quite literally, as an enemy, the "People's Republic of China" was not now an ally. Nor did the Communists become a "free" people because the United States ended the antagonism, with Chinese cooperation.

The reversal of policy altered the "game" (the relationships in the world), but the players did not simply exchange roles. Friends did not become enemies and enemies friends. Nonetheless, the reversal made an enormous difference in the distribution of enmity in the system. Where China and the United States had each previously suffered from an overload of enmity, that overload was now passed on to the Soviet Union because both China and the United States, by virtue of the change, were freer to take issue with the Soviets. So the Soviets perceived it, and so it was in fact.

As the illustration implies, the most interesting aspect of counterbalancing interests is the alternatives that have *not* been chosen for implementation but are, as it were, held in reserve. It is not at all difficult to survey the world from this viewpoint and note these reserve alternatives. Each has been "shelved," of course, because its net value is perceived as less than that of the counterbalancing interest chosen for implementation. Studying this situation reveals a great deal about the perception or concept of that particular player and also about the developments that are possible in the total system, because it leads inevitably to an assessment of the possible transformations in the distribution of enmity within the system.

To look at initial choices or at later substitutions of "reserved" or counterbalancing interests is to observe the components of a total policy, the structural unity of which is necessarily intellectual. As Henry Kissinger once put it, "You cannot conduct foreign policy except on the basis of some coherent set of ideas." The total set of integrated ideas leads to a coherently integrated total policy, in which each "subpolicy," or interest, is a piece of the whole.

It is for this reason that we have avoided, in using China as an illustration, speaking of a China *policy* as being changed, using instead the "counterbalancing interest" terminology. Speaking of "policies" toward other nations in a plural sense, meaning various policies that are being pursued simultaneously toward various nations, encourages a false notion that the individual pieces need not be integrated into a total national foreign policy. "Policy" toward individual nations is only and necessarily a subunit of a conceptual whole, so the term policy is best reserved for that totality.

We might have chosen to use a term such as "subpolicy" to denote that part of the policy directed toward China. What makes it more useful to talk of interests rather than subpolicies is the nature of the interactions among national policies. In discussing a bilateral relationship, one might say that the subpolicies of the two nations toward one another are essentially compatible, but it is far easier, and more usual, to say that they have many common interests.

In any event, apart from terminological and intellectual problems, it is not practical to have a policy or subpolicy toward another nation. Relations will be affected, willy-nilly, by all kinds of features of a national policy, including views on human rights, exploitation of the seabed, commercial air transit, pollution controls, and international law. Consequently, relations of nations toward specific other nations are never totally oriented toward those specific nations. Rather, their policies include interests of a broad, functional nature as well. Both the broad and specific (nation-directed) interests contribute to the total effect: the bilateral amalgam of compatible or incompatible interests.

The United States does not have a view of international law that it holds only with regard to Russia. It holds a view of the law that applies to Russia as well as to other countries and depending on Russia's view, contributes in that special feature toward agreement or disagreement. When all such special features (interests) are added up, it can truly be determined whether the relationship between the United States and the Soviet Union has a decidedly negative or a positive character. It follows that a change in view on either nation's part about any one or more of that nation's interests will affect the composite of their relationship positively or negatively.

The overall perception one nation has of another is not the simple result of a conscious examination of the specific interests they pursue toward one another insofar as this yields a certain compatibility or incompatibility, but it is true that a conscious reduction of antagonistic interests will affect the total net interplay. If the process is carried far enough by both sides, their leaders will begin to ask themselves why they perceived the other nation as a threat.

The argument above is, of course, at the extreme. Such drastic changes, theory apart, are not likely to occur unless the appearance of a new threat makes older enemies appear in a new light, as in the example in Chapter 4. The greater utility of our argument is in relation to third parties, looked at from the standpoint of either of the parties to a fairly stable mutual antagonism. Each party to the antagonism will soon be tempted to consider alterations in policy that will provide a more cordial relationship with certain of these third parties. Such improved relationships have many advantages, ranging all the way from reinforcement (the addition of an ally) to increased isolation of an enemy from support.

To produce such more cordial relationships with third parties means to reexamine the content of the total policy pursued toward those third parties. Where third parties have a negative net stance toward one's own nation, but the negative net is relatively small, fairly modest adjustments in the interests one pursues may completely alter the attitude of the third party. To state the point another way, the easiest way to change third-party lineups is to alter the interests one pursues toward those nations almost evenly inclined to be friendly or antagonistic, provided that the policy stance of those third parties has standing in the eyes of one's opponents. To change Albania's view toward the United States is only of consequence if it makes some difference to the Russians one way or the other. That is why we spoke earlier of a policy matrix according to which, for any given nation, one could ask the effect on a whole host of other nations of a shift on the friendship-enmity scale.

When a nation deliberately sets out to alter the total enmity it confronts, the universal currency it must use consists of the reserved alternatives, that is, the alternative counterbalancing interests *not* being pursued. It must ask what another nation would like in the environment it faces that is not there now, and then reflect on which change of interests pursued would alter the environment in the desired direction, without, of course, producing some other negative effect.

Relatively small changes in policy content can yield large dividends, because one shift can induce many others. For example, the demise of the Shah's rule in Iran increased the interest of both Israel and Egypt in making peace: Israel, because it lost the Shah's support; Egypt, because it made the Middle East situation potentially more violent at a time when Egypt needed peace for economic reasons. Saudi Arabia, now more vulnerable to a coup, became more inclined to be moderate and watchful, not seriously opposing a peace settlement.

When nations approach such forks in the road and must make important choices affecting the enmity they will confront, how well do they usually understand what they face? Do nations stumble into greater or lesser confrontations, or do they manage their great affairs? When they substitute counterbalancing interests in their policies, do they in fact change enmity in the anticipated direction?

There is great variety to be observed here; nations do in their time play many parts. Let us address this question in a systems context, using the

1920s and 1930s for specific illustrations, showing how divergent English and French reactions to Adolf Hitler undermined hopes of preserving a united front against aggression.

In the 1920s, despite the disastrous Peace of Versailles, a modest measure of progress toward a real peace in Western Europe had begun to be made. It was the era of Locarno. Spurred by two particular "men of good will," Gustav Stresemann of Germany and Aristide Briand of France, Europe at the time had achieved a certain precarious harmony.[16] Given enough time, this harmony might have taken roots.

That time was not forthcoming, as much because of the reparations and the resulting severe economic distortions as for any other reason. Instead came the Great Depression — a misery that spawned two very different kinds of national saviors, one on each side of the Atlantic: Franklin D. Roosevelt in the United States, Adolf Hitler in Germany. Both held power in nations filled with despair: a special kind of despair. In America the despair came from a crisis in confidence, as millions of workers were thrown into prolonged and semipermanent unemployment. Capitalism's promise of the good life had been broken, and anxiety prevailed. FDR's theme, as he took office on March 4, 1933, was that "the only thing we have to fear is fear itself." He meant that the resources and the strength were still there, if they could again be brought to bear on the nation's problems.

Adolf Hitler had become chancellor of Germany less than forty days earlier, on January 30, 1933, after a rigged election. He took power in a nation that, after losing World War I, was starved until the Germans, being called in at Versailles to sign a quite literally dictated peace put together by the Allies, gave in. That treaty stripped Germany of much territory, only some of it justifiably. Crippling economic obligations were imposed in the form of initially open-ended reparations. Failure to pay — quite inevitable in any case — brought on the Belgo-French occupation of the Ruhr. In the subsequent inflation, the German middle class was pauperized. When Germany began to climb out of this situation, the financial collapse of 1931 and the ensuing Great Depression again plunged it to its knees. Adolf Hitler, like FDR, restored the German people to hope and a renewed sense of national unity. Unfortunately, he also brought on the violence and death we today remember him for, but that is not how it began.

A film, *Five Minutes to Midnight*, was shown in Germany between 1953 and 1954, at a time when the country was still drab, devoid of uniforms and color, still recovering. The film showed the Nazi era. It showed it so well that for a time it was banned by the government. As the early Nazi years were being recalled, the commentator kept saying: "See those people smiling at Hitler. They are deluded. They do not know that the time is already nearing midnight [total defeat]." The commentator's overview made little impression on the audience, which was caught up in the magic memories of 1933 and 1934, when there were goals and a sense of progress. The camera panned the crowd of ecstatic faces as Hitler drove by in an open touring car.

The urgent question for England and France was how to perceive this Hitler and his Germany. The rest of Europe was more or less in disarray. Russia had lost vast territories at the end of World War I, and a Polish state had been created out of German and Russian territories inhabited by Poles (and Germans and Russians). Austria-Hungary had been dismantled. Italy, although a gainer of territory, rankled at the loss of other promised prizes, such as part of Turkey.

Europe's situation reflected a grave structural weakness. It was a situation to which the English and French response would be particularly fateful, as each nation decided between counterbalancing national interests. With Germany and Russia *both* dissatisfied with the status quo, there was a strong possibility that they could combine forces to despoil Poland and perhaps other small states to the south of Poland. In the days before World War I, when Austria-Hungary existed as a relatively strong power near the borders of both Germany and Russia, Vienna's views and policies had also always to be weighed. But now Vienna spoke for a mere 6 million people, and its policies carried almost no weight at all. Restraint on such Russo-German cooperation could only come from a league of Balkan states associated with France. Whether that, even then, would be enough was another question. France chose such alliances in the years after Versailles. England remained aloof. Where English relations with Russia stayed cool, after 1933 France moved to revive the old alliance with Russia, Bolshevik or not.

France had another choice, of course. France could have placated Germany—a course foreshadowed in the Locarno era (but where the concessions made were nominal). If it had really followed such a course, France would have had to agree to equality in armaments for Germany and probably territorial revisions, inevitably strengthening the enemy fought from 1870 to 1871 and 1914 to 1918. If Germany was not to be placated, then a Russian alliance made sense, provided Russia could be persuaded that an alliance with France was better than a cooperation with Germany.

England's policy, of course, bore on the issue. What were its choices? England could have decided that a German-Russian collaboration could be ruled out and that a policy of friendship toward both would be feasible and constructive; but in actual fact England did not think Stalin's Russia very trustworthy or forthcoming. England could have tried to stand aloof from any involvement; but history testified to the futility of such a course. More realistically, England could have sided with Germany—or with Russia.

On March 16, 1935, Hitler denounced the disarmament clause of the Versailles Treaty and openly proclaimed rearmament. At the Stresa Conference in April, under French leadership, England and Italy strongly protested the German move. (Already, in January 1935, France had made a number of colonial concessions to Italy to align it against Germany.) Then on May 2, 1935, France made an alliance with Russia, directed against Germany. Six weeks later, on June 18, 1935, England reached a naval agreement with Nazi Germany that permitted Germany to build a navy no larger than 35 percent the size of the British-controlled forces. To express it another way, England endorsed Germany's denunciation of the Versailles restrictions, while France moved in the opposite direction.

Now Italy played a card. On October 3, 1935, Italian forces began an obvious invasion of Ethiopia, in clear violation of the League Covenant, which both England and France were pledged to uphold. On October 7 the League Council branded Italy as an aggressor.

Italy could, of course, see France's need for Italian support, which would make France reluctant to quarrel with Italy, even now and even though France considered that the League Covenant should be supported if aggression (especially German aggression) were not to be encouraged. Italy might also have assumed that England would take no strong action without France. So much is obvious. What is more interesting are the possible results of such an Italian move. Italy went to Stresa to protest against Germany quite sincerely; Germany was a growing threat. In July 1934 Mussolini's mobilization of Italian troops at the Brenner Pass had frustrated Hitler's first attempt to take Austria. But if Italian troops went to Africa and became tied down there, what might happen at the Brenner Pass? Even if England and France and the League took no effective action against Italy, what were the gains and losses? Ethiopia taken; Austria endangered? Which counterbalancing interest was to be preferred? Could the Italians think one scare had finished Adolf Hitler?

With the Italians yielding to the African temptation, what were the choices for the others? From Germany's viewpoint, Italy was serving German purposes. England, which initially had tried to avoid any decisive action over Ethiopia, now joined with France in supporting the League action, although the Suez Canal remained open and no embargo of oil was attempted.

Mussolini won in Ethiopia and joined Hitler in a pact on October 25, 1936, by which time Germany had also reoccupied the Rhineland. From then on, with this switch in counterbalancing interests by Italy in an attempt at expansion, Germany and Italy were allies. England sought and reached an agreement with Italy on January 2, 1937, guaranteeing mutual respect of rights and interests in the Mediterranean and preservation of Spanish independence. On April 16, 1938, England signed a further pact with Italy, designed to reconcile policy differences.

Looked at as moves in a chess game, England might be thought through these moves to be trying to defuse enmity with Italy (true) or trying to detach Italy from Germany (highly questionable). If England were attempting a general policy of drawing back from continental involvement, its pledge on March 31, 1939 (after the Slovak crisis and the disappearance of the Czech state), of aid by England and France to Poland in case of action threatening Polish independence made no sense. This pledge was actually expanded on April 6 into a pact of mutual assistance. If England was trying to keep out of involvement, appeasement at the Munich Conference (to which Russia was not invited) made sense. But why then this sequel? If England was going to all this effort to detach Italy, why would not a greater effort to attach the Russians to the Anglo-French entente have been more desirable? Or, if England decided to support Poland—which it did—how could it do it if Russia remained uninvolved? What was the practical sense of it all?

What about Russia? Russia had a lively and justified sense of grievance, initially stemming from its territorial losses and the Anglo-French (and Allied) interventions in its civil war. Offered an alliance with France in 1935, Russia accepted, only to be ignored at Munich and to witness an agreement at Czechoslovakia's expense that Russia could only construe as an invitation to Germany to turn its threat eastward against Russia. The promises given to Czechoslovakia by England and France to uphold the security and integrity of the rest, after the Sudeten border area had been yielded, were brushed aside by Hitler's brusque conquest of the rest of Czechoslovakia in March 1939. England and France did not intervene.

Stalin, addressing the Eighteenth Communist Party Congress of the Soviet Union on March 10, 1939, stated a clear reaction:

Far be it from me to moralize . . . to talk of treason, treachery, and so on. . . . Politics is politics, as the old case-hardened bourgeois diplomats say. It must be remarked, however, that the big and dangerous political game started by the supporters of the policy . . . may end in a serious fiasco for them.[17]

It takes little imagination to see what might be in Stalin's mind. What, after all, were his options? Or could the English and the French have assumed that they could take any action (or refrain from any action) over Czech affairs and still leave relations with Russia exactly where they were before these events? In fact, the English and the French rather tardily began to negotiate further with Moscow.

The Russians suggested moving Red Army troops forward into Poland, but the Poles would have none of it. Russia pointed out that there was no advantage to Russia in being committed to Polish defense if it would have to fight Hitler only after he had already destroyed Poland. Once that occurred, Stalin very much feared he might get a paper declaration of war by England and France, but no real help. Why should he have had any greater confidence? Stalin could not help suspecting that England's pledge to Poland was bait for a Soviet commitment against Germany. Finding that Hitler was willing to divide Poland with him, he took the more tangible option. So World War II began.

Looking beyond the system framework and examining what internally lay behind these national decisions changes the perspective. The English were not being perfidious over Poland; they really meant their pledge. It was England that fought, and Russia that stood aloof. There is the irony of the whole episode. Yet can one really blame the Russians for drawing the conclusions they did?

Weighing these actions, let us see where the mistakes were made and by whom. Which actors did not perceive the realities of the system? Let us look at each actor and sum up the choices.

England made as many mistakes as any. Curiously for an avowed practitioner of the balance of power, England showed a slowness to grasp the essential weaknesses in the eastern power structure: that Poland and the rest could be defended only with the active cooperation of Russia or as a consequence of a peaceful policy by Germany. Since, in the end, England went to war for Poland, this is a highly important point. Of course, it might be argued that England could disregard events in the East so long as peace was maintained in the West. Even if that were true in power equilibrium terms, however, it would also have to be proved true in practice by policy restraint on the part of Hitler. Was Hitler bent on peace, once his "just" demands were fulfilled? To answer that question required a policy judgment by England, one that carefully examined the risks and advantages of placating Hitler (or Mussolini), especially compared to alternatives. The most crucial question here goes back to where we began: Could Britain, with its experience and knowledge of the system, have assumed that it could safely alienate or ignore Russia while hoping to placate Germany and Italy? Were not the counterbalancing interest choices clear?

What about Italy? Mussolini was not wrong to believe that England and France would not want to make war over Ethiopia. For one thing, they had similar colonies themselves. For another, they needed him — quite obviously so. Where Mussolini began to go astray was in acting as though Italy, needed by Britain and France, had no reciprocal need. Yet Italy would then inevitably have to allow Austria to pass into German hands. In return for an empire in Africa, Italy would be required to mortgage the security of its northern border at home. In view of Italy's previous experience of prolonged trouble with German-speaking powers, ignoring that danger to embark on African adventures involved significant and obvious risk. It was perfectly clear, at the time, that neither alternative was cost-free.

Russia, under communism, was not really trusted by either England or France. But neither was it trusted by, nor could it trust, Germany. Russia did understand the choices, however: either to oppose Germany or to cooperate temporarily with it. Russia did not think it could choose friendship with Germany, and it knew that war was becoming more likely. Why Russia came to believe Britain and France could not be trusted has already been indicated. Russia's need to choose between counterbalancing interests, and the nature of its choices and reasons for choosing, are all clear.

We come to France. With minor exceptions, French policy demonstrated a clear understanding that all roads could not be followed simultaneously. The French never really wavered, at least after 1933, in considering Germany the real enemy. If England was not sure who was the enemy, and neither was Italy, France had no such problem. France did have a problem, when Italy openly defied the League, of how to avoid destroying the League as a future reliance against Germany; but France was never willing, even then, to uphold the League by fighting Italy.

Poland saw the peril but refused to run the risks inherent in accepting Soviet aid. It is not clear, even in retrospect, that Poland made the wrong choice. Poland's tragedy is that its choices are always between such unappealing alternatives.

For its part Germany played the game very well in this period, especially by capitalizing on poor choices by others.

The game has its rules. They are flexible but severe, and the system does not pardon those whose hearts are right but judgment weak. The kinds of mistakes, and their consequences, shown by this comprehensive illustration may be traced in individual cases to bureaucratic roots, to moral uncertainties, or to vacillating power holders. Whatever the cause, a nation pays dearly if it misses its opportunity to contour the enmity it confronts and fails to choose its counterbalancing interest alternatives accordingly.

NOTES

1. Richard Nixon, *The Memoirs of Richard Nixon* (New York: Grosset and Dunlap, 1978), p. 696.

2. Ibid., p. 607. Italics in original.

3. Graham T. Allison, *Essence of Decision: Explaining the Cuban Missile Crisis* (Boston: Little, Brown, 1971), p. 146.

4. Harold Nicolson, *The Congress of Vienna* (New York: Harcourt, 1946), pp. 19-20.

5. John Lewis Gaddis, *The United States and the Origins of the Cold War, 1941-1947* (New York: Columbia University Press, 1972), p. 304.

6. Dean Acheson, *Present at the Creation* (New York: Norton, 1969), p. 225.

7. George F. Kennan, *Memoirs, 1925-1950* (Boston: Little, Brown, 1967), p. 315.

8. Ibid., pp. 319-20.

9. *Congressional Record*, 80th Cong., 1st sess., vol. 93, part 2, p. 1981.

10. Ibid.

11. Ibid., italics added.

12. Kennan, *Memoirs, 1925-1950*, p. 320.

13. Acheson, *Present at the Creation*, p. 225.

14. Otto Klineberg, the psychologist, says flatly: "Individuals usually share the prevailing opinions of the group to which they belong." See his book, *The Human Dimension in International Relations* (New York: Holt, Rinehart, Winston, 1964), p. 107.

15. Morton H. Halperin, *Bureaucratic Politics and Foreign Policy* (Washington, D.C.: Brookings Institution, 1974).

16. Dr. Paul Schmidt, the German interpreter, in his *Statist auf diplomatischer Bühne, 1923-45* (Bonn: Athenäum-Verlag, 1949) has given us a fascinating first-hand account.

17. Joseph Stalin, *Selected Writings* (New York: International Publishers, 1942), p. 442.

11

THE CONSERVATION OF ENEMIES

You and I were long friends: you are now my enemy, and I am
yours,

B. Franklin[1]

The fourth cardinal principle, and the name of this book, is the conservation of enemies. By setting out the proposition that a prudent nation will
not collect more enemies than it can reasonably confront, this principle provides the operational climax of our model. As a proposition it implies, as we
have reiterated many times, that enemies and enmity are, to an important
degree, matters of choice.

The initial reaction to this principle may be one of amusement, because it
sounds quaint but dated. After all, in a nuclear age what does it matter?
One nuclear enemy, sufficiently armed, has by itself the capacity to wipe
out one's own version of civilized life. Additional enemies merely equate to
additional overkill; they are either irrelevant or redundant.

Such a conclusion must be looked at very carefully. It implies that the
prime consideration for any nation contemplating war is the destructive
capability on both sides. If superiority or survival for the potential aggressor nation seems reasonably assured after comparing order-of-battle
data, it will, or ought to, attack.

Put this baldly, the proposition makes us thoughtful, as well it ought, for
it says that the decision for or against war rests upon the results of a comparative capability analysis. Is this a correct way of understanding how
nations would go to war in the nuclear age? Is it a correct way of understanding how nations in any period of history have decided for or against
armed conflict? Have the considerations that a nation contemplating war in
the nuclear age would take into account changed from what they were prior
to the nuclear age? And if so, how?

The first consideration of any prudent nation has always been whether it
could win (prevail); but a truly prudent nation would recognize from the

outset that war is unpredictable. Who would have imagined, in the Peloponnesian Wars, that Athens would be struck by the plague? It is ironical that, according to Thucydides's account, the Athenian ambassadors specifically warned the Spartans on the role of chance:

Take time, then, over your decision, which is an important one. . . . Think, too, of the great part that is played by the unpredictable in war: think of it now, before you are actually committed to war. The longer a war lasts, the more things tend to depend on accidents. Neither you nor we can see into them: we have to abide their outcome in the dark. And when people are entering upon a war they do things the wrong way around. Action comes first, and it is only when they have already suffered that they begin to think.[2]

It could be argued that the advice just recorded was impractical, that prudence is the very thing to fly out the window as soon as war is contemplated, for emotions will surely rise. Ergo, nations contemplating war are inescapably imprudent. Ralph K. White, a social psychologist, examining the Austro-Serbian confrontation of 1914, listed six misperceptions, most of them obvious and direct products of rising emotions. These were: a diabolical enemy image, a virile self-image, a moral self-image, selective inattention, absence of empathy, and military overconfidence.[3]

That may all be so, but recall our point of departure: whether, given the overkill capability in the hands of a single nation contemplating war, it would need to take into account anything more than a bilateral comparison of order-of-battle data. By definition, any such assessment would be highly dispassionate, quite unemotional, highly "scientific." One might argue that emotion might displace such an analysis, but if the decision rested upon it, the decision must be cold-blooded by definition. It would also necessarily be inadequate, because it would contemplate the events of a war fought under completely novel conditions with completely novel weapons. No one knows what that war would really be like. Nuclear war would be more unpredictable than any past war except in one single aspect. Everyone agrees it would be immensely destructive if not indeed catastrophic. The death and destruction unleashed by a nuclear attack might give rise to the spread of virulent disease and contamination, which might also destroy the attacking nation, even if it remained immune from a retaliatory nuclear strike. In Thucydides' terms, "Athens" might again be visited by the plague. Chance would intervene; which way is unknowable.

One of the most striking features of World War II, compared to World War I, is that the last phase of World War II involved the introduction of effectively used weapons of a completely new generation from that with which the war began. The list includes the atom bomb. It also includes the jet plane and rockets, the snorkel, and the proximity fuze. By contrast,

World War I saw fewer effective innovations, and none at the end. Poison gas (1915) was not exploited; the tank (1917) was misused; air power had little significant impact. Despite the series numbering, I and II, these world wars were by no means duplicates of each other. Visualize Adolf Hitler in 1939 contemplating the prospects for ultimate victory. He had fought in World War I himself. How much weight did he assign *then* to the race for nuclear weapons? How much should he have assigned? Even if the weighing of prospects is dispassionate and unemotional, it may not be accurate. War is unpredictable in this way, too.

Bernard Brodie, referring to Albert Wohlstetter's *Foreign Affairs* article, "The Delicate Balance of Terror," makes a highly appropriate comment:

This article, as is characteristic of so many writings on military technological affairs, took no account whatever of the inhibitory political and psychological imponderables that might and in fact *must* affect the conditions implied by that word *delicate*. Many things are technologically feasible that we have quite good reason to believe will not happen. It has in fact become abundantly clear . . . that the balance of terror is decidedly *not* delicate. . . . [Given] the enormous disparities in nuclear capabilities between powers . . . enormously hostile to each other . . . that fact is itself impressive.[4]

A return will be made to this line of thought in Chapter 17, which deals with the specific, technologically-inspired form of strategic analysis spawned by the nuclear age and nuclear weapons. Here our concern is only to ask whether it makes any difference at present that the weapons are nuclear. Specifically, our concern is with whether the number of enemies one confronts is of any consequence today.

We have argued earlier that it is a serious mistake to see any relationship in a multilateral world in purely bilateral terms. How would this point apply to a nation contemplating war today?

It is here that the third relatively unpredictable aspect of war comes to bear. To contemplate war on the basis of a bilateral nuclear weapon count by definition ignores third parties, some of which, at least, are nuclear-armed. Yet the very assumption the aggressor must make, to attack first, is that the initial strike can be so contrived that it will not be possible for the victim to retaliate effectively. In that case, consider the implications for a nuclear-armed third party for which security from attack by this aggressor has depended importantly upon the "victim's" nuclear armament. In such case the temptation of the third state to take action, unless the aggressor achieves complete and overwhelming surprise, will be very great. Does the aggressor dare turn its "back" on this third state?

In a prenuclear age these problems also existed. Two things have changed with the advent of nuclear weapons, the first of which everyone automatically thinks of: the vast potential destruction. But that leads to the second thing, which is different: stakes that are now so much higher that the penalties for error are enormous and drastic.

So far in this analysis of whether the number of enemies really matters, we have been describing a relatively extreme case. The more normal or usual situation of tension would be between opponents who fear one another but who are not actively seeking opportunities to make an attack.

Each could take the position, or one of them could, that nothing the other party does in terms of exercising influence or control over third states or places matters. These things do not matter, each could argue, because they would not affect the outcome of a full bilateral nuclear exchange. In that case, for example, it would become immaterial whether the West continued to hold West Berlin. It would also become immaterial whether Soviet troops continued to occupy the German Democratic Republic. If the Soviets, for example, were indifferent, then we could see them retiring behind their own frontiers while Poland and Hungary joined NATO. If the United States were indifferent, France and West Germany might soon blossom forth as new "democratic republics" while the United States retreated into isolationism.

How much likelihood is there of any of this happening? But if not, why not? What difference does it make? Is international concern over position not simply a leftover idea from a bygone age, not yet decently buried?

Nations are not, in fact, capable of this kind of indifference. There is really no need to prove that statement in any depth; almost everything we know confirms it. But what does it matter who owns Berlin? Well, it does matter. Prestige enters in. Reputation plays a part. Estimates of national willpower are involved. And projections as to future behavior are being drawn. Giving up Berlin is not just giving up Berlin; it is an announcement that one might be willing progressively to give up whole hosts of things.

Even if this were a wise course of action, it would contain one serious, inherent danger, that as concessions were made or the enemy made unresisted gains, a growing conviction would come to the passive nation that it must make a stand, draw a line. Yet the active nation, by now encouraged, would be in precisely the mood to assume that another good push was what was needed. The Czar wrote on the Russian internal documents in the Austro-Russian crisis just prior to the one that began World War I, that this would be the last time Russia would be humiliated and yield.

But if positions cannot be supinely yielded and lines left undrawn, then, calculations of power and intent must rest on more than sum totals of megatonnage and machine guns. Assets and liabilities must have to include friends and enemies — and if there are few friends but many enemies, the whole problem will start again as the opponent, convinced of superiority in these categories, presses its advantage. Therefore the numbers of friends and enemies is a fundamental part of the equation.

Everyone understands the advantages in this context of increasing the number of allies, provided they do in fact add in one way or another to the assets available. But an effort aimed at increasing one's allies yet ignoring the opposite side of the ledger is shortsighted. If the major enemy also adds allies, the tension merely increases as the opposing blocs grow and solidify. What is more effective is deliberately holding down the opponent's number of allies by making policy adjustments that satisfy the requirements of third nations. Not all reinforcements of this sort can be headed off, of course. Nations with concerns that can be adequately handled by adjustments of the first country's policies, but which will ally with its major opponent if these adjustments are not forthcoming, are the real targets of such efforts. For instance, Germany should never have let Russia, because of such trivial reasons on Germany's part, slip away after 1890 into an alliance with France.

That shift really meant a two-front war for Germany. Germany could never restore this imbalance by merely itself gaining an ally—one for France, therefore one for Germany. Germany would have had to gain, say, England as an ally, or Spain. Even then the effect would not quite have been equivalent. Besides, once France gained Russia as an ally, France was no longer isolated. France did not just gain an ally, then; France ended its psychological and military isolation. No new ally gained for Germany could balance that out. To state the point as a general proposition, it may be more important to deny the enemy an ally than to gain an ally oneself.

In this chapter our concern so far has been to demonstrate that the number (and identity, of course) of enemies does count, even in a nuclear age. We have attempted to move the argument from the esoteric assumption that weapons ratios or types mean much taken apart from a political frame of reference.

To point this out is not grounds to dismiss military calculations about first-strike potential, but rather to place those calculations in context. To be moved to commit a successful aggression against the prime enemy, the potential aggressor would probably require simultaneously: a major weapons breakthrough (plus enough time for some stockpiling while still outdistancing the enemy in technological progress), a will to conquer, some allies to encourage it to take the chance (and help discourage the opposition), some disarray and defection among its enemies, and an obvious failure of willpower on the part of its prime enemy. What would be seriously misleading would be to assume that only one part of this list counts—that intentions essentially *equal* capability.

But if enemies count, within what limits can they be chosen (avoided)? In

Chapters 5 and 6 we examined decision making from both an internal decision-making perspective and an external environmental perspective, to see the parameters of choice, especially as they affect this problem. At one extreme, if the bureaucratic paradigm is taken literally, it might be concluded that national policies are whatever comes out of the hopper of organizational procedures and opposed or allied bureaucratic interests. This would be as though the problem were merely the excuse for the decision and did not really matter. It is hard to square this thought with any notion of selecting enemies at all. At the other extreme, taking the international environment as determining national policies would be to visualize the decision makers as puppets responding to external stimuli on cue. Again, the implication is that enemies are born, not made.

Such extreme views would parallel the rigidly deterministic viewpoints, described by Erich Fromm,[5] from which the argument over instincts between the biologists and the psychologists tends to be conducted. For someone who accepts the mechanistic views Fromm argues against, national perceptions have a rigid and always predictable form determined by the perceiver's instincts or environment. (In the latter case, a nation's history would tell you precisely how that nation will act in the future. Thus policy shifts, which stem from altered perceptions — such as at the time of the formulation of the Truman Doctrine — become incomprehensible.) In terms of the cardinal principles model, if one accepts these mechanistic views, policy has no alternatives and counterbalancing interests become idle speculation. Enemies are a given.

Fromm's whole argument steers between the Charybdis of the biologists and the Scylla of the psychologists, insisting on the reality, even within bounds, of free will (in terms of the cardinal principles model, the existence of significant policy choices about enmity). Fromm does not argue that the environment provides infinite freedom of choice, but neither does he accept the notion that there are no meaningful choices to be made. I agree with Fromm; not just any choices can be made, but the choices are real. The nature of the choices is limited both by the internal political process and by the external situation, but within those parameters there remains a large area for significant choice. Whether choices become truly available for decision depends, of course, on the perceptual lenses worn by the decision makers.

It could be argued, then, that the total decision-making process has three dimensions or parts. At one end there are self-imposed parameters and constraints, whether these originate in the national peculiarities of bureaucratic politics, in organizational procedures, or in the competition of opposing pressure groups and lobbies. These constraints relate to the internal political process. At the other end there are systems-imposed constraints that derive from the nature of the multilateral system and how it functions, from the nature of its "rules." Connecting these two ends is the third dimension: the perceptual bridge occupied by the decision makers. This bridge connects the two ends because their decisions on important issues, while influenced by the internal political process, are determined by their perception of the nature of the system and their understanding of the system's rules. That perceptual bridge reflects the fundamental philosophical orientation of the decision makers; it originates in national biases reflecting the national experience, and it is fueled operationally by views of how the external system works and views on what is occurring beyond the national frontiers.

When those decision makers look outward at the system, they have some particular view as to how innate a feature enmity is to be considered. They have some view as to how constant enmity is in the affairs of men and nations across time. They have some view as to the "rules" by which nations that are prudent avoid collecting excessive enmity. And they have some view as to whether such an option is open to them in their special cases. Ideas about reality, then, prevailing in a nation, inevitably affect the entire national foreign policy process, regardless of which nation's decisions are being observed. Ideas about reality directly affect the range of options open to decision makers. They ensure that some scenarios are given more careful consideration than others. They explain why certain possibilities are frequently overlooked or discounted.

All three dimensions are necessary to provide a fully satisfactory view of the decision-making process. Where the internal perspective emphasizes the characteristics of the players and the external perspective emphasizes the game itself and its rules, the perceptual bridge that links them provides the vantage point from which any set of decision makers perceives the rules by which the game is played.

A further caution must be posted. However fascinating it may be to trace the intricacies of the way a particular national decision was made, it would be dangerous to forget that the ultimate decision represented part of a foreign policy. The internal arguments, however fierce, lead to some decision. In the nature of things, the state ultimately becomes a unitary actor at the frontier's edge. When the argument is over as to which road to take, only one road at a time can be chosen.

The cardinal principles model, which has been elaborated in these last chapters, attempts to take all three perspectives and this caution into account. The model addresses the three foreign policy conceptual questions (introduced in Chapter 5) within this framework. When it asks, first, what the decision makers want things to look like at the end of the period, it is asking simultaneously what view of reality they share. For, if not everything is possible, what things can be attempted? When it asks, second, who will then help and who will then hinder, it is asking simultaneously how the rules of the game are understood to function and why nations line up on one side or another of an issue. When it asks, third, what must the deciding nation have to contribute if it wants its goals realized, it is asking simultaneously how wide that nation understands its area of free choice to be and what is and is not possible in the system. In responding to such questions, however, the model discourages the temptation to downplay the effects of free will and range of choice.

This cardinal principles model does not contain any mechanical, deterministic working parts. We have argued that there are always third-party influences but not that those third parties or their influences are predetermined. The only part of that observation that approaches being mechanical derives from the indubitable nature of a multilateral state system, that is, that it consists of three or more independent units. We have argued that past-future linkages are vital considerations affecting policy making, because the experience of the past, necessarily digested in some form, influences the view of the future against which present decisions will be made. The only part of that observation that approaches being mechanical derives from the nature of time, that is, that the past inexorably moves through the present toward the future. Neither principle will tell us the specific nature of a policy decision, only how it will be reached.

Nor is the principle of counterbalancing national interests at all mechanical, except in the very limited sense that it is not possible to mount one's horse and gallop off simultaneously in opposite directions. The point of the principle is to call attention to the fact of choice, to the nature of that choice, and to its consequences. The choice itself is freely made by each sovereign state. That the state may rue the day or rejoice later are both possible, depending on the wisdom displayed.

Note that we make two assumptions in introducing this principle: (1) that for every important national interest in foreign policy that could be implemented, there is an alternative, and (2) that it is in the interests thus held in reserve that the potential movement in the system is to be seen. These two assumptions, however, are not very mechanical; they are better described as logical corollaries of the existence of a system—much as the simple proposition that international rules of law are binding is a presupposition for having international law at all. Without such logical rules, the system cannot function.

Finally, the principle of the conservation of enemies is mechanical only in the very loose sense that it predicts disaster for the imprudent. The principle is in no way deterministic and is now and again violated. Because free will exists among the actors, they can try both to oppose the "natural" workings of the system and to go along any policy path they pick out. Normally nations are prudent; that is not an assumption but an observation.

Looking at state behavior in light of this principle, many illustrations can be found of its being honored and a few in which it has been ignored. Chapter 4 gave us many rich examples, as England took steps to "conserve" enemies while Wilhelminian Germany plunged recklessly on. In Chapter 8 is the example of Japan, in the days before Pearl Harbor, counting up the risks of taking on the United States in combat and prudently concluding a neutrality pact with Russia, which was under threat of attack by Germany. Another example is the Chinese mainland giant, repressing its quarrel with the Soviets while American forces were on its front and flanks during the Vietnam War. Napoleon I was less prudent; so ultimately was Adolf Hitler —and their nations paid the price. Many more such illustrations are given in the chapters ahead.

It should now be clear why the cardinal principles model takes the shape it does. It represents a coherent philosophy based upon judgments about both the nature of humanity and the nature of the state system, but since the cardinal principles represent only one way to assess reality, it is desirable to look at other ways, too.

In Part IV we shall examine three other universal models of how states behave, how they arrive at policy decisions, and how they react to the behavior and decisions of other states. Each such model will be portraying a different version of reality and the nature of man. All three models — balance of power, collective security, and containment —are, if you will, metaphysical morality plays, teaching what cause brings what effect in the nature of things. They represent cosmic views of the nature of the universe. Moreover, since each is animated by a different vision of that same reality, they cannot all be correct.

NOTES

1. Benjamin Franklin, letter of July 5, 1775, to William Strahan.

2. Thucydides, *The Peloponnesian War*, trans. Rex Warner (Baltimore: Penguin Books, 1954), pp. 81-82.

3. Ralph K. White, *Nobody Wanted War* (New York: Anchor Books, 1970), p. 10.

4. Bernard Brodie, *War and Politics* (New York: Macmillan, 1973), p. 380, commenting on Albert Wohlstetter, "The Delicate Balance of Terror," *Foreign Affairs* 37 (January 1959): 211-34.

5. Erich Fromm, *The Anatomy of Human Destructiveness* (New York: Fawcett Crest, 1973).

Part IV

OTHER UNIVERSAL MODELS

Part IV

12

BALANCE OF POWER

It is a matter of dividing Europe into states almost equal in order
that, their forces being in balance, they will fear to offend one
another, and hesitate to plan too great designs.
        Attributed by the Abbé de Mably to Queen Elizabeth I[1]

A similar uncertainty dominates all operations of foreign policy
so that great alliances have often a result contrary to the one
planned by their members.
                                        Frederick the Great[2]

Any general or universal model of international relations is a representation
of reality, showing cause and effect and predicting the future consequences
of present actions. Whether the model be cardinal principles, balance of
power, collective security, or containment, in philosophical terms it must
either implicitly or explicitly do at least three things. It must, first, contain a
view of the nature of man and the sources of human behavior. It must,
second, explain the nature of the universe: how the environment or system
operates in which the states exist and have their being. It must, third, set
forth the "rules" by which these "actors" in the system should function and
by which they will either prosper or decline. These three things are
organically one, for the actors cannot function and prosper in defiance of
their own nature or the nature of the universe. In operational terms the
model must define enmity and identify enemies; it must indicate what is
considered a critical hostile act; and it must indicate a proper countermove.
Describing the functions of a general model illustrates why a "scientific"
approach, using laboriously assembled building blocks without benefit of a
general theory, will not do; that would be like assembling bricks in midair,
without either a foundation or a plan.

The balance of power model is the oldest known general theory in existence. A detailed discussion of the mechanics of the balance can be traced
back to the Indian political philosopher Kautilya, in the fourth century B.C.[3]
Many other commentators have discussed it in the centuries since, including
Demosthenes, Bacon, Vattel, Hume, Burke, Frederick the Great, and Met-

ternich. In our time it has been analyzed most effectively by Hans J. Morgenthau, Edward Vose Gulick, and Inis L. Claude, Jr.[4]

Anyone who pursues these commentaries very long will realize that the term "balance of power" has not been used in anything like an identical sense, although these commentators, old and new, share much common ground. The word "equilibrium" is central in many of the discussions, although it is not always made very clear whether equilibrium is always supposed to occur; whether, if and when it does occur, it is the product of deliberate effort or whether, if there is deliberate effort, it is common to both sides of the equilibrium-disequilibrium equation. Claude's way of addressing this issue is to ask whether the balance "process" should be conceived as "automatic, semi-automatic, or manually operated."[5] This determinism-free choice theme has already been encountered in this book, particularly in Chapters 1 and 2.

Important differences of opinion have also been voiced by these and other commentators as to whether the balance of power should be considered the product of a particular era, reflecting a political culture now past. Hans Morgenthau, for example, devotes space to what he considers to have been a moral consensus behind the workings of the eighteenth-century balance, a consensus now lost. Others have questioned whether the notion of a balance is relevant under the technological conditions of the nuclear age. Still others have argued that a particular feature of the model is critical, such as that some nation play the balancer role historically attributed to Britain.

There is also one point on which most commentators who accept the notion of a balance tend to agree: that the phenomena known so loosely under the name balance of power have existed because of human nature. Whatever their disagreements, most would agree with what James Madison said in Number 51 of *The Federalist:*

Ambition must be made to counteract ambition. . . . It may be a reflection on human nature, that such devices should be necessary to control the abuses of government. But what is government itself, but the greatest of all reflections on human nature? If angels were to govern men, neither external nor internal controls on government would be necessary.[6]

Madison went on to say that "the defect of better motives" is supplied by "opposite and rival interests."

Five specific issues arise out of these commentaries: (1) Is there still such a phenomenon as the balance of power? (2) Is it true that a (European) moral consensus used to operate, which in turn affected the performance of the balance of power system? Is that consensus now gone, since the system has outgrown Europe, and with adverse results? (3) How much is the system "automatic," and how much does it depend upon the wisdom of the actors? (4) Do the results of the system occur because important actors deliberately move to preserve the equilibrium, or are they the natural consequences in a power-competitive world of the cancellation of one set of actions by a contrary set of actions? (Does stability occur as the result of a contest between status-quo and revisionist powers or as the net effect of two opposed attempts to alter the status quo in opposite directions?) (5) In view of the actual situations they confront when the balance equilibrium is threatened, how often do decision makers perceive what needs to be done?

The answer to the first question is yes. The balance of power still exists, but it is necessary to recognize that the fundamental core of the concept focuses on actions taken by states because of the perception of enemies as a normal condition of existence in a multilateral world. Once this focus is accepted, special definitions of the balance that describe some distinctive feature as an essential precondition for a balance to exist must be looked at skeptically.

The second major question really has two parts: whether in earlier times Europe indeed had a moral consensus that was vital to the way the balance functioned and that has now disappeared, and whether the balance of power, now spread beyond Europe, really has changed its character as a consequence?

If the concept is focused on the perception of enemies as a normal condition of existence in a multilateral world, it may be asked, in other words, whether European nations perceive enmity to be more normal than non-European states perceive it to be. Do India, China, and Japan in modern times behave in patterns of reaction to enmity and hostility that are distinctively different from the European patterns? Before dealing with this question, it would be desirable to confront the issue of Europe's moral consensus.

Morgenthau and others would have us believe that in the days of absolute monarchy Europe acted with greater restraint. This is a rather curious idea —not that European statesmen of the time were not ready and eager to testify to their moderation, but in view of the record and what influenced that record.

For example, compare Louis XIV and Frederick the Great, each a great war leader, each the center of a whole array of European wars. Louis XIV fought almost incessant wars over several decades with very little permanent territorial results. On the other hand, Frederick the Great in his wars doubled Prussia. Consider the great expansion of Russia about this time, noted in Chapter 8. Can a generalization then be made that wars produced few changes?

It is true that in the eighteenth century European wars generally had limited results. Was that due to moderation or to limitations imposed by the nature of warfare? Wars fought by foot soldiers, armed with inaccurate weapons and backed by scanty logistics and uncertain finances, had their own rules. One important rule was that a battle could not be fought unless both sides wanted one. The armies had to be equally satisfied with conditions as they formed up to fire volleys across a short distance. Any dissatisfied army could easily march away and out of range, thus avoiding combat.

It is often said that the balance in Europe at the time reflected the flexible interaction of a small number of states fairly equal in power, with changes of partners as needed to preserve the equilibrium and with England balancing the scales. Until Napoleon I reorganized the Germanies, however, many states were involved in the balance — several hundred German states alone. It is true that before the partitions of Poland, for quite a long period the balance revolved around only two "superpowers," the Bourbons and the Hapsburgs. In these wars, though, England, far from being a "balancer" (willing to shift its weight to either side), recurrently sided with Austria against France. Between 1689 and 1815, England and France fought each other seven times — 60 years of war in a 126-year period.[7] To say it another way, balancing between two groups is precisely what England did not do! One need not dwell long on these points to establish that the generalizations made about the European balance of power in these centuries often lack real substance.

British Foreign Minister George Canning's observations, as often, were more precise. In a speech in 1826 he traced specific changes:

The balance of power a century and a half ago was to be adjusted between France and Spain, the Netherlands, Austria, and England. Some years after, Russia assumed her high station in European politics. Some years after that again, Prussia became not only a substantive, but a preponderating monarchy. — Thus, while the balance of power continued in principle the same, the means of adjusting it became more varied and enlarged. They became enlarged, in proportion, I may say, to the number of weights which might be shifted into the one or the other scale.[8]

A.J.P. Taylor argues that greater stability came after Canning's time.

We talk of the *ancien régime* as though there reigned then a divine stability. In fact Powers ran up and down the scale with dizzy rapidity. . . . There was no such whirligig of fortune during the nineteenth century, despite its supposedly revolutionary character. The Great Powers who launched the First World War in 1914 were the Great Powers who had made up the Congress of Vienna in 1814.[9]

The number of "players" varied enormously; some prospered and some not. So the system was far from static; its dimensions changed. Could one still argue that often the changing players accepted certain rules of restraint, such as Metternich alleged when he ruled out any Austrian alliance aimed at destroying the status quo and "aimed at dominion" as being "against holy immutable principles"?[10]

The record certainly shows all kinds of results and variations in the policy responses by European states to proposed or in-progress changes in the status quo. What is apparent is a great sensitivity, fairly widespread among the actors, as to the systems effect of changes in power or control among the units of the system. What is lacking in the record is any evidence of general or even widespread unanimity of views, backed by appropriate policy decisions, that changes had to be opposed on moral grounds. Even the policy consequences of changes were evaluated quite differently by different states and in different periods.

Quincy Wright described this sensitivity as follows:

The States were so bounded and organized that aggression could not succeed unless it was so moderated and so directed that the prevailing opinion of the Powers approved it. Such approval was generally given to the Balkan revolts which gradually disintegrated the Ottoman Empire, to the Belgian revolt which separated that country from the Netherlands, to Prussian and Sardinian aggressions which united modern Germany and Italy, and to numerous aggressions in Africa, Asia, and the Pacific which increased European empires, and extended European civilization to these areas.[11]

If there is any striking feature of the age of absolute monarchy, it is that the monarch by definition was supposed to be answerable only to God. Absolute monarchs were not much restrained by cabinet ministers or constitutions. It is a curious theory, then, that argues (as Morgenthau does) that the excesses of self-seeking human nature are constrained by equally selfish opponents, thus creating an equilibrium, but at the same time justifies any balance attained as the consequence of a moral consensus.

Morgenthau says at one point that "the balance of power of [the eighteenth century] was amoral rather than immoral."[12] But he in another place speaks of "the actual contribution that the balance of power [before and after that time] made to the stability of the modern state system and to the preservation of the independence of its members."[13] He quotes Rousseau that "Europe has exactly that degree of solidity which maintains it in a state of perpetual agitation without overturning it." Morgenthau also quotes Emmerich de Vattel (1714-1767) that "Europe forms a political system . . . the members of which, though independent, unite, through the ties of common interest, for the maintenance of order and liberty. Hence arose that famous scheme of the . . . balance of power. . . ."[14] Vattel would probably have described the nuclear club of today as a kind of confederation of power, presiding through ties of common interest and concern over the maintenance of order and peace! It does sound more elevated, expressed that way.

It should be clear that absolute monarchs could act, and often did act, in absolute and irresponsible ways. To argue that these monarchs were at most periods restrained by some consensus besides the necessity of keeping a careful eye on the others is really farfetched. (Nor would it be possible to argue that blood ties among them had great restraining effect.)

Indeed, the nineteenth century, reckoned effectively from 1815 to 1914, has three distinctive features from a balance-of-power point of view. It was the longest period of general peace in the history of the state system; it was the age of eclipse or decline of absolute monarchical power; and it was the age when the balance of power began to be centered less in Europe. With the gradual growth in popular government and the spread of the balance geographically, was there an upward trend in violence, or an increased disappearance of independent members of the system, compared with the days of absolute monarchy? The answer is clearly no.

Putting the issue even more broadly, did democracies feel less moral obligation to the "world community"? Or, to confuse the situation even more, is the present time to be considered an age of democracy, even though authoritarian governments are quite common all over the world?

Idealizing absolute monarchies and idealizing democracies are parallel forms of oversimplification. What we can be relatively sure of is that politics, under any form of government, will continue to reflect the human condition. Desire for power or fear of power, greed or ambition—these traits will determine the actions taken by those in control of state decisions. These traits will determine what occurs, plus the decision makers' perspective on cause and effect. That combination, plus the decision makers' modesty or lack of it, will determine what then happens. From time to time arrogance may come close to explaining events. Oliver Cromwell, in his letter to the stubborn Church of Scotland in August 1650, spoke in terms pertinent to the study of political behavior: "I beseech you, in the bowels of Christ, think it possible you may be mistaken."[15]

Turning to the now worldwide nature of the state system and the balance phenomena that derive from it, is it possible, observing the behavior of India, China, and Japan, to assert that that behavior is in marked contrast to the behavior of European countries during the classical period of the balance of power?

From the material that has already been covered, the second of the five questions posed earlier in this chapter now tends to answer itself. The anxiety about enemies is certainly present in the Orient today, as it was in

Europe. India, fearing Pakistan, drew nearer to Russia in the 1970s. China, fearing Russia, drew nearer to its old enemy, Japan. Such combinations and recombinations are quite typical balance behavior. Japan's actions, once it became a great power, strongly resemble those of France in an earlier time. It does not take an immersion in European culture to think in these terms.

Has the balance of power, as it exists now in Asia, been transformed by its non-European setting? Hardly. There is the same fear of domination shared by those nations not themselves tempted to try to dominate. The European consensus originated in this fear of domination, and that is where the consensus originates today, anywhere in the world.

Our third question asks how much the system is "automatic" and how much it depends upon the wisdom of the actors. To answer this question it is first necessary to be specific in defining the system. It must be clear whether a state of affairs is meant, or a set of phenomena, because authors speak variously of the *state system* and *balance-of-power system*. The state system is a structural fact, in the sense that a number of sovereign units coexist in one world, controlled by no common superior. Defined in that fashion, the state system is a factual condition or set of circumstances. From that factual condition or set of circumstances, a corollary, what I have termed the "power problem," derives: Each sovereign unit must fear the possibility that other sovereign units, each possessing some power, may take action against it. As a consequence of that corollary, each state is normally moved by prudence to analyze the possible intentions of all "neighboring" states (meaning, usually, all those that are not eliminated as possible threats by such factors as their locations or resources). The actions they take because of their perception of certain states as enemies or hostile in this multilateral state system are what I would argue is meant, at its core, by the phrase "balance of power."

What then is meant by the term "balance-of-power system"? Here the implication is strong that the recognition of enemies and hostilities by the actors induces them to respond to perceived threats in some standardized way or ways. The question about "automaticity," then, is really directed at discovering the extent of the uniformity and regularity of behavior by states in the face of perceived threats. If such regularities are observable and predominant, one would be warranted in questioning assertions that the system depends for its proper functioning on the wisdom of the actors. If all or most actors always respond in a wise fashion, there must be much more to it than a mere equal and impartial distribution of brains among the decision makers.

But if the condition or circumstances uniformly provide some degree of anxiety for every state, it can be seen even from the evidence in Chapter 4 that the perception of that set of conditions will vary state by state and case by case — this is true for reasons discussed earlier in terms of third-party influences and past-future linkages. Correspondingly, the precise policy that may appear to be prudent to a particular state cannot be foreseen; the response is *not* automatic. Because no one policy option is ever assured, it is a mistake to "mechanize" the system and think of rigidly automatic sequences of cause and effect.

A great disturber of the balance tends to be met, sooner or later, by an opposing and restraining coalition, but that may take a quarter-century of war and five attempts to form an effective coalition, as in Napoleon's day. A Talleyrand may write to his king that the balance of power is a

combination of the rights, interests, and the relations of the Powers among themselves, *by which Europe seeks to obtain* . . . that the rights and possessions of a Power shall not be attacked by one or several other Powers; [and] that one or several other Powers shall never attain to domination over Europe. . . . [16]

He may write that to his king, but having served also as Napoleon's foreign minister, he knows he means "in the long run." In the short run, all sorts of other things occur and "Europe" fails to seek anything in unison.

Does the balance preserve the independence of states? Often it does, in that the absorption of additional territory by one state automatically does pose an implied threat to the rest, which is often so perceived. It does so by changing the conditions or circumstances adversely from the standpoint of the others. The action is not automatically opposed, however. England allowed Prussia to defeat France between 1870 and 1871, knowing full well that Prussia would be transformed into the more powerful Germany by absorbing other territories. In the Polish partitions, all three neighbors shared.

It would be accurate, though, to state the point in reverse: While the balance does not guarantee the continued independent existence of every member of the state system, the conditions under which the balance necessarily functions (that is, a multilateral environment) make it a matter of interest and concern to all members when one member seizes another. The predisposition of the rest will be to set bounds to such a process of absorption or expansion. This restatement is not so far from Sir Eyre Crowe's famous definition, quoted in Chapter 3.

It is in this sense that the great emphasis in the literature of the balance of power on the principle of equilibrium must be understood. It is indeed true that these tendencies and reactions by individual states are likely to move the total system (the whole group of states involved) toward equilibrium, and have so done historically. But this is a far better protection of the system of states than of particular individual members.

No particular state is really guaranteed its *own* equilibrium (status quo). What is "guaranteed" is the reverse: that no one participant is likely to gain predominance or hegemony. Talleyrand is quite wrong about the first of his two points, because the only ones who care per se that one nation is not attacked by another or others is that nation itself and its allies. "Europe" (meaning, of course, the generalized reaction in the system) is generally indifferent at that stage, but cares a great deal about Talleyrand's second point, regarding domination by a particular power or group of powers. If there is a widespread perception that the first point will lead to the second in the specific case, action will likely be forthcoming. That is, provided it is clear to the actors what is at stake.

The fourth question is: Do the system results occur because important actors deliberately move to preserve the equilibrium, or are they the natural consequences in a power-competitive world of the cancellation of one set of actions by a contrary set of actions? To ask the question another way, Are there guardians of the status quo who profit by it and who deliberately enforce the rules, or is the result simply the natural consequence of competitive and opposed policies, with each contender quite ready to upset the balance if opportunity arises?

Here again, thinking about Talleyrand's statement is a good place to begin. Talleyrand, like Vattel and others, liked to say "Europe," furthering the impression that the powers had common intentions. In fact, there have been periods — rather exceptional ones to be sure — of which one could speak meaningfully, in a somewhat organic sense, of "Europe," such as the period following Talleyrand's statement. That period is known as the "Concert of Europe." Meeting in various congresses at close but irregular intervals, the European great powers, in the name of the Holy Alliance, dispatched one of their number to put down revolts: Austria at the Congress of Laibach in 1821 to suppress revolts in Italy, France at the Congress of Verona in 1822 to do the same in Spain. However, Great Britain disassociated itself from the system as early as 1818, and the system, representing monarchical solidarity against popular revolt, was undermined quite quickly by the Greek revolt in 1821. Then Russia, to support the principle, would have had to have supported the Ottoman Turks in oppressing fellow Greek Orthodox; instead the Russians sent an ultimatum to the Turks on July 27, 1821, and then withdrew from the brink only after Metternich reminded the czar of the dangers of supporting revolution. But, a few years later, with European sentiment now generally behind the Greeks, Russia again (April 1826) gave Turkey an ultimatum. This time Turkey yielded, on the advice of both Austria and France. Greek independence was then recognized jointly in 1829.

Increasingly, after this date, the idea of cooperation among absolute monarchs to suppress popular unrest failed as a unifying principle for action. In 1830, France itself became a constitutional monarchy, and in 1832 the British and French cooperated, intervening in Holland with forces to support Belgian independence from Dutch domination.

By the time of the revolutions of 1848, popular revolt was so widespread that no major absolute monarchy except the Russian regime was unthreatened. The Russians in that year intervened in Hungary to suppress a revolt and permit the new emperor of Austria, Franz Josef, to gain effective control of his dual throne. That the day of such gestures was really past is shown by the subsequent Austrian decision to occupy the Rumanian principalities at the outbreak of the Crimean War (1854-1856). Since these positions were athwart the Black Sea flank of Russia's usual western route to fight Turkey, Russia felt forced to refrain from attacking, and the fighting took place elsewhere, in the Crimea. So was assistance repaid with ingratitude, thought the Russians, but the very idea that "regular" politics could be long suspended, and national differences set aside in the name of the brotherhood of monarchs, was and is a quite romantic notion. Even so, the Russian aid to Austria in 1848 is about the only convincing illustration from the period of that elusive "moral consensus" so frequently mentioned.

The "Europe" whose powers contended with each other after 1848 hardly had a uniform point of view. Austria continued to cling to the status quo, afraid in a multilingual state threatened by nationalism to take any bold steps, thus continuing to delay both Italian and German unification. Prussia wanted fundamental change and, eventually, fought Austria and then France to bring it about. Italy aided Prussia against Austria for its own interests. Russia, on Bismarck's urging, seized the occasion of the Franco-Prussian War to denounce the restrictive clauses of the Treaty of Paris of 1856. England remained neutral.

It is true that the British would probably have intervened if they had seen these changes wrought by war as threatening. But it was apparent that the Germans had limited aims, so neither the British, as "balancer" of the "system," nor "Europe" really intervened. Yet later, when Germany did appear threatening, the British specifically altered policy to constrain Germany through links to both France and Russia, just as the United States also ultimately intervened in World War I, for the same basic reason.

From the sequences of events, it is evident that the kinds of actions that are "cancelled" by a contrary set of actions are those that follow from the clear perception of a particular strong nation bent upon self-aggrandizement, as was Germany at the time of World War I. However, the British actions just cited occurred in 1904 and 1907; the war broke out only in 1914; and U.S. intervention did not come until 1917. Like the coalitions against Napoleon, the coalition against Wilhelm was a rather ragged and attenuated response. "Europe" straggled into an opposition.

The point is even clearer if we look again, from this angle, at the interwar period discussed in Chapter 10: what E. H. Carr once called the "twenty-years' peace." We find England, France, Italy, and Russia never in effective agreement on actions to be taken against a Hitler, who in the end, overran three of the four and probably would have overrun the fourth if he could have crossed the English Channel. If these four were "Europe," then Europe was in disarray. Two opposite points, each valid, can be drawn from these years: first, there was certainly no unified or simultaneous response to the German threat, and second, the German threat was nevertheless in the end contained.

From these events, no sound case can be made for seeing the ultimate Anglo-German confrontation as merely the clash of two imperia, each determined to win out. The Marxists, of course, think in those terms. But throughout the period the British were attempting, even if ineptly, to conciliate and bring about peaceful change within the general perimeters of the status quo. Put another way, if the Marxist argument is correct, the English should have been eager in the 1920s and 1930s to crush Germany, or at least keep the Germans chained by the Versailles Treaty, since Germany was England's great economic rival. But the actual British policy was to oppose the ruthless Franco-Belgian occupation of the Ruhr, to argue for a more sensible reparations policy, and to agree to allow Germany to build a navy larger than the Versailles Treaty permitted. Almost simultaneously, the French made an alliance with Russia against Germany (May 2, 1935) and England made the naval treaty with Germany (June 18, 1935).

Since the Germans, as we know now, were the real threat to the status quo, Britain would have done better to have joined France. Could one argue that Britain saw itself in a power competition with *both* France and Germany and was trying to maneuver to outstrip both? Or that the British actions were designed to place the British in the role of balancer between a weak but resurgent Germany and a domineering but fearful France? In that case, Britain would have to have overestimated France and underestimated Germany. The simplest and most convincing explanation is that the British sought to conciliate the Germans to reconcile them to peace, and opposed French policy because a harsh line ruled out reconciliation.

Nor were the French really trying to destroy Germany. Rather, the French were haunted by the thought of the ultimately superior German power resources.

Arnold Wolfers, in his classic treatment of this period, *Britain and France between Two Wars*, sums up as follows:

The basic issue underlying the controversy between Britain and France was not a matter of general attitudes, but the concrete problem of Germany's power and position. How strong could Germany be permitted to become without menacing the vital interests of the two countries? The British and the French disagreed on the answer to this question; this disagreement accounts for most of the discord between them.[17]

Most interesting about the interwar period, apart from the fundamental divergence between British and French policy, is the role of Italy. The Italians, despite ambitions in Albania, had a primary interest in keeping Europe stable. Indeed, Mussolini sent troops to the Brenner Pass to keep Hitler out of Austria in 1934, the first time Hitler attempted to gain control. But Benito Mussolini had the gleam of empire in his eyes. He wanted to avenge the inglorious defeat of the Italians by the Ethiopians at Aduwa in 1896, so he set out between 1935 and 1936 to take Ethiopia, "with the League, against the League, in spite of the League," as he is alleged to have said. Such a policy ultimately brought him into tension with Britain and France and destroyed the "Stresa Front" of the three nations against Germany, and it ultimately caused Mussolini to make common cause with Hitler. In the end, for a kingdom in Africa, Mussolini helped Hitler tear up the status quo in Europe. In short, two imperia cooperated.

Ultimately, belatedly, the Anglo-French policy breach was healed; in 1939 both nations went to war against Germany in defense of Poland. But Italy by then was in the enemy's camp, and Russia, disillusioned by the Czech sellout at Munich, made its own deal with Germany.

The answer to the fourth question is that the status quo is not maintained, or the ambitions of an aggressive and expanding power contained, by equal and opposite ambitions. Nor are the "natural" status-quo parties always ready and willing to enforce the rules on behalf of the system. The ultimate ruination of Italy by Hitler's soldiers did not much help England and France, but Hitler's highhanded tactics did assist Italy to shift sides again during World War II. The German invasion of Russia, which forced Russia to the side of Britain (and Free France) was Hitler's own decision. Even the agreement of the British and French on a common policy of opposition to Hitler was forced on them by Hitler's increasingly threatening attitude. The answer these observations contribute to the fourth question is that it is the actions of the threatening power that ultimately inspire the coalition to contain the threat. The point here is like the point made earlier about whether the balance system guarantees the continued independent existence of all the members. The answer is no; what it "guarantees" is the failure of the aggressor who unwisely poses so severe a threat that, while some may fall victim, others are moved to contain it. There are no powers that naturally cooperate to preserve the status quo; cooperation results from an unmistakable threat, and often at a very late hour.

Turning now to the fifth question, in view of the actual situations they confront when the balance equilibrium is threatened, how often do decision makers perceive what needs to be done?

The record here does not yield a consistent answer, but there is a distinct trend. There is generally some initial reluctance to accept the seriousness of the situation and to take timely and adequate countermeasures. We can see this in Louis XIV's time, when France was the threat. Frederick the Great, in his time, was not always effectively opposed. This was even truer of Napoleon. World War I, so slow in taking shape, saw a much more deliberate creation of coalitions. Then, in the interwar period just reviewed, the disorganization of the status-quo powers was most pronounced.

The record shows that threats to upset the balance have frequently only tardily produced effective coalitions that contained those threats; one of the reasons for this is that to form a coalition necessitates prior agreement about the threat among the participants. But again, and just as significant to note, each threat was contained in the end. There was a time when Napoleon seemed almost unbeatable. There was a time, after Pearl Harbor, when Japan dominated the entire Western Pacific as Hitler did Europe. But those times passed, as they have in all of modern history.

Sometimes nations are quite slow to perceive what Churchill called "the gathering storm." The United States in the 1930s is an excellent example, as we shall see in more detail later; but then, England and France acted as some degree of buffer for the United States in terms of the European threat. In Asia, as U.S. perception of a threat from Japan grew steadily, there was no effective buffer, and the United States, long accustomed to discounting balance-of-power thinking, had some difficulty even formulating the threat perceived. When Secretary of State Cordell Hull in June 1938 requested the U.S. aircraft industry to refrain from selling planes to nations (Japan) that bombed (Chinese) women and children from the air, he was getting about as close as he was able to discussing the threat as he saw it, but this nonetheless was a rather indirect and generalized description of the problem Japanese actions were creating for the United States.

When World War II broke out, President Franklin D. Roosevelt, bound by U.S. neutrality legislation, on September 5, 1939, proclaimed an arms embargo against all the belligerents, including Britain and France. On September 13, appalled by the foreseeable implications for U.S. security, FDR called a special session of Congress to repeal the legislation. In his speech he described the legislation as "most vitally dangerous to American neutrality, American security, and American peace."[18] It could hardly have been true that the arms embargo was dangerous to U.S. neutrality. More convincing is the idea that it undermined U.S. security, and therefore ultimately U.S. peace, by failing to permit action in forthright balance-of-power terms. Since its leaders did not speak or think in balance-of-power terms, the United States often had difficulty during this period in even giving adequate oral expression to its foreign policy.

If the U.S. view, which we shall examine at length later, completely rejected balance-of-power thinking, it can be said that it did so in significant measure because to twentieth-century Americans the term meant an amoral, power-political approach.

Balance of power, then, is the first of the three other universal models. As the oldest, it has the most barnacles encrusted on it. Because its defenders often voiced their thoughts in antiquated phrases, it frequently sounds archaic if not obsolete. Yet, with an intellectual scraping, it becomes obvious that there is considerable merit in the view of reality exposed. It is quite clear that the balance of power — if by that phrase we mean the variety of alliance-centered actions nations take because of their perceptions of other states as enemies or hostile — is still very much with us. There is no reason to suppose it will disappear unless the multilateral state system that gives it birth first disappears.

Balance of power as a name for this generalized reaction to the power problem is therefore and inevitably still with us, because the phenomenon it names is still with us. Whether it has greater or lesser utility than the cardinal principles model as a way of visualizing relationships and accommodating the data is a question better left until Chapter 16, after the other two models, collective security and containment, have been considered.

One further comment is in order here. In the period after World War I, the implementation of balance of power ideas fell upon very bad times indeed. Apart from the increasingly important role played by the anti-balance-of-power United States, which also contributed significant uncertainties to the power-equation picture; by the war-weariness of England and France; and by the other factors mentioned, a further cause of difficulty was the existence of a competing general theory, that of collective security.

To support the implementation of this new theory, the League of Nations was established, and most of the nations of the world in the 1920s belonged to it. As we shall see, by accepting the restrictions of the League Covenant, they accepted an obligation to take certain actions not obviously in the immediate national interest and sometimes in obvious conflict with that immediate national interest. In the 1930s the principle of collective security confronted these nations with the need to take actions difficult to square with any sensible implementation of balance-of-power concepts. Two major models for national security behavior competed.

NOTES

1. Quoted in Edward Vose Gulick, *Europe's Classical Balance of Power* (New York: Norton, 1967).

2. *Die politischen Testamenta Friedrichs des Grossen* (Berlin, 1920), p. 192.

3. Kautilya is reprinted in Paul Seabury, ed., *Balance of Power* (San Francisco: Chandler, 1965).

4. See Hans J. Morgenthau, *Politics Among Nations*, 4th ed. (New York: Knopf, 1967); Edward Vose Gulick, *Europe's Classical Balance of Power* (New York: Norton, 1967); and Inis L. Claude, Jr., *Power and International Relations* (New York: Random House, 1962).

5. Claude, *Power and International Relations*, p. 43.

6. Alexander Hamilton, James Madison, and John Jay, *The Federalist* (Avon, Conn.: Heritage, 1973), pp. 347-48.

7. Thomas A. Bailey, *A Diplomatic History of the American People*, 6th ed. (New York: Appleton-Century-Crofts, 1958), p. 23.

8. *Speeches of the Right Honourable George Canning* (London, 1836), vol. 6, pp. 109-10.

9. A.J.P. Taylor, *The Struggle for Mastery in Europe, 1848-1919* (Oxford: Clarendon Press, 1954), p. xxii.

10. Prince Clemens W. L. Metternich, *Memoirs*, vol. 2, p. 485; cited by Gulick, *Europe's Classical Balance of Power*, p. 62 n.

11. Quincy Wright, "The Balance of Power," in Hans Weigert and Vilhjalmur Stefansson, eds., *Compass of the World* (New York: Macmillan, 1944), pp. 53-54.

12. Morgenthau, *Politics Among Nations*, p. 183.

13. Ibid., p. 207.

14. Morgenthau, *Politics Among Nations*, p. 210, quoted from Emmerich de Vattel, *The Law of Nations* (Philadelphia, 1829), book 3, chap. III, pp. 377-78.

15. Oliver Cromwell, letter to the General Assembly of the Church of Scotland, August 3, 1650.

16. G. Pallain, ed., *The Correspondence of Prince Talleyrand and King Louis XVIII during the Congress of Vienna* (New York: Plenum, 1881), pp. xv-xvi. Italics added.

17. Arnold Wolfers, *Britain and France between Two Wars* (New York: Harcourt, Brace, 1940), p. 381.

18. President F. D. Roosevelt addressed the joint session on September 21, 1939. *Congressional Record*, 76th Cong., 2d sess., vol. 85, part 1, p. 11.

13

COLLECTIVE SECURITY

> All concerned have tended to regard collective security as a halfway house between the terminal points of international anarchy and world government.
>
> Inis L. Claude, Jr.[1]

Collective security as a general or universal model has a far shorter history than balance of power, at least from the view of utilization. As a theory made ready to be practiced, it began when it was incorporated into a prominent place in the Covenant of the League of Nations. Woodrow Wilson was particularly responsible, with some assistance from Jan Smuts of South Africa. Its first practical application came in the form of economic sanctions in the 1930s, when Benito Mussolini openly defied the League. Handed on to the UN, when it in its turn was formed, collective security entered the UN Charter as Chapter 7. A few years later, after North Korea attacked South Korea in 1950, it was tried a second time. This time the sanctions were military in form.

In the 1950s the term also came to have a second and confusing meaning, when it began to be used extensively in the United States to describe the newly formed NATO. Because such alliances were permitted under the rubric of "regional collective security" by Chapter 8 of the UN Charter, many people remained unaware that NATO as an approach to security problems represented insurance against the failure of the UN system of universal collective security. NATO was to the UN as self-defense *in extremis* is to calling the police. What was significant here was not the presumption that an action by NATO as a whole or by some of its members *would* inevitably diverge from actions deemed suitable by a UN majority; what was significant was that it *could*. As a group less inclusive than the whole, NATO's interests were always potentially at odds with the overall UN organization. To say this is in no way to judge the utility of NATO but merely to point out its irony. The North Atlantic Alliance found easy favor with an American public that, enthusiastic about the UN, did not realize that in NATO the United States was simultaneously embracing a manifestation of the balance of power.

In Chapter 12 it was stated that any general or universal model of international relations, such as collective security, must either implicitly or explicitly do three things: it must explain humanity and human behavior; it must explain the universe (or environment or system) in which states exist; and it must set forth the "rules" by which the "actors" are to be guided in their policy decisions. To repeat from Chapter 12, these three things are organically one, for the actors cannot function and prosper in defiance of their own nature or the nature of the universe.

Elements of each of these are found in abundance in Woodrow Wilson's speeches, so we begin there. Barnstorming around the United States to "sell" the League, Wilson spoke on the evening of September 8, 1919, at the Coliseum in Sioux Falls, South Dakota: "If Germany had dreamed that anything like the greater part of the world would combine against her, she never would have begun the war. . . ."[2] Germany would not have dared to yield to ambition if it had realized that the "greater part of the world" would resist. Wilson went on, "You have either got to have the old system, of which Germany was the perfect flower, or you have got to have a new system. You cannot have a new system unless you provide a substitute. . . ."[3]

The "old system," said Wilson, was "be ready" — arm for defense. But accumulating arms would lead to "a military government in spirit if not in form." The president would become "merely a commander in chief, ready to fight the world." All of this would produce a radically different, alien United States. "Yet we cannot do without force." Wilson goes on:

You cannot establish land titles . . . and not maintain them. Suppose that the land titles of South Dakota were disturbed. Suppose the farm lines were moved, say, ten feet. You know what would happen. Along every fence line you would see farmers perching with guns on their knees. The only reason they are not perching now is that there are land deeds deposited in a particular place, and the whole majesty and force and judicial system of the State of South Dakota are behind the titles. Very well, you have got to do something like that internationally. You cannot set up Poland . . . and not have somebody take care that her title deeds are respected. You cannot establish freedom . . . without force, and the only force you can substitute for an armed mankind is the concerted force of the combined action of mankind through the instrumentality of all the enlightened Governments of the world.[4]

This was Wilson at the end of his campaign. At the beginning, on January 22, 1917, before the League Covenant had been put on paper, he had gone before the Senate of the United States and urged that "some definite concert of power" be established "which will make it virtually impossible that any such catastrophe should ever overwhelm us again." He went on:

I am proposing that all nations henceforth avoid entangling alliances which would draw them into competition of power, catch them in a net of intrigue and selfish rivalry, and disturb their own affairs with influences intruded from without. There is no entangling alliance in a concert of power. When all unite to act in the same sense and with the same purpose, all act in the common interest and are free to live their own lives under a common protection.[5]

Taking these two quotations together as representative of Wilson's thought, which they are, shows that Wilson was not an idealist in the utopian sense of believing that freedom can exist without force to maintain it: someone must take care of Poland's title deeds besides just Poland. As Robert E. Osgood summarized Wilson's thought, "Just as policemen are obliged to combat crime rather than particular criminals as their private interests may dictate, so sovereign nations would be obliged to oppose aggression as such, not merely particular aggressors under particular circumstances."[6] Wilson was fully convinced that if Germany, preparing to start the war, had realized that it faced the concerted force of the world, it would have been deterred.

With much of this, Sir Eyre Crowe might have agreed in the name of the balance of power, except that Crowe wanted to ward off the danger to independence rather than the danger to peace. Where Wilson went furthest beyond Crowe is in assuming a widespread "concert of power," a fairly universal "common interest," whereas Crowe put his trust in "an equally formidable rival, or of a combination of several countries" to maintain an "equilibrium."

If the group that opposes the ambitions of the challenger to the status quo were sufficiently broadened, ultimately it would equate to Wilson's proposition about a "common purpose." In that sense it is not too far from Henry Brougham's advice that

other states, though not either attacked or threatened, ought to make common cause with the one which is placed in more immediate jeopardy; and for this plain reason, that its overthrow will further increase the power of the aggressor, and expose them to the risk of afterwards being assailed and conquered.[7]

Brougham is, of course, speaking about the balance of power. If the balance mechanism fails to work effectively when the challenge is small or slight, it will take much more counterforce in the end to contain it. Napoleon is a case in point.

When we realize that Wilson was arguing his thesis at a time when a great coalition *had* come into effect to restrain German power, we can see why he so readily made one of his most basic assumptions: the existence of a group of nations prepared to "unite to act in the same sense and with the same purpose." Wilson, a student of U.S. congressional government in his academic days, was not a persistent observer of international relations. Like most

Americans of his time, he had not really studied the system thoroughly. Thinking in a U.S. context, always ready to deprecate the balance-of-power alliance formula, and convinced that armed unilateralism was not a viable choice, Wilson urged an alternative that did not seem so radical to him. He wanted, in effect, to institutionalize what Brougham meant about coalitions. What Wilson did not see at the time of his Senate speech was just how "selfish" the separate (and clashing) interests of his wartime partners were. He found that out when he negotiated with them at Versailles. Perhaps the difference between his 1917 and 1919 formulations can be attributed to this; in 1919 he spoke of "concerted force" — Brougham might have said that — but in 1917 he spoke more confidently of a common purpose and interest providing a common protection.

This difference, if it represents a change in Wilson's thinking, relates to one of the fundamental questions about collective security. How common and widespread and timely are the purposes and interests of the states in providing a common protection? They almost surely band together when there is no practical alternative, as in the coalitions formed against Napoleon and Wilhelm, but is it possible to institutionalize this ultimate response to make it available at earlier stages, when the challenge is not so unmistakable? Also, will the challenge always arise as a threat to the "land deeds"? Will all states have a similar or equal interest in preserving either the status quo or peace?

With his attention newly focused on the international environment, Wilson thought he saw the beginnings of a concert of power and a common purpose. These, he assumed, would become more and more manifest with the passage of time, as democracy spread. Providing an institutionalization through the structure of the League of Nations and its Covenant would merely speed up the process.

So Woodrow Wilson was less of an idealist, in a second sense, than we are accustomed to think. He believed that he was institutionalizing existing tendencies, providing a better mechanism for their expression through the socializing and centralizing processes of the League. This "community of mankind" was a real community, not one that had to be invented. What it needed was a place to be housed.

True, this would produce change of a sort, in a desirable direction and on an accelerated basis, but it involved no feigning of good motives or a pretence at better behavior until a future time when habit would have replaced art. A League would accelerate the change already in process. Like a good Marxist, Woodrow Wilson, too, believed in his own optimistic version of inevitability. To him it seemed inevitable that once "selfish rivalries" leading to intrigues and "particular" alliances had effective competition, they would never survive.

Woodrow Wilson knew that people sometimes proclaimed him an idealist. He said, in his Coliseum speech, "Well, that is the way I know I am an American." To him, America was "the only idealist Nation in the world." In the "records of that [American] spirit . . . is this authentic tone of the love of justice and the service of humanity."[8] As to the psychology of resistance to the League concert idea, it was the mark of those who

know physical force and do not understand moral force. Moral force is a great deal more powerful than physical. Govern the sentiments of mankind and you govern mankind. Govern their fears, govern their hopes, determine their fortunes, get them together in concerted masses, and the whole thing sways like a team. Once get them suspecting one another, once get them antagonizing one another, and society itself goes to pieces. We are trying to make a society instead of a set of barbarians out of the governments of the world.[9]

But again, Wilson was preaching this message in an atmosphere ultimately rare in the annals of international affairs. He spoke in the context of a world recently galvanized by an immense military struggle, a world in which many of the people had been forced to choose up sides rather than hold aloof. He himself headed a people that had preferred neutrality. When World War I began, Wilson had proclaimed that the United States would be neutral "in thought, word, and deed." But now he was preaching the message of a convert, convinced that the old way would not do, that holding aloof would always encourage the ambitious aggressor.

But the extreme dichotomy induced by or reflected by a world war is a relatively rare occurrence in international affairs. Wilson was generalizing rather loosely. Is it true, for example, that any aggression anywhere ultimately proves a threat to everyone, unless stopped at an early phase? Does aggression thrive on success as mosquitoes thrive on swamp water, spreading, spreading?

That belief was widespread between World War I and World War II. Historians and political scientists in the 1940s and 1950s, analyzing the "failure of the League" in its efforts at collective security, at times contributed by the very sequence of treatment (Manchuria, 1931; Ethiopia, 1935, 1936; Munich, 1938) to the notion that these represented a causal series. Sometimes a simple cause and effect sequence was suggested or implied. For example, the most popular text then in use, Frederick L. Schuman's *International Politics*, said in 1941: "In their first great test in dealing with aggression by a Great Power, the League members failed to restrain the lawbreaker and protect his victim. Following Japanese occupation of central Manchuria on September 18, 1931" — and here follows detail on Manchuria. "Italians and Germans dreaming of empire *were not slow to grasp the lesson* of these events" — and here follows detail on Ethiopia and Munich.[10]

About as widely used as Schuman, in courses in international relations in the 1930s and 1940s, was Simonds and Emeny's book, *The Great Powers in World Politics*. Here is how it refers to Manchuria and Austria:

In the Manchurian affair, for example, Japan had to give in or the other Great Powers had to join in the application of force. But Japan would not obey the law and the other nations would not enforce it. . . .

The *consequences* of the failure of the League in Manchuria and in the London and Geneva Conferences were fully disclosed in the Austrian crisis of July, 1934.[11]

In other words, the failure of the League to act in Manchuria led nations in Europe to assume that the League members would act ineffectively there, too.

In a book published in 1962, Richard W. Leopold writes:

Historians have long asserted that the chain of events leading to the Second World War began in Manchuria in September, 1931. . . . There and then the League of Nations suffered a blow from which it never recovered, as its inability to check this resort to force encouraged other dissatisfied governments to violate the Covenant and subvert the Versailles settlement.[12]

Presumably the first bad example helped lead to the next — but is this true? Can one conclude, for example, that the failure of the British and French to take any decisive action far away in Asia, to cope with the rather ambiguous circumstances of Manchuria, would also lead them to draw back from decisive action at home in Europe under clearcut circumstances?

For that matter, not only was the Manchurian case not a clearcut issue, but neither was the Ethiopian case in its first stage (the Wal-Wal incident). And Hitler's challenge in reoccupying the Rhineland was not perceived by England, at least, as a clearcut issue. After all, the Rhineland was German. So we have three cases, in the first of which Japan had a treaty right to maintain armed forces in the actual territory of Manchuria, in the second of which Italian troops at Wal-Wal had been in effective occupation for years, and in the third of which German troops were reentering undisputedly German territory. No one of the three cases could lead a reasonable person to conclude that no effective resistance to a clearcut aggression anywhere could be expected. It would depend on the circumstances.

Certainly, these actions by three of the great powers in fact introduced further uncertainties into the situation in Europe. But the League logic was not based upon great-power expansive or aggressive action alone. Any successful aggression, by anyone, was seen as an ultimate undermining of the structure of peace. But is this true? Even if there was a causal connection between the successive expansions or aggressions by Japan, Italy, and Germany, does it mean that aggressions by less strategically situated states (for instance, some Latin American middle power) somehow ultimately reproduce an equivalent state of crisis in world affairs? Will any three aggressions do? by any Nations X, Y, and Z?

The problem here is fundamental. When we later discuss the domino theory, a direct descendent of this early sequential aggression, crisis acceleration idea, the issue will recur. Despite the fact that important decisions by important nations have been based in the twentieth century on the truth or falsity of this idea, the idea itself remains insufficiently explored in international relations theory.

Even at the height of the crises represented by World War I and World War II, any number of nations sat out the whole conflict, either completely (remaining neutral), or by merely nominal belligerency. How can anyone convince nations in this category that they must be prepared to sacrifice to repulse an aggression on the far side of the world?

The idea carries somewhat more conviction for large and medium powers, who typically do get caught up in struggles of world war dimensions, and it carries complete conviction for those small powers that, in every such world crisis, achieve prominence as victims. This second group fluctuates, however. So, stripped of verbiage, the organized community of mankind, a phrase so easily falling from the tongue of Wilson and many others, is a rather ill-defined group unequally affected by events.

The great variations in economic and military power among the hundred and fifty or so sovereign states of the world (less in number, of course, in Wilson's time), must also be taken into account. Some are able, if so disposed, to exercise power at a distance, but most are not, at least in the form of military force.

Woodrow Wilson glossed over these problems, largely because he felt that once the new institutions had been put in position and placed in operation, the overwhelming power nominally arrayed against any potential aggressor would effectively deter most aggression from even being attempted. Since defeat would be so certain, why try? Wilson did not literally waive the prospect of use of force, but he was sure that force would be a rare resort. When Wilson submitted the Covenant of the League to the Paris Peace Conference on February 14, 1919, he said, "Armed force is in the background in this program, but it *is* in the background, and if the moral force of the world will not suffice, the physical force of the world shall. But that is the last resort, because this is intended as a constitution of peace, not as a league for war."[13]

Because physical force was to be the "last resort" and "moral force" was almost certain to suffice most of the time, the very offering of the pledge would largely obviate the need to honor it. The spreading of the burden was to be so wide that the yoke would be light and everyone could feel that, at the small price required, it would be highly worthwhile to be involved. It is like an insurance scheme in which, in addition to full coverage at reasonable costs, most of the premium is also refunded to the customers.

But once let an issue begin to have costs or clearly be approaching that point, and the whole question changes focus. Reconsideration and backsliding become inevitable — the UN experience with the Korean "police action" is an indication. Very early in the history of the League, once the initial euphoria had blown away, and even before any issue with clear costs was raised, the founders had to come to terms with the repudiation of the Covenant by the United States. As a direct response, movements were soon on foot to amend the obligations of the Covenant through "interpretations." In each case the initiative came from a nation or nations that were either too close for comfort to the troublemaker or far enough away to feel safe regardless of the League's decisions.

In the Second League Assembly in 1921, Denmark, Norway, and Sweden, neighbors of Germany, cosponsored "interpretations" of Article 16 of the Covenant, and their resolutions were adopted on October 4, 1921. Article 16 had provided for automatic economic sanctions against any covenant-breaking state, followed by a recommendation by the Council of the League of Nations as to what armed forces might be required. But the fourth paragraph of the resolutions instead said: "It is the duty of each Member of the League *to decide for itself* whether a breach of the Covenant has been committed."[14] Article 16 had also provided that the economic sanctions were to be immediate, but the ninth paragraph of the resolutions specified that "in the case of certain States, the effective application of the economic sanctions" could be postponed "wholly or partially," but only "in so far as it is desirable for the success of the common plan of action, or reduces to a minimum the losses and embarrassments which may be entailed. . . ."

Article 10, which Wilson considered the "heart" of the Covenant, was also proposed for interpretation, but the motion failed by one vote. By Article 10 the members had undertaken "to respect and preserve as against external aggression the territorial integrity and existing political independence of all members of the League." The proposed interpretation said the League Council, in implementing force, "shall be bound to take account, more particularly, of the geographical situation and of the special conditions of each State." The interpretation added: "It is for the constitutional authorities of each Member to decide . . . in what degree the Member is bound to assure the execution of [the Article 10] obligation by employment of its military forces."[15] Very little comment is needed. This resolution, incidentally, was sponsored by Canada and vetoed by Persia in 1923.

This chapter is not really concerned with the practice of collective security or with the mechanisms provided and how they functioned. Some detail has been included simply to show that nations confronted with the possibility of having to suffer by virtue of their membership in the League immediately began to water down their obligations. Similarly, with the UN, members have carefully refrained from entering into agreements with the Security Council that specify forces under UN command in the event of sanctions. As is well known, the Korean War was fought entirely with ad hoc voluntary contributions, and to this day no forces agreement, relinquishing national sovereignty in favor of "police actions," has ever been concluded.

If this treatment were concerned with technical points, we could indicate the role of the veto and other features that in fact limited the obligations of members of the League, and now limit those of UN members, to less than is implied by a philosophical statement of the collective security model. There are already many good treatments of these points.

Inis L. Claude, Jr., after a lengthy discussion of collective security, concludes that collective security as a doctrine "is obsolete—it envisages a system which might have been feasible in an earlier period . . . but can hardly be expected to operate effectively in the setting which has been produced by the transformations of recent years."[16]

One such transformation, the nuclear, will occur to everyone. If India, possessing nuclear weapons, should commit an aggression on Pakistan, can third states in Europe or the Americas or Africa be expected to respond with armed force to protect the Charter of the UN? Most people today will answer no. Even alliance partners, presumably faced with an acknowledged common threat, eye one another skeptically when such a scenario is mentioned.

There are still other fundamental assumptions and problems with this model. It assumes, for example, that "aggression" is a clear and unambiguous term and that it will be obvious when aggression has occurred. Wilson, in his talk of "land deeds," made no allowance for such situations as the one that would develop in Manchuria, assuming that aggression was a question of foreign troops crossing a well-defined frontier. He would have been quite amazed to find out how many frontiers are now ill-defined or unagreed upon. He would have been absolutely astounded to find out that neither the League nor the UN would even be able to define the term "aggression" until December 14, 1974—over fifty years after the League began functioning. Even then, the definition necessarily lacks precision. As the preamble to the definition points out, "whether an act of aggression has been committed must be considered in the light of all the circumstances of each particular case."[17] It is therefore inconceivable that every nation will judge the event by identical standards, although that does not exclude agreement in flagrant circumstances.

Collective security thinking portrays human nature as peaceful and benevolent, provided the environment or system is properly organized. It describes the policy requirement: to be prepared to act even before the danger is at one's own door, but in the double assurance that such sacrifices will be few in number and easy as a burden because all humankind assists — if any sacrifice is really needed at all.

There is automaticity here, too, as in the balance-of-power model, but the automatic feature is more subtle: it consists of an innate love of peace and a ready acceptance of responsibility for the affairs of others. That the world has failed to meet these utopian specifications is also true.

In an important sense, the collective security model represents the first intellectual policy response on the part of the United States to playing a role in modern world affairs. Rejecting the balance of power, it sought to put international affairs on a better footing. When collective security faltered in the late 1940s, and even more in the 1950s, the United States supplemented it with an even greater commitment to yet another model, that of containment, to which we now turn.

NOTES

1. Inis L. Claude, Jr., *Swords into Plowshares: The Problems and Progress of International Organization*, 4th ed. (New York: Random House, 1971), p. 246.

2. *Addresses of President Wilson*, Senate Document No. 120, 66th Cong., 1st sess. (Washington, D.C.: 1919), p. 83.

3. Ibid.

4. Ibid., p. 85.

5. *Congressional Record*, Senate, January 22, 1917. Reprinted in "Official Documents Looking toward Peace, Series II." *International Conciliation*, No. 111, p. 62 (February 1917).

6. Robert E. Osgood, "Woodrow Wilson, Collective Security, and the Lessons of History," in Earl Latham, ed., *The Philosophy and Policies of Woodrow Wilson* (Chicago: University of Chicago Press, 1958), p. 189.

7. Henry Brougham, 1st Baron Brougham and Vaux, *Works*, vol. 8, (London and Glasgow: 1857), pp. 69-70.

8. *Addresses of President Wilson*, p. 86.

9. Ibid., p. 88.

10. Frederick L. Schuman, *International Politics*, 3d ed. (New York: McGraw-Hill, 1941), pp. 232-35. Italics added.

11. Frank H. Simonds and Brooks Emeny, *The Great Powers in World Politics* (New York: American Book Company, 1935), pp. 548-49. Italics added.

12. Richard W. Leopold, *The Growth of American Foreign Policy* (New York: Knopf, 1962), p. 486.

13. Ray S. Baker and William E. Dodd, eds., *The Public Papers of Woodrow Wilson, War and Peace*, vol. 1 (New York: Harper, 1927), p. 426.

14. See *League of Nations Official Journal*, Special Supplement No. 6 (October 1921), pp. 24ff. for text. Italics added.

15. *League of Nations Official Journal*, Special Supplement No. 14 (September 1923), p. 27.

16. Inis L. Claude, Jr., *Power and International Relations* (New York: Random House, 1962), p. 192.

17. *Yearbook of the United Nations, 1974* (New York: United Nations, 1977), vol. 28, pp. 842-46.

14

CONTAINMENT I

You have a row of dominoes set up, you knock over the first one, and what will happen to the last one is the certainty that it will go over very quickly. So you could have a beginning of a disintegration that would have the most profound influences.

Dwight D. Eisenhower[1]

If the balance-of-power model was invented long before the United States came to exist, and the collective security model by contrast had some distinct admixture of American thinking, containment can be described as almost purely American in intellectual origin and concept, even though Americans thought of it as a universally valid model. It was, in effect, the second American attempt to replace the balance of power with a more congenial system.

Although for decades containment had a vigorous hold on the whole of American thought about national security affairs, in discussing it today, it is not easy to revive the sense of life and meaning it once conveyed. Where the more recent shock to Americans at Russia's invasion of Afghanistan has revived part of the cold war atmosphere, the old unquestioned belief in containment has not revived with it. To explain the emotional and intellectual hold that containment used to have, to anyone who does not remember it, is like trying to explain why the United States felt it necessary to fight the Vietnam War. Although these events are hardly long past, they already have a curious deadness. A new page has been turned. Yet a look at containment is by no means an antiquarian exercise. The kind of restless spirit that wants to remake the world in another image has been a recurrent feature of American life and may well break out in new directions in the future. So it behooves us to understand ourselves.

As a system of thought, containment properly begins with the Truman Doctrine already quoted in an earlier chapter, with its very American blend of realism and idealism in its twin emphases.[2] Truman's geopolitical emphasis on Greece and Turkey seemed sound enough as he called on Americans to look at the map and see what would happen if those nations passed under unfriendly control: "Discouragement and possibly failure would quickly be the lot of neighboring peoples striving to maintain their freedom and independence."[3]

As we know, the more philosophical emphasis on "two ways of life" traces back to George Kennan's "long telegram," which Dean Acheson calls a "truly remarkable dispatch. It had a deep effect on thinking within the Government, although Government response with action still needed a year's proof of Soviet intentions as seen by Kennan." Acheson quotes Kennan that "at the bottom of the Kremlin's neurotic view of world affairs" were centuries of insecurity. Marxism furnished justification for the Soviet "fear of [the] outside world. . . . In the name of Marxism they sacrificed every single ethical value in their methods and tactics." Kennan, says Acheson, predicted Soviet attempts to divide the West.[4]

Acheson also records that Kennan, asked about the Chinese question, "stated frankly that he did not know [whether] the Chinese Communist Party, like others, was subservient to Moscow [and] he hesitated to accept it as established truth."[5] Kennan was not prepared to lump all Communist movements completely into one category, and neither was Acheson, who as late as January 1950, explaining the fall of China, argued that "What has happened in my judgment is that the almost inexhaustible patience of the Chinese people in their misery ended. They did not bother to overthrow this government. There was really nothing to overthrow. They simply ignored it throughout the country."[6] Until the Korean War, explanations about China lacked the automatic assumption of a Moscow-run Communist conspiracy.

Later on, a great deal of controversy would arise as to just what Kennan had in mind in his argument. His famous article by "X" in *Foreign Affairs* argued that the Soviets assumed an "innate antagonism between capitalism and socialism." Therefore, "If the Soviet Government occasionally sets its signature to documents which would indicate the contrary, this is to be regarded as a tactical maneuver permissible in dealing with the enemy (who is without honor) and should be taken in the spirit of *caveat emptor.*"[7] The implication is clear: The Russians are deceitful, not to be trusted. After pointing to the Kremlin belief in its own "infallibility," Kennan said bluntly that the United States

must continue to expect that Soviet policies will reflect no abstract love of peace and stability, no real faith in the possibility of a permanent happy coexistence of the socialist and capitalist worlds, but rather a cautious, persistent pressure toward the disruption and weakening of all rival influence and rival power.

Kennan said that "exhibitions of indecision, disunity and internal disintegration" within the United States had "an exhilarating effect on the whole Communist movement [sending] a thrill of hope and excitement . . . through the Communist world. . . ." Notice that Kennan's focus has shifted from Russia to the "whole Communist movement," the entire "Communist world."

Kennan's prescription was for the United States to enter

with reasonable confidence upon a policy of firm containment, designed to confront the Russians with unalterable counter-force at every point where they show signs of encroaching upon the interests of a peaceful and stable world. [Such a policy would] promote tendencies which must eventually find their outlet in either the break-up or the gradual mellowing of Soviet power.

Kennan, looking back, saw "serious deficiencies" in the article.[8] One was "the failure to make clear that what I was talking about when I mentioned the containment of Soviet power was not the containment by military means of a military threat, but the political containment of a political threat." (Kennan in the article had said "counter-force," not "counter-pressure.") Another weakness was the "failure to distinguish between various geographic areas, and to make clear that the 'containment' of which I was speaking was not something that I thought we could, necessarily, do everywhere successfully. . . ." Or should do everywhere. "My objection to the Truman Doctrine message revolved largely around its failure to draw this distinction."[9]

Walter Lippmann, in a small book, *The Cold War*, published in 1947, took on Kennan's argument and showed what he thought were the problems with it. Lippmann pointed to the "disturbing fact . . . that Mr. X's conclusions depend upon the optimistic prediction that the 'Soviet power . . . bears within itself the seeds of its own decay. . . .'"[10] Lippmann found little "ground for reasonable confidence in a policy that can be successful only if the most optimistic prediction should prove to be true."

Lippmann wonders whether the Western world can operate a policy of containment: "At the root of Mr. X's philosophy about Russian-American relations and underlying all the ideas of the Truman Doctrine there is a disbelief in the possibility of a settlement of the issues raised by this war." Lippmann is talking about the U.S. perception of the Soviet Union and the Soviet attitude. By Kennan's own words, quoted earlier, Lippmann is correct. Kennan has described communism as unwilling to make a good-faith, permanent settlement of the issues. Containment, according to Kennan, is a fight to the point where Moscow "mellows" and concedes defeat.

Lippmann points out:

The history of diplomacy is the history of relations among rival powers, which did not enjoy political intimacy, and did not respond to appeals to common purposes. Nevertheless, there have been settlements. . . . There would be little for diplomats to do if the world consisted of partners, enjoying political intimacy, and responding to common appeals.

Lippmann continues:

The method by which diplomacy deals with a world where there are rival powers is to organize a balance of power which deprives the rivals, however lacking in intimacy and however unresponsive to common appeals, of a good prospect of successful aggression. That is what a diplomat means by the settlement of a conflict among rival powers. He does not mean that they will cease to be rivals.

Lippmann argues that a "genuine policy would . . . have as its paramount objective a settlement which brought about the evacuation of Europe." Lippmann ends his argument with this advice:

In our conflict with Russia [our policy should] aim to redress the balance of power, which is abnormal and dangerous, because the Red Army has met the British and American armies in the heart of Europe. The division between east and west is at that military boundary line. The meeting of those armies caused the division. No state in eastern Europe can be independent of the Kremlin so long as the Red Army is within it and all around it. No state in western Europe is independent while it is in effect in the rear of this military frontier.

Lippmann grants the need "to hold the whole Russian military machine in check," but that is merely a phase in "a mounting pressure in support of a diplomatic policy which has as its concrete objective a settlement that means withdrawal."

Looking back, there is much to be said for Lippmann's warnings, but we shall not evaluate them here. Ironically, some years later, in the 1950s, Kennan was to advocate a "disengagement" of forces from the Iron Curtain line. Dean Acheson was almost sputtering in anger (in my presence) as he read the news report about Kennan's "reversal."

Whatever was initially intended by containment, it soon reduced the United States, even in Europe where it was most successful, to the appearance of merely preserving the status quo, rather than changing it in positive fashion to end the "unnatural" division of Europe. Whether in fact a diplomatic "deal" to achieve East-West disengagement was ever possible, is a difficult question.[11] Europe was stabilized by the Marshall Plan and the North Atlantic Alliance, but the "fall" of China in 1949 and the outbreak of the Korean War in 1950 seemed sufficient proof to enough Americans of a "Communist conspiracy" that the struggle between "two ways of life" now became worldwide and even more intense. The issue bulked large in the U.S. election of 1952, and to some even containment seemed insufficient.

The Republican party platform for 1952 denounced the wartime agreements with the Russians at Tehran, Yalta, and Potsdam as "tragic blunders" and charged that the agreements abandoned captive peoples in Latvia, Lithuania, Estonia, Czechoslovakia, and Poland to "fend for themselves against the Communist aggression which soon swallowed them." All "secret understandings such as Yalta" were to be repudiated, along with "the negative, futile and immoral policy of 'containment' which abandons countless human beings to a despotism and Godless terrorism...." The aim was to "set up strains and stresses within the captive world which will make the rulers impotent to continue in their monstrous ways and mark the beginning of the end."[12]

Louis L. Gerson, the relatively sympathetic biographer of John Foster Dulles, remarks: "One should have no question who wrote the above. The style, tone, ideas, hope—all pure Dulles." He adds: "Eisenhower showed little enthusiasm for liberation" and in his speeches was always careful to add the phrase "by peaceful means."[13]

From today's perspective it is readily apparent that "liberation by peaceful means" and "containment" represent a distinction without any real difference. As policies they were hardly in logical contradiction. What is significant, however, in the development of U.S. thinking is that the election of 1952 was already a contest between two brands of containment, one posing as more hawkish than the other. In parallel fashion, what is significant about the Eisenhower-Dulles years as they affected the containment concept is that the model was applied outside Europe. The United States on September 8, 1954, became a member of the Southeast Asia Treaty Organization (SEATO), along with Britain, France, Australia, New Zealand, the Philippines, Thailand, and Pakistan. By it each party recognized that "aggression by means of armed attack" in the area "would endanger its own peace and safety" and agreed to "meet the common danger in accordance with its constitutional processes." A special "Manila" protocol, attached to the treaty, included Cambodia, Laos, and South Vietnam within the treaty's protection. Congress, in March 1957, also passed the so-called Eisenhower Doctrine, authorizing the president to give economic and military assistance to any nation in the Middle East threatened by international communism.[14]

These measures alone were a vivid indication of an enlargement of the area in contest between the "two ways of life." But there were also additional U.S. treaties in Asia, with South Korea and Taiwan. "Crises," once centered in Europe, now occurred in other areas, too. The Eisenhower Doctrine was invoked in the Lebanon crisis in 1958. "Brinkmanship" was employed in Asia.[15] In Dulles's own words,

if you are scared to go to the brink, you are lost. We've had to look it square in the face—on the question of enlarging the Korean war, on the question of getting into the Indochina war, on the question of Formosa. We walked to the brink and we looked it in the face. We took strong action.[16]

Note how Asia-oriented our crises had become.

We are not trying to weigh policy here, but only to show the development of an idea, of the policy model called containment. The acute British observer Dennis W. Brogan wrote in 1952 of the American "illusion of omnipotence."

This is the illusion that any situation which distresses or endangers the United States can only exist because some Americans have been fools or knaves. . . .

This illusion of omnipotence is best illustrated by a very common American attitude toward the Chinese Revolution. In this attitude — apparently the dominant one at the moment — there is a curious absence of historical awe. . . . The Communist triumph in China is discussed as if it were simply the result of American action or inaction. . . .[17]

Brogan speaks of "the attitude of mind of those who have complained that, at Yalta, F.D.R. 'permitted' Russia to become a Pacific power. Russia was a Pacific power before the United States existed. And she was and is an Asiatic power, which the United States is not."[18] Brogan throughout discusses the U.S. frustration that the containment-liberation slogans reflected. The "lack of historical awe" grew more pronounced as the United States activated containment to cope with areas ever farther away and relatively unknown. The Korean War period almost coincided with the period of Senator Joseph McCarthy's prominence — another indication of unrest and confusion.

Many Americans, even at that, considered Dulles lacking in vigor. In 1958, in a widely noted article, David Shea Teeple argued that U.S. television, then dominated by Westerns, was "telling a story that our diplomats and political leaders should watch." He counted twenty-five Westerns between seven and ten P.M. in the Washington, D.C. area. Teeple heaped scorn on the timidity characterizing U.S. policy, asking

would Wyatt Earp stop at some frontier equivalent of the 38th Parallel when the rustlers were escaping with the herd? Ridiculous. Would Marshal Dillon refuse to allow his deputies to use shotguns for their own defense because of the terrible nature of the weapon? Ha! Would the Lone Ranger under any circumstances allow himself to be bullied and threatened by those who sought to destroy the principles by which he lives?

Teeple sums up:

The American public . . . wants to abandon the fuzzy-minded philosophy that can see nothing but grey, and return to the days when things were either black or white, right or wrong.[19]

Teeple closed by suggesting that TV Westerns be made compulsory viewing for U.S. diplomats.

It should be clear that in the United States the 1950s represented both a hardening of prevailing attitudes toward the outside world and a significant extension of politico-military involvement. That the United States ended the Korean War and refrained from the temptation to take part in the Indochinese War is also true. Obligations widened; prose was invoked freely; but actions stayed prudent.

By the time John F. Kennedy took office, the Soviet launching of *sputnik* had severely shaken American confidence in a direction so far considered impregnable: America's technological lead. The feeling was strong that the United States had become stagnant at home and unimaginative abroad. Criticism of U.S. inaction during the Hungarian uprising in 1956, which also made a mockery of Dulles's rollback rhetoric, was still heard. Some voices advocated a less sterile and negative policy toward China; others wanted positive steps incompatible with improved Chinese relations.

The Kennedy administration, for many reasons, was fated to be activist. Kennedy's own inaugural address made no secret of that intent: "Let every nation know, whether it wish us well or ill, that we shall pay any price, bear any burden, meet any hardship, support any friend, oppose any foe, in order to assure the survival and success of liberty." These are rather truculent and certainly open-ended propositions.

Because of the Bay of Pigs fiasco and because Laos was in crisis soon after Kennedy's inauguration, the hard-line action orientation won out. On March 23, 1961, Kennedy was warning on Laos that "armed attacks by externally supported Communists" had to stop. "If these attacks do not stop, those who support a truly neutral Laos will have to consider their response. The shape of this necessary response will, of course, be carefully considered, not only here in Washington, but in the SEATO Conference with our allies...." Roger Hilsman, reporting these events, adds quite correctly: "The implication was war."[20]

The Vienna meeting on June 3 and 4, 1961, was a harsh confrontation between Kennedy and Khrushchev. The Cuban missile crisis in October of the same year intensified the confrontation to breaking point. Hardly more than a half year after taking office, Kennedy was in an important sense the prisoner of events, given little opportunity to break out of the old containment mold. Although he did successfully initiate nuclear disarmament steps with the Soviets, in Europe he had to confront the Berlin Wall and in Vietnam he had sent new thousands of "advisers" — 16,000 (some say 17,000) by the time of his death.

President Johnson, years later, looking back on the wreck of the Vietnam War, said that he had only been following where his predecessors, from

Truman through Kennedy, had led. In the Dominican Republic crisis in the spring of 1965, Johnson said he did not intend to sit on his hands in a rocking chair while communism extended itself further in Latin America. In Asia he saw himself in the situation of meeting the Communist challenge or capitulating. That he actually and overtly committed U.S. troops in combat in Vietnam was, in his view, only one more step in the steady evolution of American thinking and action.

In his memoirs Johnson argues this point at length. For example, he cites Eisenhower's remark in 1953, soon after taking office, that "aggression in Korea and Southeast Asia are threats to the whole free community to be met by united action."[21] He quotes President Kennedy's State of the Union message of January 1962: "The systematic aggression now bleeding that country is not a 'war of liberation'—for Vietnam is already free. It is a war of attempted subjugation—and it will be resisted."[22]

Johnson, sensitive to the charge that he misled the American people on what to expect if he were elected over Goldwater, cites his remarks of August 12, 1964, to the American Bar Association in New York:

Some say we should withdraw from South Vietnam, that we have lost almost 200 lives there in the last four years and we should come home. But the United States cannot and must not and will not turn aside and allow the freedom of a brave people to be handed over to communist tyranny.

This alternative is strategically unwise, we think, and it is morally unthinkable.[23]

So Johnson prepared himself to take one more step and commit combat troops.

Townsend Hoopes quite accurately wrote of Johnson that his "exposure to the subject [of foreign policy] as a member of relevant House and Senate Committees had been long, but superficial."[24] Hoopes goes on to write: "In matters of war and peace he seemed too much the sentimental patriot, lacking Truman's practical horse sense, Eisenhower's experienced caution, Kennedy's cool grasp of reality."[25]

That is one way of explaining why Johnson went further, although along a path prepared by his predecessors. Hoopes makes another significant observation:

What seemed in retrospect to have made large-scale military intervention all but inevitable in 1965 was a fateful combination of the President's uncertainty and sense of insecurity in handling foreign policy, and a prevailing set of assumptions among his close advisors that reinforced his own tendency to think about the external world in the simplistic terms of appeasement versus military resolve. The President seemed, from the beginning to the end, uncomfortable and out of his depth in dealing with foreign policy.[26]

President Johnson's chief political adviser was, of course, Dean Rusk. Hoopes says of Rusk that he

seemed the very embodiment of the embattled Cold Warrior with convictions rooted in the Stalinist period. . . . He was, moreover, possessed of a special mania about China and of a knack for arguing by dubious analogy. Not only in public, but in private conversations with colleagues and with President Johnson, Rusk expounded his thesis that Communist China was actively promoting and supporting aggression in Vietnam, that aggression in Vietnam was not different from Hitler's aggression in Europe, that appeasement in Vietnam could have the same consequences as appeasement at Munich.[27]

Dean Rusk heard this charge so often that he once responded that "he was not the village idiot; he knew Ho was not Hitler, but, nevertheless, there was an obligation to stand."[28] But Hoopes is correct on the main point. Rusk, testifying before the Senate Committee on Foreign Relations on February 18, 1966, made his views perfectly clear, arguing that the United States was in Vietnam to prevent

the expansion and extension of Communist domination by the use of force against the weaker nations on the perimeter of Communist power.
[I]n the course of your hearings . . . some objection has been raised to the use of the term "Communist aggression" [but] we should not confuse ourselves or our people by turning our eyes away from what that phrase means. . . . The Communist world has returned to its demand for what it calls a "world revolution," a world of coercion in direct contradiction to the Charter of the United Nations. . . .
So what we face in Vietnam is what we have faced on many occasions before — the need to check the extension of Communist power in order to maintain a reasonable stability in a precarious world.[29]

Interestingly, George Kennan, testifying before the same group only eight days earlier, had said that

if we were not already involved . . . in Vietnam, I would know of no reason why we should wish to become so involved. . . . Vietnam is not a region of major military, industrial importance. It is difficult to believe that any decisive developments of the world situation would be determined in normal circumstances by what happens on that territory. . . .[30]

Kennan termed our military involvement there "unfortunate."
There is surely dramatic irony here! The "father" of containment, surveying its Vietnam offspring, says, "I know not this child." Yet from the beginning, from Kennan's long telegram to Johnson's use of combat troops in Vietnam, is a logically continuous route. That Johnson entirely changed the

nature of United States commitment, and escalated the confrontation into a war from which the United States was to find it difficult to withdraw, was a practical development of tremendous importance, but Johnson is in the end correct when he cites the thought patterns and policy "appreciations" of his predecessors. He merely carried them on.

Since in this chapter it has been necessary to devote considerable space to showing the development of containment as a system of ideas, the focus of the next chapter will be to critique it as a model.

NOTES

1. Dwight D. Eisenhower, news conference, April 7, 1954. *Public Papers of the Presidents: Dwight D. Eisenhower, 1954* (Washington, D.C.: Government Printing Office, 1960), p. 383.

2. For the doctrine, see *Congressional Record*, 80th Cong., 1st sess., vol. 93, pp. 1980-81.

3. Ibid., p. 1981.

4. Dean Acheson, *Present at the Creation*, (New York: Norton, 1969), p. 151.

5. Ibid., p. 202.

6. Dean Acheson, "Crisis in Asia—An Examination of United States Policy," Department of State *Bulletin*, vol. 22 (January 23, 1950), p. 113.

7. This and following quotations are from X, "The Sources of Soviet Conduct," *Foreign Affairs* 25, no. 4 (July 1947): 571-82.

8. George F. Kennan, *Memoirs, 1925-1950* (Boston: Little, Brown, 1967), p. 357.

9. Ibid., p. 359.

10. This and following quotations are from Walter Lippmann, *The Cold War* (New York: Harper, 1947), pp. 11-14, 60-62.

11. For a detailed account of the diplomacy as it revolved around the German question, see Frederick H. Hartmann, *Germany between East and West: The Reunification Problem* (Englewood Cliffs, N.J.: Prentice-Hall, 1965).

12. Quoted in Louis L. Gerson, *John Foster Dulles*, vol. 17 of *The American Secretaries of State and Their Diplomacy* (New York: Cooper Square, 1967), pp. 87-88.

13. Ibid., p. 88.

14. Ibid., p. 298.

15. The term comes from the famous *Life* magazine article of January 16, 1956, "Three Times at Brink of War: How Dulles Gambled and Won."

16. Quoted in Gerson, *Dulles*, pp. 302-3.

17. Dennis W. Brogan, "The Illusion of American Omnipotence," *Harper's* 205 (December 1952): 21-28.

18. Ibid.

19. David Shea Teeple, "TV Westerns Tell a Story—Our Diplomats Should Watch Them," *Human Events* 15, no. 10, sect. 2, March 10, 1958.

20. Roger Hilsman, *To Move a Nation* (New York: Doubleday, 1967), p. 91.

21. Lyndon Baines Johnson, *The Vantage Point* (New York: Holt, Rinehart, Winston, 1971), p. 49.

22. Ibid., p. 58.

23. Ibid., app. 3, p. 575.

24. Townsend Hoopes, *The Limits of Intervention*, rev. ed. (New York: David McKay, 1973), p. 8.

25. Ibid.

26. Ibid., pp. 7-8.

27. Ibid., pp. 16-17.

28. David Halberstam, *The Best and the Brightest* (Greenwich, Conn.: Fawcett, 1973), p. 770.

29. Dean Rusk, "The United States Commitment in Vietnam: Fundamental Issues." Testimony before the Senate Committee on Foreign Relations, February 18, 1966. Department of State *Bulletin*, March 7, 1966, pp. 347-48.

30. Hearings before the Committee on Foreign Relations, U.S. Senate, 89th Cong., 2d sess., *Supplemental Foreign Assistance Fiscal Year 1966 — Vietnam*, p. 331.

15

CONTAINMENT II

President Johnson frequently assured his listeners in press conferences that if only they could see the many cables on his desk
each day they would understand as he understood, and as they in
his mind clearly failed to understand, what was really going on in
Vietnam.

Bernard Brodie[1]

Containment is crystal clear about the nature of humanity: human beings
love freedom. Totalitarian movements, such as communism, seek to
enslave humanity; therefore communism is opposed to the deepest wellsprings of human striving. Communism is imposed from without or from
above, but it is unnatural. It is unnatural not just in the West or in modern
industrial, advanced societies but regardless of culture, regardless of
geography, regardless of economic condition.

Containment is equally clear about the nature of the environment. Where
communism has prevailed (temporarily), the peoples so enslaved are forced
into a way of life opposed to freedom and a struggle between the "Free
World" and the "Communist bloc" ensues. In this struggle some may hold
aloof out of a mistaken sense of "neutralism," but they are simply mis-
guided. It is the human condition to want freedom and to oppose those who
would take it away. Thus international politics can be understood as a
struggle between Free World states and the Communist bloc, each led by a
champion (Washington or Moscow), supported by lesser allies. In
Washington's case, however, the allies are freely associated, whereas in
Moscow's case the arrangement is forced. (Since China is obviously so huge
and unmanageable, sometimes the Moscow-Peking relationship envisaged
was that of senior partner, junior partner.)

Containment, from these observations, yields policy guidance. Since
communism is aggressive, as is well known, and seeks world revolution, it
will seek gains anywhere the resistance is soft, but particularly on its immediate periphery. If these attempts by subversion and force to expand the
Communist orbit are not resisted, a crisis of confidence will occur among

the remaining potential victims, who by their disarray will make the task of further aggression easier. The Munich experience shows how critical it is to hold the line.* Therefore the Free World must be prepared to fight anywhere the Communist world attacks, whether it be in Germany or the Middle East, Korea or Vietnam. On the one hand, each attack is as important as any other because of the domino effect (meaning one loss ultimately can be fatal). On the other hand, while the Free World does not more or less automatically win if it resists aggression successfully, it can expect a "mellowing" in the heart of the Communist world if enough Communist attempts are frustrated. Exactly why the odds vary, with the Communist side ceded the better chance if the West does not remain vigilant, is not altogether clear in containment thinking.

Thus the policy prescriptions come down to this: Organize the Free World and arm against the attack, expecting that attack at unlikely places and inconvenient times and meanwhile building economic strength. When the attack comes, resist it by force, because otherwise the domino effect will occur. In short, fight Communists who attack at the times and places of their choosing: any Communists, at any time, at any place. What is left for decision to the Free World is little more than the choice of weapons. The rest is automatic, speaking in conceptual terms.

It is significant to remember where this line of thinking begins and where it ends. Both the beginning and the ending deserve extended comments. We have just seen where it ends: in an automatic disposition to resist Communist aggression anywhere. It begins, however, with American observations about the nature of communism.

Communism's most striking feature, as Americans perceived it, was its *automaticity*. Much in communism in the 1950s clearly did fall into that category, including communism's basic claim to future triumph. Even at the time, however, this automatic feature was overemphasized in the American perception, and it was to be seriously overstated after Khrushchev's revisionism.

Lenin in 1913 wrote an introduction to Marxism (translated by Max Eastman) that brings out this strong automatic emphasis. Lenin said:

The historic materialism of Marx is one of the greatest achievements of scientific thought. The caprice and chaos reigning up to that time among opinions about

---

*Compare this thought with the observations in Chapter 11. While containment emphasized holding the line, it was indifferent to the geopolitical implications of the particular territories held. The line's importance arose only from demarcating the "free" and "unfree" worlds. In a fundamental sense, then, containment was really ageographical. Note that U.S. strategic theory at the time was also substantially indifferent to geography in its strategic implications — a point explored further in Chapter 17.

history and politics were here replaced by a strikingly whole and symmetrical and scientific theory, showing how out of one setup of social life, another higher one develops in consequence of a growth of the productive forces — capitalism for example out of feudalism.[2]

A world that had intellectually accepted Darwinism was receptive to Marxist "scientific" thought, which predicted more or less "inevitable" further developments. As Lenin said, "The genius of Marx lay in the fact that he was able . . . to make and consistently carry out the inference to which the whole of world history leads." This automatic theme is very pronounced in Friedrich Engels's statement in January 1888. He described Karl Marx's concept that "the whole history of mankind . . . has been a history of class struggles [forming] a series of evolution" that had reached a stage "where the exploited and oppressed class (the proletariat) cannot attain its emancipation . . . without, at the same time, and *once and for all*, emancipating society at large from all exploitation, oppression, class-distinction and class-struggles."[3] Engels adds that "this proposition . . . is *destined* to do for history what Darwin's theory has done for biology. . . ."[4] Engels was quite confident that Marx had established a scientific basis for predicting future developments in society.

Engels and Marx, like Lenin, were describing a historical process with a definite, anticipated ending, when "once and for all" society will be emancipated. In a fundamental historical sense this process was seen as automatic and ultimately inalterable. Yet, as their writings and intense lobbying efforts show, the inevitability of this process also had to be helped along by specific individuals or groups doing some specific things. One of Lenin's most interesting books, called *What Is to Be Done?*, took up exactly this question — the way to be sure that the inevitable happens without undue delay. His solution was to organize the most "mature" workers, who best comprehend the nature of the class struggle, to form the vanguard of the working class. Since the masses are slower to understand what needs to be done, that vanguard should lead events.

Thus communism in practice would be what Inis L. Claude, Jr., speaking of the balance-of-power model, would call not a fully automatic model but a semiautomatic one. The end would be inevitable, but the process would take some hands-on assistance.

In the United States in the 1940s, at the time when containment as a model was evolving, the automaticity and rigidity of Communist doctrine were taken for granted as implying automatic Soviet aggressive intent. Lenin's famous statement of March 18, 1919, was quoted recurrently in U.S. discussions of policy issues concerning Russia:

We are living not merely in a State, but in a system of States, and the existence of the Soviet Republic side by side with imperialistic States for a long time is unthinkable.

One or the other must triumph in the end. And before that end supervenes, a series of frightful collisions between the Soviet Republic and the bourgeois States will be inevitable.[5]

Lenin, of course, had been thinking primarily in terms of *being* attacked. Soviet armed strength at that time was very weak.

Another favorite often cited was Lenin's statement that "In the end . . . a funeral requiem will be sung either over the Soviet Republic or over world capitalism. This is a respite in war."[6] This, like the previous statement, dates from the days when the Soviets were simply trying to survive, but both statements were frequently understood in the 1940s as clear evidence of future Soviet aggressive intent.

From the Soviet viewpoint, capitalism's very existence guaranteed active hostility toward socialism, up to and including aggressive war. From the U.S. viewpoint, the friction originated in the domination of Soviet policy by an idea system that saw confrontations and conflicts as inevitable.

Obviously, it was farfetched to assume that actual Soviet policy in the 1940s would necessarily be governed by statements made by Lenin many years earlier under conditions of capitalist "encirclement." The U.S. approach, however, did have real grounds in fact and logic for perceiving inflexibility and hostility, grounds we have already cited. The main other thing to see is that the Soviets, while well aware that they could take "one step backward, two steps forward" when confronted by changing odds, were simultaneously perceiving their enemy (the capitalist world) as foredoomed to rigidity in policy and in action. The Soviets knew their own tactical flexibility, but they believed in their opponent's tactical rigidity.

After all, communism was supposed to win because capitalists could not help behaving automatically as capitalists. If capitalists were indeed free to cease exploiting the workers and make social reforms, the incentive and cause for revolution would melt away. Thus communism's inevitable victory was entirely derivative from the inevitability of capitalist behavior.

When we look at the problem that way, the most fully automatic part of communist thinking is capitalist behavior; this behavior "inevitably" creates a winning situation for the proletariat, which the proletariat in its turn may fail to exploit if it is not properly organized and ready.

So what we really had at the onset of the cold war and the evolution of the containment doctrine was a relationship between two superpowers, each convinced of its own tactical flexibility but equally convinced of its opponent's inflexibility. Each thought of its actions predominantly in defensive terms; more important, each saw the other as inflexibly aggressive. When the United States tried to overcome Soviet suspicions, it only raised more. It is not surprising that the relationship deteriorated.

Once views hardened, it was difficult to thaw the images. Even when

Communist thought underwent a highly important revision in 1956, the United States took no serious account of it. When the United States took containment to the extreme length of a combat role in Vietnam, it was still thinking of communism in the old Leninist-Stalinist framework. Yet the change in communism was of radical dimensions. Let us see how that came about.

We have already quoted two statements by Lenin about war. Lenin had become fixed in these views by virtue of his experience with Western intervention in the Russian civil war at the end of World War I, but the views had originated in academic study as Lenin prepared his *Imperialism: The Highest Stage of Capitalism.*[7] There Lenin argued that the finance stage of capitalism, which marked the pre-World-War-I years, was its last stage, since it was accompanied by a frenzied competition among the capitalist powers to annex colonies that would ultimately destroy capitalism itself. The enormous accumulations of empire by many of these states between 1875 and 1905 seemed to give credence to Lenin's argument. In any event, it was obvious to everyone that the day was arriving when either the capitalist nations had to rest content with the colonial possessions they already had, since few if any were left to be taken, or take each other's. Lenin thought they would not — could not — call off the competition. The result inevitably would be war, as capitalist fought capitalist for additional prizes and capitalism destroyed itself. Lenin had no doubt that World War I, when it came, reflected this analysis.

Lenin's thesis was never questioned in the interwar period. It remained not only the orthodox Communist explanation of international (as contrasted with civil) war, but also the sole Communist explanation of such wars.

In the cold war period, which was also the nuclear age, Stalin found no reason to depart from Lenin's argument. Stalin, like Lenin before him, insisted that war remained "inevitable." In his *Economic Problems of Socialism in the U.S.S.R.*, published in September 1952, Stalin took note in Chapter 6 of "The Question of the Inevitability of Wars among Capitalist Countries." Some comrades, he said, were arguing that

wars among capitalist countries have ceased to be inevitable. They consider that the contradictions [sources of tension] between the camp of socialism and the camp of capitalism are greater than the contradictions among capitalist countries, that the U.S.A. has made other capitalist countries sufficiently subservient to itself to prevent them from going to war with one another.

Stalin wrote bluntly, "These comrades are mistaken." He went on: "It is said that Lenin's thesis that imperialism inevitably gives birth to wars should be considered obsolete. . . . This is not correct."[8] Stalin, in so many words, was denying the ultimate significance of what appeared to be a bipolar cold war. The main contest, according to him, remained capitalist versus capitalist, with Soviet territories as a possible prize to be sought in the process. More critical to the comrades Stalin labeled as mistaken was that Stalin in effect was accepting the inevitability of nuclear war.

But "these comrades," mistaken or not, took control of Soviet policy after Stalin's death. In February 1956, Nikita S. Khrushchev argued bluntly that "there is no fatal inevitability of war" between Russia and the West because, he said, "the socialist [Communist] camp is invincible."

He spelled out an astonishing new doctrinal flexibility: communism might now be expected to come to power in some nations without a "revolutionary class struggle." The working classes "in a number of capitalist and former colonial countries" might even win stable parliamentary majorities through free elections.

Of course in countries where capitalism is still strong and where it controls an enormous military and police machine, the serious resistance of the reactionary forces is inevitable. There the transition to socialism [communism] will proceed amid conditions of an acute revolutionary class struggle.[9]

Khrushchev's revisionism was both remarkable and radical in three respects. First, he rejected the traditional Leninist thesis that capitalists, competing for profits, would war on one another (and attack "peaceful socialist" states as well). Second, Khrushchev, in sidelining that whole idea, described capitalists as one bloc and socialists as another, adding that the capitalist bloc, observing the strength of the socialist bloc, would not dare to attack. Third, he heaped on top of that another radical thought: that the working class could come to power peacefully in a number of countries.

Even today, the sweeping impact of these changes tends to be undervalued. Taken together, they totally revised extremely important Soviet Communist assumptions about the nature of their principal adversary. That adversary, the United States, was suddenly seen through Khrushchev's eyes as capable of reaching rational decisions outside the blinders of class bias, as able to observe the Soviet Union, assess its strength, and arrive at the logical conclusion that starting a war with the Soviets has no utility.

Logically, if capitalists can use their brains and their actions are not automatic and inevitable, nothing else that Marx and Engels predicted as inevitable is necessarily foreordained. In a strict logical sense, Khrushchev's revisionism makes communism's victory no more inevitable than its defeat, unless the Soviet camp is indeed too strong to be defeated.

Whatever the philosophical nuances of Soviet revisionism, though, there can be no doubt that it implied significant changes in attitude. For it followed that the United States and its allies were for the first time conceptualized by the Soviet authorities as able to think rationally and admitted to be subjected to many and diverse pressures.

That the new acceptance of capitalist flexibility derived from a practical Soviet concern does not cheapen its meaning. The practical concern was that, if war is inevitable (as traditional Marxism insists), then millions upon millions of the proletariat are going to die in the holocaust. As the point was expressed in the September 1960 *Kommunist* (the Russian theoretical monthly):

The working class cannot conceive of the creation of a Communist civilization on the ruins of world centers of culture, on desolated land contaminated with thermonuclear fallout, which would be an inevitable consequence of such a war. For some peoples the question of socialism would in general cease to exist: they would physically vanish from the planet. It is thus clear that a *present-day nuclear war in itself can in no way be a factor that would accelerate revolution and bring the victory of socialism closer.*[10]

The Chinese reaction to Khrushchev's ideological revisionism, which helped widen the Sino-Soviet split, is somewhat complicated and only of peripheral concern here. It is notable, however, that while Mao liked the two-bloc emphasis in the new propositions, he disliked intensely the implications of Soviet-American rapprochement for China and for the Third World. He accused the Russians, in effect, of saying: "I've got mine, Jack. You others shift for yourselves."

At this remove it is possible to appreciate the irony in the intellectual contradictions between the perceptions then current in Washington (observing Moscow) and in Moscow (observing Washington) in the early months of 1956, while Moscow claimed a new flexibility. The disparity between these perceptions might well have disappeared shortly had not that same Khrushchev, now "soft" in theoretical terms, immediately begun to pursue a very hard line in actual policy. Precipitating the 1958-1959 crisis over Berlin, Khrushchev lumbered into the Cuban missile crisis of 1961. Looked at in this perspective, it is not surprising that the United States was slow to appreciate the change in Soviet thinking. Less excusable was the slowness in U.S. appreciation of growing Sino-Soviet tensions. In those tensions the ideological feature was only one factor, but the dominant image of monolithic communism held by the United States again retarded comprehension.

The preceding analysis shows the extent to which the containment model is a mirror image of communism. Communism (and its "goals") provide the threat; containment provides the response. Thus if containment is inflexible, it is because communism is inflexible. America did not start the cold war; the Russians did.

But a simple mirror image does not explain why communism, for all its inflexibility, should conceive of "one step backward, two steps forward" as a perfectly reasonable response to no-win situations of a less obviously crucial sort, while the United States was regarding any one loss as fatal (the dominoes), regardless of where. From this point of view there is a crucial difference between the "inflexibility" of communism and the "inflexibility" of containment. Whereas the United States found it necessary to fight in Vietnam, the Soviet Union did not use its troops overtly in real combat after World War II until the Afghanistan affair. And not only did the United States fight in Vietnam, but it fought without any real assessment in a positive sense of what goals were to be achieved or how much the war was worth fighting. When Senator Claiborne Pell (D.-R.I.) asked Secretary Rusk on January 28, 1966, during Rusk's testimony before the Senate Foreign Relations Committee, whether he could see any satisfactory end to the Vietnam venture, he replied: "No, I would be misleading you if I told you that I know where, when, and how this matter will be resolved."[11] A little later he added: "The nature of a struggle of this sort . . . is, of course, substantially determined by the other side."[12]

In other words, the enemy was to be permitted to choose where the war would be fought, how long it would be fought, and perhaps even how it would be fought. The U.S. role was reduced to that of an automatic response: send the troops because an aggression has been committed. The U.S. role was automatic. It was open-ended (the United States had declared it would prevail whatever it cost, which depended on how long and hard the enemy fought). It was also negative (designed to prevent the change communism was attempting to bring about).

These characteristics of the containment model show it to be, above all, one in which the ramifications, subtleties, and consequences of policy decisions conspicuously do not have to be thought through and context and occasion do not count. Summing up all the "movable parts" of the model, we have the following pieces: Communism is inexorably aggressive, and the Communist bloc will seek weak points on its perimeter where it will plunge forward when opportunity presents. This must be stopped because otherwise the unity of the Free World will be undermined as potential victims hurry to make peace with the aggressors. Thus any war, anyplace, under these circumstances is a critical war since its vital character does not derive from its geopolitical setting but from its predicted psychological impact. Thus, while it may seem odd not to consider the conflict in a cost-effective way and think through some positive goals, it is the event itself (the aggression) that is significant, and also the events that will follow that event if nothing is done. The price if this sequence is followed is incalculable. Thus whatever price the enemy establishes by its effort is worth paying, since the stakes are really "winner take all." That is what President Johnson thought he saw in all the cables on his desk.

What stands out from a bald listing of the parts of this model is how cut-and-dried, how mechanical these containment propositions are. There is a rigidity, a pronounced tendency to think in black and white terms: Free World versus Communist bloc. There is also a startling simplicity in outlook: a belief that freedom is so central and all-inclusive a motive for behavior that it overrides any combination of other motives, and a belief that free peoples have some natural affinity for one another that makes them tacit or actual allies. There is a lack of historical underpinning in these views, even an absence of awareness that they need proof. There is an almost complete insensitivity to the actual strategic implications of geography and geopolitics; instead, every piece of terrain is considered as important as any other.

That many Americans would believe all this, is highly interesting. As will be seen in Part V, there are some good reasons why we did.

NOTES

1. Bernard Brodie, *War and Politics* (New York: Macmillan, 1973), p. 211.

2. V. I. Lenin, Introduction to Karl Marx, *Capital, The Communist Manifesto, and Other Writings*, Max Eastman, ed. (New York: Modern Library, 1932), pp. xxi-xxiii. Italics added.

3. Friedrich Engels, "The Method and the Call to Action," in ibid. pp. 318-19. Italics added.

4. Ibid., p. 319. Italics added.

5. V. I. Lenin, "Report of Central Committee at 8th Party Congress" of March 18, 1919, *Selected Works*, vol. 8, p. 33.

6. Lenin, *Collected Works*, vol. 17 (1923), p. 398.

7. Lenin, *Imperialism: The Highest Stage of Capitalism* (New York: International Publishers, 1939). The book was written in 1916.

8. Reprinted by Leo Gruliow, ed., *Current Soviet Policies* (New York: Praeger, 1953), pp. 7-8.

9. *New York Times*, February 15, 1956.

10. As cited in Zbigniew Brzezinski, "A Book the Russians Would Like to Forget," *The Reporter*, December 22, 1960.

11. Hearings before the Committee on Foreign Relations, U.S. Senate, 89th Cong., 2d sess. *Supplemental Foreign Assistance Fiscal Year 1966 — Vietnam*, p. 32.

12. Ibid., p. 36.

Part V

THE CONSERVATION
OF ENEMIES

16

MODELS: A SUMMING UP

It has never occurred to most Americans that the political principles by which they themselves lived might have been historically conditioned and might not enjoy universal validity.

George Kennan[1]

The four models we have examined, like the national policies they foster, can be looked at through either end of a telescope. By noting which models appeal to which nations, much can be learned about how those nations and their decision makers see reality. Comparison can be made between what Robert Jervis calls the "'psychological mileau' (the world as the actor sees it) and the 'operational mileau' (the world in which policy will be carried out). . . ."[2]

Looking through one end of the telescope (the view from the other end will be described later in this chapter), we can see that national policy decisions are made on the basis of the information available, as it takes on meaning by being fitted into national patterns of thought. An excellent illustration is President Harry S. Truman's reaction when Secretary Dean Acheson telephoned to say, "Mr. President, I have very serious news. The North Koreans have invaded South Korea."[3] Despite the standing appraisal of the Joint Chiefs of Staff as to the limited value of defending South Korea, Truman took immediate and far-reaching action.

The Joint Chiefs memorandum of September 25, 1947, had concluded that "the United States has little strategic interest in maintaining the present troops and bases in Korea." Those troops were "a military liability" unless substantially reinforced. Moreover, any "offensive operation the United States might wish to conduct on the Asiatic continent most probably would by-pass the Korean peninsula." Even an offensive enemy move in the peninsula could best be neutralized by "air action [which] would be more feasible and less costly than large-scale ground operations."[4]

Truman's reaction to Acheson's phone call paid almost no attention to the points covered in the Joint Chiefs memorandum. Neatly combining

American assumptions about the world common to both the collective security model and the containment model, Truman later wrote:

In my generation, this was not the first occasion when the strong had attacked the weak. I recalled some earlier instances: Manchuria, Ethiopia, Austria. I remembered how each time that the democracies failed to act it had encouraged the aggressors to keep going ahead. Communism was acting in Korea just as Hitler, Mussolini, and the Japanese had acted ten, fifteen, and twenty years earlier. I felt certain that if South Korea was allowed to fall Communist leaders would be emboldened to override nations closer to our own shores [and] no small nation would have the courage to resist threats and aggression by stronger Communist neighbors. If this was allowed to go unchallenged it would mean a third world war, just as similar incidents had brought on the second world war.[5]

And so the die was cast and a war began to avoid the consequences Truman was sure inaction would have caused.

When the United States is seen reacting in this way, we know it stems from American beliefs on the one hand, and what American leaders observe and comprehend as the situation on the other hand. As with any belief structure, ideas prevalent in the American culture about human behavior and cause and effect in human affairs shaped its leaders' comprehension of the nature of the environment and the interaction occurring in that environment. Because these ideas vary from culture to culture, members of one culture have difficulty understanding the points of view of those in other cultures.

Studies of crises confirm this view. Snyder and Diesing report that in a crisis "the chances of a message getting through untarnished to *someone* in the receiving government are about four in ten." They call this figure "very approximate" and go on to say that the

total correct interpretations could be raised higher by including more minor messages . . . but the total of misinterpretations could also be raised by starting our count in the pre-crisis build-up phase. The general pattern is for misinterpretations to predominate early in a crisis and to give way to correct interpretations at the end. . . .[6]

Ole Holsti, in his case studies, parallels Snyder and Diesing. He also found that differences in perceptions among decision makers decrease as tension increases.[7] As the nature of the conflict or crisis becomes clear, cultural bias may become less significant and permit informed decisions.

Arnold Wolfers, in a much quoted remark, argues that certain situations were obvious enough to surmount *any* cultural biases:

Imagine a number of individuals, varying widely in their predispositions, who find themselves inside a house on fire. It would be perfectly realistic to expect that these individuals, with rare exceptions, would feel compelled to run toward the exits. . . . Surely, therefore, for an explanation of the rush for the exits, there is no need to analyze the individual decisions that produced it.[8]

Robert Jervis says of Wolfers's comparison that different leaders see fires sooner, later, or not at all.[9] (Compare Chamberlain and Churchill, for instance.) This may be the most significant point of all. It involves perception, and this is what models, and their less full-blown cousins, theories, are all about.

That is why, throughout this book, we have stressed the overriding importance of perception. Errors in perception are very costly, and none of the models we have examined can escape running those risks. Each model both *describes* and *prescribes*, correctly or incorrectly, depending on the view of reality it contains. The description it "feeds back" into the decision-making process tells the decision makers the nature of the problem faced. The prescription it suggests looks ahead to the consequences and, to do that, necessarily has to include some assumptions about the way the system operates, what moves the various players are making, and why they are making them.

Before the models are summarized and compared and contrasted on major points of description and prescription, a few specific aspects of game theory, operational theory, and deterrence theory should be discussed, since all three of these theories consist largely of propositions about the extent to which it is possible to visualize and analyze an opponent's reaction in advance. Each of our models, as we have seen, necessarily makes a similar claim, even if not with the precision of game, operational research, or deterrence theory. Examining the theories first will help to determine how much any model may validly claim to predict the future for purposes of present decisions and what the parameters of that much abused word, prediction, are.

The problems with game theory (and decision theory) are discussed in a stimulating study by Alexander George and Richard Smoke.[10] They point out that even that most elementary distinction in game theory between "zero-sum" and "non-zero-sum" is clearer in logic than in fact. They also point to a number of what they consider to be simplifications and distortions connected with decision theory and game theory. The first is what they call the "necessary assumption . . . that each side is a *unitary* and *purposive* player" in which "'the player' perceives a situation, consults 'the' national interest and constructs 'his' payoffs, and then selects the strategy that will maximize 'his' utility." George and Smoke say "this simplification does great violence to . . . reality," since any meaningful decision is "the product of tugs-of-war among institutions within its society or bureaucracy, and of the personal and self-interested maneuverings of many top decision-makers."[11] Graham Allison is then cited, as might be expected.

George and Smoke, examining rationality as another key assumption of decision theory, argue that four difficulties arise at this point. First is the fact that "it is notoriously difficult to construct an unambiguous and consistent ordering of values." Second is the problem in assessing possible outcomes:

Decision theory presumes that the cells define the outcomes and that the payoffs within each cell define the players' valuations of the outcomes. But the real policy-maker will often find it difficult to define the principal, possible outcomes of an actual situation. Thus even if he knows his values — his preferences among various hypothetical outcomes — he may have difficulty in estimating the various actual outcomes possible and in connecting these unambiguously to his values.[12]

Third is the problem of trying to decide "what actions on one's own part are likely to generate any particular outcome."[13] Fourth is the problem of information.

All of these considerations, say George and Smoke, also apply to one's estimations of the opponent's payoffs: "In the real world the opponent does not provide one with a matrix, his own half filled in; yet critical choices depend upon one's reconstructing the opponent's probable subjective payoffs."[14] And, we might add, knowing the opponent's view of reality. Many of these observations are warranted. George and Smoke are quite right to criticize the familiar matrix of game theory, with mathematical "values" and "payoffs" calculated and neatly written in. Situations involving nations in crisis or enmity are rarely seen in identical terms by all the actors. (It does not often or easily happen that the participants, in Wolfers's terms, simultaneously see that the house is on fire.) Even if they do, the problem will certainly change focus quite soon as the enemy does unexpected things and chance intervenes. But that does not mean one should abandon gaming insights or forget that policy is always calculated in terms of yielding some advantage, even if it does not turn out that way.

It is also true, as George and Smoke argue, that the nation, represented by its leaders as they attempt to arrive at a decision, often has interests that may be at odds in the given situation or crisis as that situation or crisis is perceived. (In Wolfers's terms, what may appear as an argument over what fire equipment to use and how to fight the fire may be in reality an argument over whether it is better to choose to save the house or save the people in peril — including oneself.)

For this reason, George and Smoke are certainly right in rejecting the notion of "the" (single) national interest that can be identified and implemented. Nevertheless, in any argument over any policy decision, competing claims to embody the national interest will confront each other, each claim supported by its own rationale and clientele. Since the term "national interests" represents only names given to alternatives, to say "we shall implement the national interest" necessarily means the same as "we shall pursue the alternative we think is best."

One does not effectively grapple with the implications of what was just said by pointing to bureaucratic or organizational competition for advantage within the government or by pointing to the "irrationality" of that competition. Such observations, by stressing the way decision is reached (which may include quite irrational aspects), tend to obscure the more important consequences that flow from the decision. Decisions may be made on a split basis within the state, but they will not be pursued that way. A nation does not cast a two-thirds vote for and a one-third vote against a resolution in the UN; whatever the argument within the state, the state casts a single vote. Regardless of who has chosen the path that decision marks out, the state must now pursue it, because a state cannot go down two different paths at the same time. That is the most important thing that can be said about decision making.

Once that path is chosen (in incomplete knowledge and with disagreements in most cases), all kinds of things may happen. As Thucydides tells us, the plague that swept Athens during the Peloponnesian War altered everything, but who could have foreseen it? Or, as the Spartan King Archidamus said, speaking of that supreme category of decision making, the decision to go to war:

Spartans, in the course of my life I have taken part in many wars, and I see among you people of the same age as I am. They and I have had experience, and so are not likely to share in what may be a general enthusiasm for war, nor to think that war is a good thing or a safe thing. . . . We are trained to avoid being too clever . . . and [know] that it is impossible to calculate accurately events that [in part] are determined by chance.[15]

Karl von Clausewitz went further. He wrote that "Everything in war is very simple, but the simplest thing is difficult. The difficulties accumulate and end by producing a kind of friction. . . ." By friction, Clausewitz means the effect of the unknown, the unexpected, the unplanned for. "Countless minor incidents—the kind you can never really foresee—combine to lower the general level of performance, so that one always falls far short of the intended goal." For example, "Fog can prevent the enemy from being seen in time, a report from reaching the commanding officer. Rain can prevent a battalion from arriving, make another late by keeping it not three but eight hours on the march, ruin a cavalry charge by bogging the horses down in mud, etc."[16]

Anyone who has been in combat knows that all this is true. It is a reminder that, in judging the future consequence of present decision, as each model purports to do, we are far from dealing with scientific predictability.

Operational research (OR) theory, which is a form of applied game theory, is somewhat less restricted in predicting results, but only because it eliminates two of the greatest sources of uncertainty. In OR the cultural factor can frequently be eliminated. Only actual performance is pertinent, and usually it is weapons interactions that are counted. (If, for instance, Japanese pilots, for cultural reasons, had been easier to shoot down during World War II, it would not have altered kill ratio data.) Nor is the multilateral environment factor significant when the weapons of two different nations are compared. (If the Soviets need some of their tanks against the Chinese, that does not alter the way a one-on-one engagement of a U.S. and a Soviet tank will turn out, in probabilistic terms.)

But what any good systems analyst will argue, quite correctly, is that the definition of the problem is crucial, worth infinite pains. It is appallingly simple to study a problem quite unwittingly out of context, or to focus on the wrong issue.

To illustrate,[17] in the early stages of World War II, U.S. merchantmen traversing the war zones were being armed, but the United States still had a shortage of guns and gun crews. Was it better to continue equipping merchant ships with at least a gun on the fantail, plus a small navy gun crew to serve it? Or was it better to save the scarce guns and crews for destroyers and destroyer-escorts? A study was made; it found that the plane-kill record of guns on navy escorts was much better than that of navy gun crews firing guns from merchant ships.

That might easily have ended the analysis, until someone pointed out that the objective of putting guns in one place or the other was not to see which shot down the most planes but to see whether merchant ships equipped with such guns had a better survival rate. Once restated properly as a problem, the answer leaped out: merchant ships so equipped, rotten shots or not, had a substantially greater rate of survival. Apparently the enemy planes had an easier go at those ships without guns.

Operational research tells us that in the statement of the problem is where things can go badly astray, and the relevance of this to the models can be seen. It is precisely in the statement of the problem that the models differ most radically—a point we shall come back to.

Deterrence theory assumes that action and reaction tend to follow clearly discernible psychological patterns. It assumes that the meaning of move and countermove can be "signaled" to an opponent in such a way as to render a situation unambiguous. The opponent can consequently be persuaded or compelled to react in some rationally predictable way.

There are significant problems with deterrence theory, not the least of which is the potential contradiction between its emphasis on signaling and communicating intent and the fact that most deterrence theory is concerned with the bilateral relations of the two superpowers, who happen to perceive situations very differently and are far from having the same signal book. Even worse, as will be seen in the next chapter, to the extent that deterrence theory focuses attention on a bilateral relationship in a multilateral environment, it runs a serious risk of introducing distortions into the analysis. Another problem with it is noticeable from Thomas C. Schelling's very influential work, *The Strategy of Conflict*. Schelling is almost silent on the question of how different cultures influence decisions.[18] He is concerned, and very ably oo, with reactiono on the purely psychological and intellectual level, but does not make it clear how far that can be taken without distortions.

The comments on deterrence theory by George and Smoke are especially interesting. They point to its narrowness.[19] They also point to features common to both deterrence theory and to the balance of power:

It is slightly surprising, in retrospect, how many of the concepts of contemporary deterrence theory — commitments, and how to reinforce or escape them, signaling, comparatively fine calculations of opposing forces, the fear of escalation and the use of that fear as a deterrent, the mutual assumption of rationality — were implicitly part of the diplomatic practice of the balance-of-power system, without being articulated in this kind of terminology.

La plus ça change, la plus c'est la même chose. George and Smoke conclude that eighteenth- and nineteenth-century diplomatic and military history, while offering "a rich lode of empirical material for the expansion and refinement of contemporary concepts," has "not been studied systematically from such a [contemporary] perspective. . . ."[20] And, we might add — and even more to the point — neither has deterrence theory (which assumes a novel world) really sought to validate itself against the ancient wisdom. Deterrence theory might become less mechanical if it took historical experience more into account.

Certainly many of the approaches to enmity encountered in these theories are unduly simple in stressing action and response, rather than the essential ambiguities and confusions prevalent in an anarchic state system. In this scientific age, there may be a recurrent temptation to simplify society to resemble Pavlov's dog: salivating on cue. Whether this temptation represents the computer made flesh is hard to say. Perhaps we have tried to absorb the characteristics of the machines we have made.

Much of the concern in these chapters has focused on the nature of humanity, on the problem of the real nature of the universe or environment, and on how and why national policy is made. These three concerns, by a quite logical and parallel development (since they are central) are what these models also try to explain.

We could discourse about whether a human being is "good" or "bad," but this is of limited utility. The real question is how a person's mind arrives at judgments. When people look at their environment, they may or may not see it as it is. What we know from what an individual perceives is what that individual is like and may do. Those who think people are not to be trusted will undoubtedly see the environment as filled with untrustworthy people and will make their plans and policies accordingly. It is human nature to be partial to one's self: "When, after their victory at Salamis, the generals of the various Greek states voted the prizes for distinguished individual merit, each assigned the first place of excellence to himself, but they all concurred in giving their second votes to Themistocles."[21] Our natural confidence in our own (sometimes misunderstood) good motives does not prevent us from being properly skeptical of the motives of others. The models faithfully follow the logic of this point.

A relatively unpleasant national experience will compound the tendency among the leaders to be suspicious of others and to feel also that what is encountered in the here-and-now is planned, perhaps maliciously. Quite regardless of whether "capitalism" wanted to eliminate "communism" in the 1930s and 1940s, communism was bound to see it so. When immediately at the end of World War II the United States tried to reassure the Russians of its good intentions, such actions, if anything, raised Soviet suspicions. The Russians "knew" the United States was hostile just as surely as they "knew" from the dialectic that it was "scientifically inevitable" that communism would triumph. In Einstein's terms, the Soviets had their own view of what made the watch tick.

Consequently, it would be expected that a widely held theory that has retained popularity over a considerable time, such as the balance of power, would have a general view of human nature and of the environment that is widely shared. (That is the other end of the telescope from the one given in the second paragraph in the chapter.) In reverse terms, when a model is encountered that arouses narrower enthusiasm, such as collective security or containment, it is plain that the experience and background of its leading advocates has probably been rather divergent from the common stream. That, indeed, has been true of ideas prevailing in the United States.

No one model can sum up the whole truth, quite apart from the fact that the models themselves observe different "truths." No model can include the whole of reality because by definition it consists only of the main parts as they link together. So they all leave more out than they include. It is worthwhile indicating the special strengths and weaknesses of each.

Containment is fairly radical, as models go, especially in its tendency to visualize two "camps" separated by their appreciation or lack of appreciation of freedom. The model is radical because it is framed in terms of two worlds and yet we know there is not only a "third" world of developing nations but even a "fourth" world of those without oil or real resources. Many able commentators have pointed out the weakness of a proposition that assumes that starving nations value freedom above food. Indeed, containment has enough weaknesses to make one prone to dismiss it as an organizing concept prescribing policy — until one remembers that the most powerful state of its time accepted its descriptions and followed its prescriptions for a long period of time and at great national expense.

Containment has one other overriding weakness: not only does it not encourage prioritization of enemies, but it asserts that judgments on this point are unnecessary and, indeed, impossible. Since all Communists are joined together in aggressive intent, all are equally enemies. The logic of that belief is that containment troops will have to be deployed anywhere and everywhere "freedom" is threatened. There are problems with such a view — problems like the Vietnam War.

Collective security, the other U.S. favorite, has the fairly obvious defect that anyone who commits aggression against anyone anywhere becomes an enemy of all "peace-loving" peoples, meaning particularly the United States. Again there is the striking refusal to permit or encourage any prioritization of enemies. Like containment, collective security makes the occasion for war automatic. Again the United States is supposed to deploy its forces whenever aggression occurs.

Both of these models are fairly silent on cost considerations. The costs of the police action (Korea) or the war (Vietnam), however high they may be, are supposedly a quite small finger-in-the-dike price when compared with what would need to be paid to stop the flood at a later time.

One of the great advantages of the balance-of-power model is that it encourages broader thinking, such as the connection between policy content and accumulation of enemies. Those who may think of the balance in terms of a two-bloc form may not as quickly see its variations (as in Bismarck's time). Properly addressed, however, the balance-of-power model permits discriminations stemming from a prioritization of enemies by any party. Chapter 4 indicated in detail how this is done.

American audiences do not understand the balance-of-power model well, and any number of U.S. chief executives and secretaries of state have "known" that it was a nefarious foreign construct not suitable as the policy of a democracy, and have not refrained from saying so. The model contains features that are uncongenial to the American temperament; especially because it suggests, when it is working, a fairly stable and prolonged tension. When the balance is in fact "balanced," neither side prevails: progress is suspended. It also suggests behind-the-scenes manipulation instead of proceeding, as Wilson said, "in the public view." Moreover, to many the balance of power now seems quite inappropriate as a prescription for action because it is a formula from the prenuclear age.

American contemporary strategic thought, by assessing relations in bilateral acultural terms such as "mutual deterrence" and "mutual assured destruction," has often appeared to deemphasize what third parties may add to or subtract from the bilateral equation. American policy has not, of course, been that extreme, even though American strategic thought often has. But the question of what is added to or subtracted from the bilateral nuclear equation by coalitions like NATO or the Warsaw Pact does not by any means have only one obvious answer.

Overall thinking by U.S. decision makers has wavered between (1) the more broad-gauged view that NATO and the Warsaw Pact, and places like Berlin between them that may be in contest, are important and (2) the view that the nuclear equation, expressed bilaterally, as in the SALT negotiations, is the only thing that counts. The parallelism between the heavily mechanistic or abstractly psychological views associated with bilateral nuclear theory and the U.S. preference for general theories like containment, which are highly automatic in defining the enemy, is an area we shall explore in the next chapter.

We now return to the cardinal principles model. Three claims can be made on its behalf. At a minimum the model makes clearer, especially to an American audience, the nature of the central phenomena that the traditional balance-of-power model addresses. The main difference is that the balance-of-power model focuses on an "equilibrium" in the system, which can be achieved through the redistribution of power, while the third and fourth cardinal principles focus on the security of the individual actors through wise counterbalancing interest choices made in order to achieve the redistribution of enmity. But calling attention to the process of selecting appropriate "reserved" counterbalancing interests and substituting them in policy in order to reduce enmity with third states emphasizes an additional point that traditional balance thinking does not. For selecting such interests requires an intellectual process of prioritizing enemies.

When the first two cardinal principles, third-party influences and past-future linkages, are taken together, the cardinal principles model also provides a perspective on how actors perceive their environment and come to believe some things and reject others. Of all the models, the cardinal principles may be the best able to do this. All in all, it also survives fairly well the criticisms levied at game theory and decision theory.

On the other hand, the cardinal principles model is fairly silent about capability. The model does not exclude capability analysis, but neither does it explicitly call attention to that aspect, as threat analysis and deterrence theory do. By emphasizing the circumstances in the total environment, the cardinal principles model actually tends to de-emphasize bilateral relationships, whether military or broader. While the cardinal principles can readily be supplemented in this respect as needed, in doing so it is important not to go too far. We have already pointed out, in a preliminary way, the difficulties that occur at that point. In the next chapter we shall expand on the problems implicit in what is there called "weapons-oriented theory," as the last step before the final summation and an assessment of the American perspective and attitude toward the problem of enmity.

NOTES

1. George Kennan, *Soviet American Relations, 1917-1920*, vol. 1, *Russia Leaves the War* (New York: Atheneum, 1967), p. 12.

2. Robert Jervis, *Perception and Misperception in International Politics* (Princeton, N.J.: Princeton University Press, 1976), p. 13.

3. Harry S. Truman, *Memoirs*, vol. 2, *Years of Trial and Hope* (Garden City, N.Y.: Doubleday, 1956), p. 332.

4. Quoted from ibid., p. 325.

5. Ibid, pp. 332-33.

6. Glenn H. Snyder and Paul Diesing, *Conflict among Nations: Bargaining, Decision Making, and System Structure in International Crises* (Princeton, N.J.: Princeton University Press, 1977), pp. 316-17. See also Richard Ned Lebow, *Between Peace and War: The Nature of International Crisis* (Baltimore: Johns Hopkins University Press, 1981), pp. 101-18.

7. Ole Holsti, "Individual Differences in 'Definition of the Situation,'" *Journal of Conflict Resolution* 14 (September 1970): 303-10.

8. Arnold Wolfers, *Discord and Collaboration, Essays on International Politics* (Baltimore: Johns Hopkins University Press, 1962), p. 13.

9. Jervis, *Perception and Misperception*, p. 20.

10. See Alexander George and Richard Smoke, *Deterrence in American Foreign Policy: Theory and Practice* (New York: Columbia University Press, 1974).

11. Ibid., p. 72.

12. Ibid., p. 74.

13. Ibid., p. 75.

14. Ibid.

15. Thucydides, *The Peloponnesian War*, trans. Rex Warner (Baltimore: Penguin Books, 1954), pp. 82-85.

16. Karl von Clausewitz, *On War*, ed. and trans. Michael Howard and Peter Paret (Princeton, N.J.: Princeton University Press, 1976), pp. 119-20.

17. For this illustration I am indebted to Dr. Frank Shoup, formerly of the U.S. Naval War College faculty in Newport, R.I.

18. Thomas C. Schelling, *The Strategy of Conflict* (Cambridge, Mass.: Harvard University Press, 1960).

19. George and Smoke, *Deterrence*, p. 591.

20. Ibid., pp. 13-14.

21. Edward S. Creasy, *The Fifteen Decisive Battles of the World* (New York: Heritage Press, 1969), p. 111.

17

WEAPONS-ORIENTED THEORY

The First Lord . . . talked of "shield and sword," "striking power," "capability." It was a curious abstract language, of which the main feature was the taking of meaning out of words.

C. P. Snow[1]

Lord Snow, in the headnote, is describing a fictional Parliamentary debate in the late 1950s, a debate using the whole body of theory that has arisen because of nuclear weapons. This body of theory has given rise to "a curious abstract language" indeed: second strike, first strike, counterforce, countervalue, and so on. These terms, most of them, do have fairly precise meanings among the initiated; yet because of their very narrow, often mechanical focus and the fact that they discuss cataclysmic events, they convey less than they are intended to convey. By comparison with such overall and universal models as balance of power, collective security, and containment, these terms emphasize only relatively special and limited aspects of international relations. If they make any assumptions about human nature, it is to the effect that humans tend to approach problems on a rational basis and that their reactions to nuclear weapons problems will tend to be the same and universal, once the problems have become clear. In other words, these theories go beyond discounting cultural influences and ignore them altogether. Indians, Chinese, Russians, Americans, Brazilians, Germans are considered to react in identical ways if they possess nuclear weapons or are responding to those who do.

As to the environment, these theories tend to ignore any third parties and focus almost entirely on bilateral relationships.

Finally, their policy prescriptions are given in psychological rather than political terms.

As a consequence, for anyone who takes the cardinal principles as a fairly realistic guide to approaching problems, such weapons-oriented theories are quite inadequate. They ignore offhand both past-future linkages and third-party influences, encouraging the leaders in a particular culture to assume that any foreign leaders will react in much the same way they would themselves. They also discourage thinking through of such important questions as whether two nuclear armed powers in a "bilateral" confrontation can act as though conditions at their flanks and rear are irrelevant. Because so much of this contemporary theory ignores the balance of power in favor of the "balance of terror," indeed thinks one *succeeded* the other, there has been little attempt to integrate the new thinking with the old.

Glenn Snyder is a very definite exception. He says, "The balance of power theory is still generally valid. . . . The new military technology has not terminated but only modified the balance of power process."[2] Much or most of contemporary strategic theory, by contrast, simply busies itself with capability-derived issues, much of them weapons-oriented, and assumes the rest is old hat.

It is not absolutely clear why these theories developed in this way. Bernard Brodie points out that most of the intellectual leaders in this development were "singularly devoid of history" in their background. As systems analysts, "they were trained to be highly scientific in one area of limited application, but that did not incline them to be comparably scientific or even worldly wise in the larger area where . . . it becomes important to consider motivations and emotions as well as mechanics."[3]

Colin S. Gray's explanation is very similar to Brodie's, and they are very likely right. Gray, after mentioning that long-range nuclear missiles "seemed to many people to destroy the validity of the old, familiar geopolitical concepts," says that traditional "strategic *and* international political theory and experience . . . tended to be ignored" in grappling "with the exciting and apparently novel problems posed by the galloping revolution in weapons/transportation technology." Gray adds: "With few exceptions, the scholars and officials who have given direction to American thought and policy in the fields of foreign policy and strategy since the mid-1950s have been people heroically ill-versed in history and geography."[4] The broad-gauged notions of a Nicholas Spykman or a Halford Mackinder or an Arnold Toynbee have received short shrift.

The narrowness and inadequacy, as well as the strongly mechanical flavor of the prevailing conceptualizations of strategic problems can be illustrated briefly (1) in terms of general theory, (2) in respect to strategic doctrine, and (3) in reference to intellectual approaches predominating within the U.S. government.

By theory we mean here the academic thrust of the argument. As Alexander George and Richard Smoke point out in their thorough study of deterrence, deterrence theory was, paradoxically and simultaneously, "historically bound in a manner unrecognized by most deterrence theorists" and yet "ahistorical." While "the state-of-the world assumptions of deterrence theory remained largely implicit, . . . the prescriptive content" assumed that the actors were not "imbedded in any particular historical configuration or, at least, not one subject to variation and change."[5] Not only was such "normative-prescriptive deterrence theory" ahistorical in emphasis, but it was also "apolitical." The apolitical assumption of such theory was that commitments, if made, are unequivocal; but in real life, commitments necessarily "vary in strength and scope, *depending upon judgments about interests.*"[6]

Achieving credibility, as George and Smoke say, "is secondary to and dependent upon" the issues and interests at stake. Of course, a nation can make a pledge to aid a weaker ally more credible "by taking actions that would increase the damage to its interests" if it did not honor the commitment.[7] But that ignores the "prior question" as to the utility of promising to do something otherwise questionable in interest terms.

In their conclusion, George and Smoke point to "the narrowness of deterrence theory" and the need for "a broader theory which encompasses deterrence as one of a number of means that can be employed" to control potential conflict.[8] To their criticisms should be added the overemphasis of deterrence theory on bilateral relations (really, confrontations), the acultural approach of the theory, and its great stress on capability-derived conclusions.

Deterrence theory is not an isolated case in this respect; it is quite typical of a quarter-century of thinking. It is no accident that such mechanically abstract thinking has flourished at a time when containment has been the predominant "grand" strategy. Deterrence and containment have the same common features, downplaying geography, nationality, and personality.

Michael Howard, in his invaluable survey of the development of post-World War II strategic thought, remarks that "the major American contributions" between 1956 and 1957 attempted to "reintegrate military power with foreign policy, stressing, in contradiction to the doctrine of massive retaliation, the need for a 'strategy of options.'"[9] Howard is referring to the effort to resolve (1) the feeling that it was futile to engage in mutual and full-scale nuclear destruction with (2) the contradictory feeling that wars would continue to occur and continue to be fought with the weapons to hand. This effort usually led theory in the direction of "integrating" possible use of tactical weapons with a cold war posture toward the Russians. "Reasonable-sized" nuclear wars began to be envisaged.[10] Such speculations in no way restored geography, nationality, and personality to prominence; ideology and the physical performance characteristics of weapons continued to be emphasized.

Between 1959 and 1960, Michael Howard goes on to say, "a slight but perceptible change of emphasis" was apparent. This change was "the work

[of] physicists, engineers, mathematicians, economists and systems analysts. . . ." The net result was, of course, to weight the discussion even more toward physical characteristics. Howard concludes that these people, analyzing the technical problems of deterrence, began to recognize that "certain elements" were common issues for both superpowers and that both sets of "leaders faced comparable problems." As a consequence, says Howard, while some cold warrior scholars still saw the conflict as "between the Archangel Michael and Lucifer," for others it became a conflict between "Tweedledum and Tweedledee." In short, the problems of the United States equalled those of the Soviet Union and vice-versa. This division of opinion in no way restored geography, nationality, or personality to the discussion, however. Instead it led to the conclusion that if the United States and the Soviet Union faced a similar problem, they would see it and react to it in a similar way, which was correct up to a point — but only to a point.

The center of gravity of the debate now shifted to the more or less technical problem of whether the "balance of terror" could be stabilized. From there the logical sequence led to the concept of "invulnerable second-strike" forces, primarily hidden at sea. The logic, now familiar, ran: If he cannot destroy me in a first strike because part of my retaliatory forces are beyond his reach, I can destroy him when I respond. So he has no incentive to strike first. The development of this thinking was to be of great importance in reorienting U.S. policy. Ultimately, it was to lead to the conclusion that a finite number of offensive weapons would "suffice," provided they could not be destroyed with impunity. This development was important. Had it not occurred, the very worry and concern felt in various nations about "balance of terror" instability could alone have triggered a much higher rise in tensions, a much more unbridled arms race, and an even greater preoccupation with the dubious formula, "If he can, he will."

Second-strike thinking therefore made a valuable contribution, by helping to lead to a more stable bilateral relationship in the weapons systems area. But, even more than other deterrence theories, it drew attention away from an adequate consideration of how geography, nationality, or personality related to the total ("grand") strategic discussion.

Howard, in concluding his survey, remarks on "the extent to which the quality of strategic thinking in the nuclear age is related to an understanding of international relations, on the one hand, and of weapons technology on the other." He is quite correct that the political understanding without the technical knowledge, or vice versa, will not do, but the fact that he expresses that opinion does not bring about the condition he endorses. With the United States playing such a leading role both in the development of strategic theory and in the creation of new and unprecedented weapons systems, plus a rather vigorous foreign policy, what could be expected was that the predilections, shortcomings and strengths of the United States would be reflected in all aspects — which is what happened.

Military strategic thought in the United States moved steadily away from the "one big blast" school of thought, toward a controlled ladder of escalation with delicate nuances of destructive capability, both in delivery ("surgical" air strike) and in kind (big bang down to small). Soviet military thought continued disposed toward the more plodding, more pessimistic, and simpler notion that nations would use what they had available in order to avoid defeat. The two nations were speaking for themselves whether they limited it explicitly to that or not. In any event, the Soviets never bought the notion that it was possible to have a "token" war, using nuclear tactical weapons on an implicitly limited scale; yet the Soviet reaction should have been a warning that strategic notions are influenced by national experience, and that what seems an accurate generalization about national behavior will reflect the attitudes formed in a people by historical experience in a particular geographical setting.

In the realm of doctrine, the same ahistorical, apolitical, and other tendencies abounded, and the same conflict with reality emerged. Let us tabulate the sequence of major doctrinal propositions and then comment on them. In doing so, there is no intention of dismissing doctrine as irrelevant to strategic problems. From a practical standpoint, doctrine, at least in the large sense, governs the very composition of forces and selection of weapons systems, not to mention targeting. But that is not to say that any doctrine is of equal value and utility compared with any other. Just because doctrines have practical consequences, it is necessary to scrutinize them at least as severely as the theories that beget them.

We shall begin with the National Security Council decision paper known as NSC-68, in 1950, which concluded that by 1954 the Soviets could mount a nuclear strike on the United States and might hope to catch most of the Strategic Air Command on the ground; therefore, it said, a greater strategic and NATO conventional effort would be required. The Eisenhower "new look" at the problem resulted in NSC-162/2 of October 1953, which became known popularly as "massive retaliation." The United States would no longer meet Communist attacks with local conventional counterforce but would "depend primarily upon a great capacity to retaliate instantly" at its own discretion.

But once the Soviets also acquired a certain massiveness, doubts about "massive retaliation" began to be raised. De Gaulle, for example, wondered out loud whether the United States would be willing to accept nuclear devastation as a result of a French action that aroused a Soviet response. At the same time doubts were being expressed about having only one option. By Kennedy's time the United States was hastening to build conventional forces to allow it to deal with "contingencies" below a full nuclear engagement, especially because of the conviction that the very equality of reciprocal destruction resulting from a nuclear exchange now put more premium on the less than nuclear.

The shift under Robert McNamara to the new strategic doctrine in NATO of "flexible response" was accompanied by creaking and groaning all the way. West Germany, for example, feared that the Russians would be well launched toward the Rhine while the NATO nations were still shrinking from the necessary. The longer the wait, the more West Germany would be devastated by its own allies once the blow fell. But shift NATO did, at which point de Gaulle withdrew France from the integrated features of NATO. That is, France remained a member of the alliance but expelled NATO institutions and infrastructure from French soil. Most of these were then crammed into Belgium and Holland, while French military cooperation with NATO began to be haphazard or at least irregular.

Once the transition had been made, the military effect was drastic. West Germany is only a hundred miles wide at its narrowest, and Belgium and Holland are completely inadequate in area for logistics backup. The action by France forced NATO strategically into the position that any Soviet attack across the Iron Curtain would have to be repulsed in very short order by a fairly full resort to nuclear weapons. Flexible response and controlled escalation became phase stations on the short road back to massive retaliation.

Did NATO then alter its doctrine to reflect the new reality? Not at all. Emphasis continued to be put on finding the new conventional forces needed to balance the Soviet threat, but no NATO European nation is actually much interested in doing so, particularly so long as U.S. troops are deployed in Germany. Indeed, there are many good political reasons why it would be of little use to redebate NATO military strategy. At the same time, the formally approved strategy has little resemblance to the real situation. It is considerably tidier than the reality.

Discussing intellectual approaches within the U.S. government, in Chapter 8 I mentioned the U.S. definition of the "threat." Recall that I wrote that the term itself is not included in the *Dictionary of Military and Associated Terms* published by the Joint Chiefs of Staff, but its two elements, capability and intentions, are separately defined and cross-referenced to one another. Capability is defined as "the ability to execute a specified course of action. (A capability may or may not be accompanied by an intention.)"[11] Intention is defined as "an aim or design (as distinct from capability) to execute a specified course of action."[12]

Capability is clear enough as a definition, even though beset with great problems in any practical sense of "how much is enough." Intention is vague and problematic on its face — sufficiently so that Admiral Thomas H.

Moorer, former chairman of the Joint Chiefs, publicly stated his skepticism about "announced or estimated intentions."[13] Aims and designs, he thought, cannot be considered very stable things. They can change overnight, or at least quite quickly.

A senior U.S. flag or general officer, going by the book, who pursues the definitions to this point, is perfectly warranted in concluding, as Moorer did, that the significant element in any analysis of threat must be capability rather than intention. If the threat has two parts, with one easily changeable and the other quite slow to change (and therefore also not easily impro-vised), it behooves the prudent planner to keep an eye steadfastly focused on comparative capabilities—in the jargon of the trade, on "net assess-ment."*

These definitions and their implications help to explain the divergence of perspective that necessarily occurs within the U.S. government as military men and diplomats respond to what we earlier called "top-level" problems.

The first difference in perspective is that military thinking quite naturally and inevitably begins with bilateral assessments, while the normal political assessment really ends with the bilateral assessment. Where the military starts by comparing numbers of U.S. and Soviet missiles or submarines or armed forces and then calculating plus or minus factors for the "allies" on both sides, the political assessor, if viewing the problem from the perspec-tive of the cardinal principles, normally starts by observing the degree to which third parties impose constraints on either side. From a political point of view, the bilateral relationship always and inevitably includes a multilateral dimension, but from a military point of view, and especially under conditions of actual warfare, the bilateral relationship (of the two in-dividual nations or the two warring blocs) is the real thing. The tanks and missiles that count are the ones in use or ready for use by the belligerents, not the ones in the hands of the nonbelligerents.

The contrast here between the military and the political view is not ab-solute, but it is marked. Military strategists have to be aware of a possible new front opened if a new nation enters a fray, but their preoccupation is with the slugging matches they are already carrying on. The most critical influence politicians may be able to bring to bear, however, will stem not from their own deterrent capabilities but from what they can stir up, en-courage, or just let grow in their potential enemies' rear. The typical

---

*Lord Salisbury must have encountered this attitude in his time, because he wrote to Lord Lytton (June 15, 1877): "But I think you listen too much to the soldiers. No lesson seems to be so deeply inculcated by the experience of life as that you should never trust in experts. If you believe the doctors, nothing is wholesome; if you believe the theologians, nothing is innocent; if you believe the soldiers, nothing is safe."

military assessment will not exclude feint and deception, let alone the end run around the flank, but ultimately the enemy has to be confronted and directly and physically deterred because he by his actions is already committed to the use of force. The typical political assessment, while not excluding direct power or pressure, finds it more efficacious to rely heavily on increasing enemy anxieties.

To express the point crudely but usefully, the military strategist understands the utility of a dagger in the back but believes in the punch to the jaw. The political strategist studies how to direct the dagger toward the back in order to avoid the need for a punch to the jaw. If a Pentagon military staff analyzes a threat, it will advocate more missiles. If a State Department civilian staff analyzes the threat, it will in these postcontainment days advocate another trip to Peking. These are not really antagonistic concepts if properly orchestrated.

The second difference between the normal political and military perspectives is that the political is much more relative. Look at the military aspect first. If the United States and the Soviet Union should fight, they would use some or all of the weapons they possess. The range is exactly that: from some to all. While indefinite, it is also specific, with the extremes absolute. If war once begins, only the range of violence is not foreseeable. Each will kill a certain number of the enemy. And what will influence the range of weapons used is almost certainly predictable: whether one side can inflict nonreturnable damage. So the military problem, while containing important variables, is not very relative in its basic parameters. The enemy is the enemy. It is not half-friendly of the enemy if he refrains from killing every one of us.

But consider the political perspective, especially the implications of sharing a border. China and Russia, for example, are hardly likely to be friends for very long at a time in view of the long disputed frontier they share and their mutual ability to inflict important harm on the other. The temporary exceptions prove this rule, for it was only during the days of an anti-Chinese policy by the United States, accompanied by a massive military deployment on China's flank, that Soviet-Chinese policy was close. Thus friendship and enmity, from a political perspective, are relative. Here is the greatest difference between the military and the political perspective, for the military strategist plans for a confrontation with a defined enemy, while the political strategist contemplates a choice of enemies (within, to be sure, certain constraints).

There is a third difference in perspective, which can lead to divergent operational assumptions if it comes to fighting. Particularly where the war is not popular, it will almost certainly lead to a political-military split over how to fight it.

Consider two types of situations. First, suppose two countries by rather narrow margins decide to fight one another. Once the fighting begins, it is conceivable (but unlikely) that the fighting, paralleling the decision to resort to it, will be desultory and half-hearted. But the reverse is far more likely. Military operations have their own logic, and the closeness of the initial decision to fight, while it may induce political caution against extending the war, will not normally affect the intensity with which the military operations are carried on. So even for wars that have, or are seen to have, marginal utility, the military does not approach them in the expectation of fighting a one-handed battle but will fight to win battles at the least cost to itself.

But the political analyst, if judging that the political will of one of the parties is ambivalent, will see the fighting largely from the point of view of its political consequences. In Vietnam that meant that the Communist political advisers, seeing the ambivalence in the U.S. attitude toward the war, used military means first and foremost to achieve political results. That is why the Tet offensive, although costly in casualties to the Viet Cong, was so useful to them and worth the price. While the U.S. generals, counting casualties, pronounced it a U.S. victory, it really turned out the other way around. President Johnson, noting the domestic unrest, refrained from mobilizing the reserves, thus "tying the hands" of his own military, as they saw it.

In coalition warfare this point has even greater relevance, for it is safe to assume that some among the enemy bloc are less dedicated to the prospect of ongoing struggle. Where this is so, it can be more effective from an overall standpoint to work on the political will of the "detachables" rather than to win on the battlefield as such.

A military analyst, following out the logic of the problem from the military point of view, notes the forces of the enemy, especially their equipment and deployment, and then makes the prudent assumption that the enemy will fight hard. If the enemy does not fight hard, so much the better. To try to reduce the effective opposition, the military strategist may try to knock out the weaker or fringe allies of the major enemy, but knows that will have only a limited usefulness. Eventually the major enemy's forces will have to be faced. The military instinct is to concentrate on the main enemy capability.

A political analyst, however, noting a group of nations that is apparently hostile, begins by assuming that in fact some are 51 percent opposed, some 85 percent opposed, some almost completely opposed. By altering his approach or the contents or the substance of his proposition, the more loosely attached members of the enemy coalition can be peeled away. To change 51 percent hostile to 49 percent hostile does not take any great effort. If enough of the group is removed, the psychological effect on the core of opponents remaining can be quite devastating. The political strategist's instinct is to concentrate on the weaker or fringe states, to detach or neutralize them.

The divergence between the military and political viewpoints arises out of equally sensible observations on the part of each. In politics there is frequently almost as good a reason to do the alternative, while on the battlefield defeat is never as appealing as victory. Military strategy seeks to cultivate situations in which one's own strength is superior and concentrated while that of the enemy is inferior and scattered. But where the military strategist's thinking is applied to lines of supply and reduction of enemy effective strength at the point of battlefield impact, the political strategist is trying (1) to reduce what the enemy gains in allies, and (2) increase the opposition the enemy encounters by confronting it with still other opponents. From an analytical viewpoint, the military and the political strategists do not see the problem as the same problem.

The total intellectual picture (theory, doctrine, divergent professional perspectives) makes one wonder whether deterrence theory, with its capability orientation, became that way as its theorists looked at the problem with this military bias, or whether the military got the habit from the theorists as they consulted with each other in the early post-World War II years. In any event, Moorer's contention that "intent" can change radically overnight cannot withstand serious analysis in light of what is required for intent to change. This is close to the core of the question raised by the whole of nuclear weapons-induced theory. What should be considered significant in determining policy? Is it simple weapons ratios and comparisons? Should it be broadened to take into account the organizational and bureaucratic infighting of each antagonist? Should policy decisions be regarded as an amalgam of weapons relationships and bureaucratic interests?

The new theories do not really come to terms with the old thinking at all. As we have pointed out, weapons-oriented theory has little or nothing to say about third parties, about the circumstances in the world environment existing when two nations fear and face each other's nuclear arsenals. Yet it is of primary importance to assess whether the policy actions of two nuclear-armed antagonists are influenced in any significant respects by third parties. Is the Soviet Union as willing to confront the United States in a crisis when an unfriendly China is at its back? Do terms such as "back" and "flanks" have real meaning in a nuclear age, when the emphasis is on the direct, station-to-station, impersonal exchange of missiles? Does what is at one's flank or back still matter significantly? Or is the effect of a bilateral nuclear exchange the only thing that matters? Such questions, raised in passing in Chapter 11, require serious answers.

There are many reasons for believing these to be the most significant theoretical questions of our time. Their implications really should be thought of under two quite different sets of conditions: that of active warfare and that in which no overt resort to significant violence has yet occurred.

Consider the American-Soviet nuclear balance. Disregarding the effects of nuclear weapons in the hands of third nations for the moment, if war comes, the military logic of reliable intercontinental ballistic missiles (ICBMs) being possessed in large quantities by both sides is that each can destroy the other with "sufficiency," regardless of whether either has allies, forward land positions, or naval fleets. Reduced to those dimensions, each would still "enjoy" mutual assured destruction (an overkill capacity x-times greater than necessary).

Scenarios for such a war in strictly military terms could have two opposite but equally rational conclusions. Conclusion One would be that destruction would be relatively equal and very extensive; therefore nothing would be gained by resort to nuclear weapons and there would be no such resort. Wars instead would be fought by conventional forces; fleets would engage at sea; and so on. Allies and forward land positions would remain prime factors in the balance, and Berlin would have to be defended to retain West Germany's confidence. Conclusion Two would be the reverse of Conclusion One. Conclusion Two would say that no concern over Berlin, no worry about Soviet penetration of the Middle East or the Indian Ocean is justified from a military point of view, since if Russia had most of the third world in its pocket, it would not alter the nuclear equation one iota and that is the only thing that counts. Conclusion Two, at its most basic, would be arguing that policy derives (or derives importantly) from strategic nuclear weapons ratios per se.

Few military planners are willing to risk the future by a categorical, once-for-all choice between Conclusion One and Conclusion Two. Also, NATO can hardly be indifferent to the fate of Berlin without splitting the alliance, and it is a fact that two (some say three) of the severest crises between East and West have originated over Berlin. Deterrence theorists would argue that places like Berlin retain "significance," but not in their own right — rather as places where willpower and determination are or are not shown. Berlin's significance thus shifts to its psychological meaning as a "signal" of intent.* *Where* the contest of will occurs appears secondary in deterrence theory.

Both Conclusion Two and deterrence theory make light of third-party considerations; yet, supposing that any ultimate U.S. war with Russia would be nuclear, can there be any doubt that Russia would be far more

---

*Of course, on the tactical nuclear level the thinking is not quite so cavalier.

likely to follow a policy leading to that result after the United States had dismantled its alliances and discarded its political assets? Would not a Russia triumphantly playing a prime hegemonic role in the Middle East and the Indian Ocean area be more tempted to challenge the "weak" United States with "only" a few thousand nuclear warheads?

It is possible to approach the third-party issue from a somewhat different point of view. If there were an all-out nuclear war, one could argue that third parties would not count significantly because they could only increase already unacceptable damages, raising casualty figures above what was already purposeless.

The argument of the Committee on the Present Danger, in 1979 in reference to SALT II, made much of the propositions that (1) the U.S. Minutemen were becoming vulnerable, (2) Soviet "first-strike" weapons were being developed to take them out in a counterforce strike on our silos, (3) if this occurred, the United States would be forced to resort to its Polaris-Poseidon "countervalue" (population-centered) weapons, and (4) this would produce a Soviet countervalue rebuttal while the Soviet silo-based nuclear arsenal was essentially undamaged but the U.S. arsenal was substantially destroyed.*

If this argument is correct, even nations that had suffered casualties (like the 5 to 10 million for the United States in the first strike in this scenario) would continue to assess reaction "options" rationally rather than simply retaliating in hot blood. If that is indeed true, in a full bilateral Soviet-American nuclear exchange, the Soviets might hesitate before a subsequent Chinese ultimatum even if the Chinese arsenal were only capable of killing another few million Russians. It is hard to know, and it would certainly be risky to assume one view or the other as proved.

The before-hostilities case is perhaps a little clearer. The Russians would probably pay heed to even a limited Chinese nuclear capability at Russia's back. With a million or two Russians at stake, the Soviets are not likely to assume that, because they could not cause even greater losses, the Chinese simply did not count. Moreover, no matter how many potential nuclear death formulas were paraded before the Soviet leaders by their military and technical experts to prove the Chinese to be a minor consideration, it would be understandably awesome for the Soviets to discount the importance of a neighbor almost 1 billion people strong. It is hard to imagine any leaders in any nation able to shut out that awesome statistic in preference for assured kill figures of supposedly crippling dimensions. It is hard to imagine any Russian leader taking the Chinese problem so lightly as to be willing to go to war simultaneously with that neighbor and with the United States. Nothing is impossible; the question is whether it is probable.

---

*In 1981, essentially the same debate continued, with the MX missile and the "window of vulnerability" as its new features. The basic argument was unchanged.

The theory of deterrence says that the Soviets are restrained by the nuclear and conventional capability in the hands of the United States. It does not allow for additional deterrence of the Soviets when Chinese hostility is added to their list of woes. It has not tried to address even more complex issues such as what amount of U.S. capability, plus what amount of Chinese hostility, equals effective Soviet deterrence. Cross-hatching the two, mixing them in various proportions, represents a strange proposition, one "not invented here" and therefore thought by many to be irrelevant.

Complicating the formula still more, could identical Soviet policy decisions (with the identical decision makers and the identical weapons ratios on each side) be assumed under circumstances of, first a Communist bloc well disposed to follow Moscow's lead, including Peking, and second, Moscow at odds with the Communists of both Eastern Europe and China? If Germany or Japan were added to or subtracted from the effective list of Soviet enemies under these two contrasting situations, would that make any further difference?

Any of these changes ought to make quite a difference, but that difference would stem from alterations in exterior circumstances, in the world environment. The difference would go far beyond demonstrating resolves by signals sent in a crisis to allow one side's willpower to be accurately recorded by the other. Places like Berlin and third parties like China would not appear then in the calculations as a kind of random "happenings," of interest merely from their psychological impact, but would be seen in their own right as factors affecting decisions.

If "announced or estimated" intentions, to use Moorer's phrase again, are seen as easily altered policy decisions, one must probe more deeply into the method of stating the threat. Capability asks, "Is this nation able?" Intentions, in the Joint Chiefs' formulation, asks, "Would it like to?" But the two parts, taken together, leave unaddressed the significant and pertinent question, "Does it dare to?" If that question is addressed at all, it is done by rounding back on to capability analysis, with the assumption, which of course may well be true as far as it goes, that a certain ratio of imbalance in weapons will tip the decision scale to "attack." This assumes that decisions to attack or not to attack represent mainly judgments of enemy capability and enemy willpower, whereas, if the preceding analysis has utility, the third part of the threat analysis, the part unaddressed that should be asking, "Does it dare?," should lead to at least as much consideration of the conditions prevailing at the attack-tempted nation's flanks and rear. Threat analysis, in this view, should have three parts: capability (what is in its hands), intentions (what is in its head), and circumstances (what is at its back), with no one of the three looked at in isolation.

Again, as before, the reality we see is the one we program ourselves to see, through our experience and our preconceptions. If our thinking is too heavily influenced by weapons considerations and we come to believe that the policy decisions of our opponents essentially derive from the number, quality, and ratio of our weapons, we will misperceive our problem in significant ways.

Referring to weapons as "first-strike" and "second-strike" is particularly unfortunate because it so strongly suggests that the weapons themselves have (automatic?) roles to play, that the weapons themselves have intentions. What the terms were invented to describe, however, was sets of conditions under which certain types of weapons would have utility. Such conditions of presumed utility have typically been examined only in a very narrow frame of military-psychological interaction. As such, they have many of the virtues — and many of the defects — of a strategic war game in which one nation's leaders play both sides in a scenario they wrote themselves.

It is not wrong to think this way for certain narrowly defined purposes. It is, to the contrary, highly useful to consider specifically what effect changes in capability can have on policy. In Chapter 16 we even argued that the cardinal principles need such a supplement. The caution given here is that such weapons-oriented theory should not be elevated from its useful partial role in evaluating strategic problems to the implicit status of one of the universal models.

NOTES

1. C. P. Snow, *Corridors of Power*, from *Strangers and Brothers*, 3 vols. (New York: Scribner's, 1972), vol. 3, p. 256. The quote is, of course, fictional — but apt.

2. Glenn Snyder, "The Balance of Power and the Balance of Terror," in Paul Seabury, ed., *Balance of Power* (San Francisco: Chandler, 1965), p. 186.

3. Bernard Brodie, *War and Politics* (New York: Macmillan, 1973), pp. 475-76.

4. Colin S. Gray, *The Geopolitics of the Nuclear Era*, National Strategy Information Center, Inc. (New York: Crane, Russak, 1977), pp. 11-12.

5. Alexander George and Richard Smoke, *Deterrence in American Foreign Policy: Theory and Practice* (New York: Columbia University Press, 1974), pp. 553-54.

6. Ibid., p. 556. Italics added.

7. Ibid., p. 559.

8. Ibid., p. 591.

9. Michael Howard, "The Classical Strategists," *Adelphi Papers* 54 (February 1969): 18-32.

10. For the most prominent illustration, see the book that first made Henry Kissinger known, *Nuclear Weapons and Foreign Policy* (New York: Harper, 1957).

11. U.S., Department of Defense, Joint Chiefs of Staff, *Dictionary of Military and Associated Terms*, JCS Publication 1, September 3, 1974, p. 58.

12. Ibid., p. 177.

13. In conversation with the author in 1975 in Newport, R.I., he was even more emphatic.

18

PERSPECTIVES, CONCLUSIONS, AND EVALUATION

In science . . . novelty emerges only with difficulty, manifested by resistance, against a background of expectation. Initially, only the anticipated and usual are experienced . . . [Then comes an] awareness of anomaly . . . in which conceptual categories are adjusted.

Thomas S. Kuhn[1]

We have tried to show that dealing with policy problems is in the first instance an intellectual task: it involves thought. But as Kuhn warns in the headnote, thought is more structured than the thinkers assume. Freeing ourselves of preconceptions and achieving "objectivity" requires a realization of how much our conceptual insights may be bound by culture. But that realization comes slowly to Americans. The last thing Americans tend to be sensitive about (and this includes American scholars) is the degree to which viewpoints and emphases popular in the United States represent a peculiarly or predominantly American point of view. Frequently we Americans discuss in universal terms what is really only true or mostly true of ourselves.

Since we Americans are not self-conscious about our biases in approaching problems — indeed, we tend to believe that being "scientific" has eliminated bias — we have special difficulty in seeing our own uniqueness and realizing where our approach to problems differs from the "norm." Americans have particular difficulty in realizing how much these intellectual habits account for and compound problems, since we do not think of those patterns of thought as in any way abnormal. Even the notion of being "conditioned" by environment and national experience is foreign to the way Americans think.

Yet the way we think has a fundamental effect on the way we act. It is obvious from the record that, as colonial days and their dangers receded from the national consciousness, Americans forgot how to think in balance of power terms. We even forgot most of the vocabulary of *Realpolitik*—a language we once understood well. Bit by bit and link by link we developed a Janus-like notion about international affairs, one face emphasizing a romantic and sentimental idealism, balanced on its obverse side by cynicism concerning the motives of foreigners.

Conscious of its increasing power and accomplishment, when the United States returned to active involvement in world affairs (beginning with the Spanish-American War), it took a generally "no nonsense," direct approach to problems. As problem-solvers with a problem-solving bias, Americans tended to ask what should be done, rather than what result should be brought about. Taken for granted were (1) that the problem could be solved and (2) that the United States had what it took to solve it. Noticeably absent from this activist approach was any real concern about costs. Equally absent was much interest in the advantages of *not* doing something—like, for example, allowing China to have more freedom by withdrawing from its flank, thereby exerting significantly greater pressure on the Russians.

Americans tended to look at the issue without much regard for its historical context: we are a forward-looking people. We gave little consideration to its geopolitical dimensions: our deterrence theory is noticeably two-dimensional, as is our threat analysis. And we tended, in our actions as in our thinking, toward a direct and concentrated attack on the problem, such as a cross-channel invasion of Normandy in preference to a peripheral strategy.

These intellectual predispositions encouraged us rather naturally in a confrontation approach. In our globalist phase after World War II, this approach was to produce a distinctly openhanded approach to enmity. Far from ranking our enemies to discriminate among them, we lumped them together in that amorphous group known as the Communist bloc. As a consequence, neither of our two Asian wars was fought against a primary enemy of the United States. The United States did not think in the terms that came quite naturally to the Chinese, whether Communists or non-Communists: "Chairman Mao, using the revolutionary dialectical method . . . clearly differentiates who is the principal enemy, who is the secondary enemy, and who is a temporary or an indirect ally."[2]

To think in terms of the prioritization of enemies is then not a natural pattern of American thinking. To think in terms of what Belgium's Paul-Henri Spaak once called "a hierarchy in international obligations" is equally uncongenial to the American approach, which revels in the great open-ended commitments implied by either collective security or containment. To many Americans, Spaak's further comment must appear downright small-minded: "The nations of a continent cannot reasonably be asked to consider with the same realism and . . . judgment affairs which directly concern them and events which are taking place thousands of kilometers away. . . ."[3] Spaak's thought is certainly very far removed from John F. Kennedy's determination to maintain an activist role and "bear any burden," as discussed in Chapter 14.

That "game plan" brought an active involvement in geographically remote affairs. Many foreigners may have agreed with President Johnson's remark in 1965 that this was "the clearest lesson of our time. From Munich until today we have learned that to yield to aggression brings only greater threats."[4] But far fewer non-Americans would likely in consequence have decided to fight a Vietnam War halfway around the earth.

Two quotations sum up the difference in attitude. Thomas Jefferson said that "The ordinary affairs of a nation offer little difficulty to a person of any experience."[5] Bismarck, by contrast, said, "Man cannot create the current of events. He can only float with it and steer."[6] Bismarck implies that quite a bit of experience is required merely to break even.

All of which is to suggest that the intellectual habits which so drastically shape the way the United States approaches problems in foreign policy, precisely because they are so ingrained and unconscious, stand sturdily in the way of any easy appreciation of how we handle the problem of enmity and enemies.

Robert Lieber, quoted before, points out that game theory has the special merit of encouraging thinking about the relationship two enemies have: although they are not objects of mutual affection, they are objects of mutual concern, and the threat they are to one another is real. He is right, for the most basic problem of all in the American attitude is not to believe in enmity at all, except impersonally as a form of social disease to be eliminated with progress. We did not fight the Germans in World War II; we opposed Nazi tyranny. We did not oppose the Russians in the cold war, only godless communism. As long ago as Teddy Roosevelt we had the same approach. He once said: "I like the Russian people but abhor the Russian system of government and I cannot trust the word of those at the head."[7]

It is noteworthy that both the collective security and the containment concepts picture the enemy as a sort of minority culprit (temporarily under the control of bad men?) struggling against more socially conscious majority elements. The thought is that aggression, the sin in collective security, represents a minority challenge to the majority's status quo and that being Communist and authoritarian, the sin in containment, represents a repudiation of humanity's innate love of freedom. To threaten the peace, to undermine the status quo, to restrict freedom, is all seen as abnormal behavior.

To argue as we have just argued may seem to some to overstress the importance of things intellectual as the shapers of policy choices. But it is dangerous to underrate the truth of what Oliver Wendell Holmes once said: "Every idea is an incitement. It offers itself for belief and if believed it is acted on unless some other belief outweighs it or some failure of energy stifles the movement at its birth." Americans are a very energetic people.

These preliminary remarks can be reduced to two essential points: (1) that Americans, in thinking about problems, conceptualize with particular stresses, omissions, and biases (our perceptual lenses for viewing the world are not plain glass) and (2) that the thinking that goes into the handling of a problem, especially a policy problem, is itself a vital part of the policy process.

While these points are preliminary, they are also critical, since they focus on the vital role of perspective. As Thomas S. Kuhn, Albert Einstein, and Karl von Clausewitz all insist, it is not possible to simply study the facts and see how they arrange themselves. We arrange them ourselves in patterns our culture and experience encourage. Since the American culture and experience have some unique and many unusual features, the patterns we impose on the phenomena can take some odd or at least unusual shapes.

So much for what is unusual in the American approach. Turning now away from a particular culture, let us summarize in connected fashion and from a more universal standpoint the conclusions that have been reached about the nature of enmity and the handling of enemies. After that, we shall close this book with an evaluation of the U.S. foreign policy record from this special point of view: How well have we handled enmity and enemies?

The early chapters brought out a number of very old and very fundamental controversies: whether human beings have instincts or merely habits and how much they are free to choose. These issues, stated in conventional philosophical terms, are the same issues that recurred later in the book, expressed then in political language, when we asked how such models as the balance of power and collective security suppose the system to operate, and why; or how the freedom of decision makers to make choices would be seen as constrained by the "rules" of the system. All the important questions underlying approaches and responses to enmity and enemies reappear in diverse disciplines using different terminologies, but they are still the same questions. To each of these questions and riddles we have sought answers.

First, when we asked whether enmity might conceivably disappear sometime in the future, as a consequence of altered human behavior, we were unable to arrive at a categorical answer. It is not impossible to visualize such a development, because a few great past changes in human behavior, such as the almost universal abolition of slavery, can be documented. On the other hand, we showed much evidence that humans have a present and historic tendency to divide into groups. Psychologists believe that this tendency is a significant root of suspicion and anxiety directed against other groups, that "other" groups mean "potentially rival" groups. Historians, for their part, furnish innumerable illustrations of this effect. So while enmity might disappear, that is highly improbable.

Second, if the probable continued existence of enmity must be reckoned with, it is still possible to think of it as increasing or decreasing. Is this true? Raising this issue makes it necessary to be entirely clear about what enmity is. Is it important operationally as a feeling, increasing or decreasing in intensity, or is it important as an effect that is clinically observable in the relations of particular nations? Our essential reply is that the emotional aspects deriving from the psychological alienation innate in "groupness" are real and have real effects in driving the system's tension level higher or lower. This same tension-altering effect might conceivably be described as increasing or decreasing enmity per se, but we have not resorted to this explanation for two reasons. The first reason is that it is really the expectation of violence that increases when enmity "increases." It is the *tension* which really alters. The second reason is that it is far more useful to think of enmity as a constant allocated and reallocated within the system through a series of policy choices, with the result of increasing or decreasing the number of enemies confronted. Otherwise, we would need another term for that.

Lumping enmity and enemies into a synonymous lockstep wastes the opportunity to make some important distinctions, including the proposition that an enemy is one against whom one contemplates the possibility of actual hostilities, while enmity is the degree of antagonism or opposition one is confronting. These are two quite different although related concepts. If the term enmity is restriced to our use of it, the flow of relations in the policies of two or more countries become clearer from either a bilateral or a multilateral (systems) point of view. Bilaterally, the extent of common and opposed interests and their fluctuation can be examined as new decisions are made; in that case, the amount of enmity is the same as the degree of opposed interests. Such new decisions, shifting the specific bilateral relationship one way or the other, usually arise out of reappraisals of the condition of relations with third parties. We can see them therefore as deliberate decisions to reallocate systemwide enmity. Or, to say it more simply, nations with an unduly large share of the system's enmity revamp policies to improve relations with marginal opponents.

Such terminology avoids the necessity of speaking more loosely of bilateral relations becoming "worse" or "better" and integrates such change (usefully, it is to be hoped) into a systems framework. This would seem more appropriate than talking lamely of "half-enemies" and "two-thirds" enemies.

To sum up, when discussing the relations of particular actors, we have used "enmity" to mean the degree of opposed interests, "enemies" to mean nations with which opposed interests predominate, and "tension level" to mean the expectation of resort to violence. As to the assumption that, from a systems viewpoint, enmity can best be regarded as a constant, we do not insist that this is demonstrably true, but only that it provides a highly useful vehicle for analysis.

If the two theory propositions about enmity are united, a certain degree of enmity, observable in a bilateral relationship in the form of opposed interests, can be visualized as a "share" of the total enmity in the system. A nation, through policy choice, can increase its share of enmity by maximizing its opposed interests with other parties, with the probable* operational result of having a greater number of enemies.

Third, even if by such a method of analysis it is assumed that policy choices will affect the enmity-enemy equation, it is necessary to decide whether other "objective" factors, such as the nature of frontiers or the location of a state, also produce significant change in that equation. But, in exploring this possibility, we were in fact unable to find any factor as important as policy choice itself.

Fourth, operational support of these theories was found in detailed consideration of a case study in which a nation that was accumulating too many enemies made conscious policy decisions, the effect of which was to reallocate enmity rather drastically in the system.

Fifth, in view of the importance of policy choices, it became necessary to explore the nature of decision making, to inquire into the murky question of how much free will a nation has and how many of its choices are in effect imposed on it by the "rules" of the system.[8] Unfortunately, inquirers into this problem have not been eager to relate these two aspects. We have tried to show that much of what is said today about decision making suffers from what we have described as the American bias and from a tendency to make inadequate distinctions between ordinary bureaucratic procedure and crisis management, or at least high-level decisions. Ordinary bureaucratic procedure involving the handling of less-than-vital issues often proceeds in a fashion insulated from the outside world, whereas the nature of a crisis lays a premium on putting provincialism to one side. The "rules" of the system may never overcome the insulation of ordinary procedure; that is, no matter what the rules of the system may be, they simply do not impinge significantly on the problem. But for important issues the reverse is true. The top-level decision makers typically illustrate the rational actor model, as modified by their own notions of the meaning of what they see and hear.

---

*"Probable" because it is impossible to exclude altogether the highly unlikely case in my formulation in which a nation increases its opposed interests with any number of other nations without changing the number of nations with which it has *predominantly* opposed relations.

It is not their personal ambition that tends to count here, or their "representational" function to argue the views of some section of the bureaucracy. If there is a distortion as they view the crisis, chalk it up primarily to the effects of culture, to their model image.

Sixth, in following through these theories, one returns again and again to the question of the nature of reality and the problems innate in perceiving that reality free of bias. Each age has its intellectual fashions, so much so that certain features of the environment that may go unnoticed in one age may be emphasized in another. It is striking to watch the evolution of thought itself, such as the connections we sketched between Darwin and Marx, to see how certain propositions seem to be "obviously" true at a given time. The obverse is also highly important: those who stress aspects not already popular and accepted have a double burden. To the restriction these fashions impose on perceptions must be added the constrictions, noted in the first part of this chapter, that national or cultural biases bring to the problem. The total effect is to make truth an operational variable, depending upon the century and the people concerned for the way it is perceived. The "real" truth remains, of course, unaltered by these distortions, but that "real" truth also remains unknown.

Seventh, and here we must again stress Kuhn, Einstein, and Clausewitz, it would be a grave distortion to assume that policy makers first observe a "real" situation and then make objective decisions. The policy makers are equally unable to observe any "real" situation and to make any "objective" decisions about it. The order they see in the problem (its features, its presumed causes, its assumed effects) is not, or not necessarily, innate in the problem addressed, but is brought into a focus by some perceptual lens. This lens we have called a "model," and we examined four of them, one the author's own invention and three with some historical baggage to them. Arranged in terms of American preferences and prejudices (and leaving the cardinal principles for the moment aside), they span a spectrum from the traditionally disliked balance of power to the more usually popular collective security and containment.

The point here is that competing models exist, each with a different lens for viewing "reality." Decision makers choose models that are direct reflections of their nations' historical experiences and cultural biases. If Americans abhor the balance of power but revel in collective security and containment, this does not add to an understanding of "reality" but goes far toward an understanding of Americans.

Eighth, it is here that the models and the U.S. approach to policy problems in general and to the question of enmity and enemies in particular, inevitably cross paths. We can look at these models simultaneously as different telescopes for observing the universe or, by peering through the other end of each telescope, discover the nature of the viewer. Each view has value.

Ninth, the models, because they describe "reality," each have to do three things: (1) they must portray a view of human nature; (2) they must explain the environment and indicate the nature of its rules and the extent of free choice left to the decision makers; and (3) they must predict the future consequences of present decisions, in view of both human nature and the nature of the environment. While these models may overlap, that is, in the case of one or more of these three features, yield the same observation or advice, they are nevertheless quite distinct intellectually. For example, although the balance-of-power model, the collective security model, and the containment model all "advised" U.S. action to stop the North Korean assault in 1950, each came to its advice by a different reasoning. In most cases, though, the models will yield contrasting advice.

Where these models differ most dramatically is in their description of the greatest disaster that can befall, the worst thing to fear, the thing therefore to prevent. For the balance of power, Tacitus's statement that "power is never stable when it is boundless" sums it up: equilibrium is the most usually quoted goal, but the aim is to avoid the effects of disequilibrium. Or, as Montesquieu put the point in *The Spirit of Laws*, "The real power of a prince does not consist so much in the facility he meets with in making conquests as in the difficulty an enemy finds in attacking him,"[9] which usually means in policy guidance terms to cultivate one's neighbor's neighbors and thereby restrain neighborly ambition. The worst mistake is to allow foreign power to grow too greatly, unrestrained. Both collective security and containment, by contrast, see unrestrained aggression as leading to the worst disaster, because aggression (in containment's case, Communist aggression) is supposed to spread its effect like a disease. The identity of the aggressor is of no real consequence; anyone will do. The cardinal principles model sees the collection of an unneeded and excessive number of enemies as the greatest disaster, predicting that it leads straight to great cost and risk of defeat. To sum up, the balance-of-power model advocates regulation of power; the containment and collective security models advocate regulation of aggression; and the cardinal principles model advocates regulation of the number of enemies.

The cardinal principles model, which we have examined at greatest length, was not put forward with any claim to an exclusive insight into "reality." It was put forward at greatest length for two reasons. First, because it is the author's own and fits the needs of the analysis. Second, and more importantly, because it is the product of repeated attempts to explain to American audiences (especially, and predominantly, of decision makers) that they ought to take into account what American preferences in models tend either to omit or to minimize. Just as with any of the other models, it will be likely to appeal to decision makers in direct relation to their own cultural biases.

Tenth, it is worth considering very carefully why American preferences in models are what they are. It is also necessary to reach some conclusion about the comparative weaknesses and strengths of these models before weighing and evaluating the American record. For if, as illustration, containment is really acceptable and "realistic" as a guide to decision making, a policy that aligns the United States against all Communists (seen as a bloc) has to be praised. But if, by contrast, it confronts the United States with unnecessary enemies, in weighing the record it has to be condemned. So the way one assesses the record is inseparable from the way one views the models.

Throughout this book we have come across a decided American tendency to think in line-flow, push-pull, input-output, mechanical and/or functional terms. We have described these tendencies as natural in view of the American experience. There is also an ingrained preference for direct dealing, confrontation, and face-to-face relationships, with a minimum of protocol, ceremony, or frills. Finally, there is a strong feeling in most Americans that problems can be solved, that they ought in most cases to be solved through compromise, and that their resolution otherwise should be guided by presumably universal standards of justice and equity. All of these features, with the exception of the last group, tend toward an engineering or management image of reality. Including the last set of features overlays the engineering-management approach with a moralistic veneer. Add now the lack of historical awe ("Americans look to the future, not the past") and the lack of geographical awe (the airplane or the missile can go anywhere in a short period of time), and the viewpoint becomes worldwide without any of the nuances that variety of culture and location in the world ought to introduce. Then add the great national power and energy of Americans, and one finds some definite model preferences.

Distaste for the balance of power runs throughout U.S. history, including the colonial period. Even when we practiced balance-of-power politics, we did so only out of necessity and certainly with no zest. The colonial founding fathers knew the vocabulary of *Realpolitik* but did not themselves like to use it, at least in foreign affairs. As the necessity to deal with balance politics receded, our leaders gladly put it from them. In the whole documentary record of U.S. diplomacy, few things are more striking than both the avoidance of use of the term "balance of power" and the avoidance of balance-of-power vocabulary. The reason is, of course, not hard to come by: it is the natural tendency of a society that knowingly and consciously turned its back on the Old World to create a brave society in the New.

As to collective security and containment, those successive attempts by Americans to displace the "obsolete" balance of power, it is worth remembering that containment was only a second-best option. The collective security concept had (and retained) first allegiance. Put another way, Americans preferred the collective security notion, which is enshrined in international law, to the notion of containment. It was only when collective security showed problems that it had to be supplemented with an anti-Communist refinement. Perhaps, though, what these models had in common is of greatest importance. They both included optimistic views about human nature. Human beings loved peace and freedom. Both models described an environment where aggression constituted the occasional threat. Each counselled an immediate and overwhelming response to that threat, containment because of the domino motif, collective security to discourage repetition or imitators. Each assumed that a prevailing power was available, containment because it was backed by the whole Free World, collective security because it represented "the organized might of mankind."

Eleventh, what, we may ask, did these two models tend to ignore, understate, or distort? There were a number of things, beginning with the assumption of both models that every nation had a natural interest in taking part, in taking sides. In collective security, "neutral" meant refusing to carry out the obligations of membership; in containment, not being in the Communist orbit was seen as meriting automatic inclusion in the Free World contingent. Yet any number of nations — indeed, a growing number — saw these choices as Tweedledum-Tweedledee, and as not serving their national interests either way. A second problem with these models was that they attempted to align the national interest of the United States with suppression of aggression anywhere in the world, as though these were synonymous terms. And yet it was by no means self-evident that the committing of aggression by someone somewhere was a valid blank check on American blood — it was not even obvious that shedding American blood in defense of free peoples was worthwhile. A third problem was that American decision makers, under either formulation, were left with little or no choice in their response to aggression. Furthermore, both models were silent on the question of proportionality: When was enough enough? When did the punishment fit the crime?

Consequently, both models prescribed fairly automatic and rather costly reactions to certain events initiated outside the borders of the United States, with the implication that the United States was to take action even if the scene was half a world distant. That meant in turn that any area, and any event in that area, became as important as any other area or any other event, merely by the kind of happening it represented. Provided it was an "aggression," reaction was mandatory. Both models assumed universal reactions, with nations confronted with what was assumed to be obvious cases and categories. That left judgment out of account. It rejected any hierarchy of interests. It put any enemy on the same level with any other enemy by excluding priorities from the list. It ignored troublesome questions such as what to do if one's own allies commit aggression or what to do if two or even three dangerous situations develop simultaneously and one cannot afford to turn one's back to deal with a more flagrant but obviously less threatening offender.

In short, these line-flow, input-output, mechanical ways of visualizing world problems, and the foreign policy decisions necessary to cope effectively with them, ignored the complexities of international politics and sidelined analysis in favor of action.

Twelfth, to cope with the intellectual deficiencies of these formulations by putting the balance of power forward as a substitute is not a satisfactory solution in the United States since the balance of power has never been very congenial to American thinking and, as we showed, it is itself riddled with ambiguities. Yet the core of the wisdom of the balance of power, as all its great practitioners have known, is to control the power problem by complicating the posture of the major potential disturber of the peace, achieving this by undermining the tranquility of its flanks and rear, or, even better, isolating it entirely. It is really to translate this thought into an acceptable American idiom that the four cardinal principles evolved.

They were evolved in reverse order from the sequence in this book. First came the fourth or culminating principle, the point of the exercise: the conservation of enemies. To Americans too fond of thinking initially and absolutely instead of tentatively and relatively of objectives, this made sense because it indicated the result wished at the end of the evolution. Then, to show how that result was obtainable, the other operational principle of counterbalancing national interests was pressed into service. By emphasizing the element of choice, both for and against, this cardinal principle showed that selection and rejection of interests resulted in an array of more-friendly, less-friendly nations and that a proper selection of interests could remove the incentive for third nations to ally with an enemy. The principle of counterbalancing national interests restored free will to the problem and rejected the rigid determinism of both of the models preferred by the United States.

To leave the principles at that point, however, would have been to encourage the false assumption that all nations approach the assessment and selection of these counterbalancing interests with the same values and attitudes. Moreover, without a continual reminder that every bilateral relationship is ultimately only a part of the greater, multilateral whole, these counterbalancing interest considerations would become too narrowly construed. Out of these needs grew the two "perspective" principles of third-party influences and past-future linkages.

As a single model, the four cardinal principles sought then to express in an American idiom the positive features to be derived from traditional balance-of-power thinking, while discouraging the mechanical, cost-be-damned refusal of the collective security and containment models to distinguish, rank, and prioritize. The cardinal principles model assumes that nations are supposed to and normally do make effective choices to enhance their national security and that they function most effectively when they minimize the number of enemies they confront. It assumes that piles of weapons, however high and however nuclear, do not really define a relationship, that in the contemporary world, as in the prenuclear world, second parties are constrained not only by first parties but by third parties.

I would argue, then, that the cardinal principles model and especially the principle of the conservation of enemies is a valid yardstick against which to judge the national security performance of the United States, that it describes norms that are reasonable and relevant. If this argument is accepted, what then can we say of the record of U.S. policy? How well have we solved the operational riddle of where to deploy and where to draw the line in defense of the nation under the best obtainable conditions? Because, if the objective is to keep the number of enemies minimized, and the method of doing so is to utilize the cardinal principles intelligently (which is best done by remembering the effect of third-party influences and past-future linkages), the practical game plan will still necessarily involve decisions on where to deploy and with whom to ally. The deployments and alliances are the tactical evidences of the strategic concept governing the policy.

In the colonial period, once the thirteen states had raised the banner of revolt, the record shows a highly realistic appraisal by the revolutionary leaders of the problem faced: the French alliance was vitally needed and sought with no hesitation. The record shows how carefully after independence was achieved the first U.S. presidents were prepared for their duties, serving apprenticeships as secretary of state. Experienced leaders were required, for Europe's powers were all around the weak, new United States. Popular passions in the early years, with a pro-French party pitted against a pro-English party, raised the prospect of much mischief, especially in view of this situation, but Washington's farewell address indicated quite clearly that he recognized the danger. The quick seizing of first opportunity to jettison the "entangling" French alliance and resume full discretion over our own affairs is striking. In the first few decades, leaders of neither political party allowed any good opportunity to expand the national domain to slip by unutilized—and such expansion was a prime prerequisite for growing national strength (and automatically also produced a receding threat perimeter as Europe's powers transferred such territories to the infant United States).

In accomplishing the continental territorial expansion, which was essentially complete with the Treaty of Guadalupe Hidalgo in 1848 (supplemented by the Gadsden purchase of 1853 and the acquisition of Alaska in 1867), the United States fought Great Britain, France, and Mexico — one at a time. That the United States contemplated the possibility of fighting *both* Great Britain and France in the War of 1812 is also a fact. It would have been a serious mistake; even fighting just Britain went poorly. The United States was saved from a serious situation only by more important British concerns abroad. It is also true that the United States, facing the Mexican War, was foolhardy enough to threaten the British simultaneously, thus exposing itself to the threat of a two-front war in the north and in the south.

Yet there is no denying the overall success of what was done, and there is no denying that the United States in fact avoided fighting more than one enemy at a time. On the whole, a sound security policy was continued from one administration to another, designed to consolidate the national power base, expand the national territories, and encourage the withdrawal of the European powers from the American scene. Clausewitz's caution that war must serve political ends was not forgotten in any of the early wars of the United States; the military operations were obviously designed to serve clear political purposes.

From 1847 until 1898 the attention of the United States was focused inward and its foreign policy limited, but with the Spanish-American War the United States first encountered a serious national security problem for which the solution was not obvious. On the earlier question of expansion, different tactical answers were possible and different moral judgments could be made as to the methods used, but the strategic wisdom of what was done was really beyond dispute. The infant republic very likely would either grow or die. But now grown to strength and power, capable of far-flung deployments, the republic had to face a more complicated strategic issue: Where should the defense perimeter be drawn, and how much enmity was it desirable to cultivate or tolerate in the process? The acquisition of the Philippines was a fateful step, providing for one thing a vantage point on the edge of Asian continental affairs. Whether the acquisition was a mistake is a more complicated issue. It probably was, but the answer given is closely intertwined with the judgment one makes of the subsequent continuing involvement with continental Asian affairs. Acquiring the Philippines meant fighting Spain, but no other nation was involved in the fighting, meaning that the American habit up to that point of fighting only a single enemy was continued intact.

The reaction of the United States to the outbreak of World War I demonstrated that we were largely without any overall strategic concept by which to guide our decisions. War planning in those prewar years was still frequently directed to the contingency of a war against England. After 1903 and the creation of a Joint Army and Navy Board, color-coded plans were produced for hostilities with Japan, Great Britain, and a German invasion of the Western Hemisphere: Plan Orange, Plan Red, and Plan Black, respectively.[10] In our diplomacy we "tilted" toward England and subsequently fought Germany — still only one enemy at a time, since although the Germans had allies, the United States did not fight them — but we entered that war without any clear articulation of our strategic intentions and objectives. The closest we came was the Fourteen Points, which if they were stripped of their moralistic clothing and rephrased, were not devoid of sensible notions. If the Versailles settlement had actually conformed to the Fourteen Points, a viable balance of power probably would have emerged, particularly since fewer nations would have had serious grievances to nourish.

Woodrow Wilson's address to Congress, enumerating the points, began with a preamble in which he said: "What we demand in this war . . . is that the world be made fit and safe to live in; and particularly that it be made safe for every peace-loving nation which, like our own, wishes to live its own life, determine its own institutions. . . ."[11] That is a somewhat indirect way of saying it, just as the earlier indirect expression of anger over German curtailing of our "freedom of the seas" could be translated into a concern over the actions of an ambitious Germany upsetting the balance of power. It was not unreasonable to rest U.S. national interests at this time on the foundation of a stable balance of power constructed through the avoidance of "a peace of victors." The United States had a demonstrably greater interest in a Germany not too drastically upset by the peace settlement than in one seeking a new war. There was no reason why the United States should instead have cast Germany in the role of permanent enemy. The United States, looked at geopolitically, would prosper if *no* nation gained such a predominance as to unsettle world affairs. Where the United States had unquestionably benefited from the stable balance of 1815-1914, it could no longer expect that stability as an unearned increment but now had to begin to make a more positive contribution on some sustained basis.

It is in this regard that the United States, in seeking to insulate itself in isolationism and neutrality acts (in a unilateralist stance) after World War I, helped to bring on exactly what it feared. Not that the U.S. action was necessarily definitive, the one way or the other; World War II really originated in the shortsighted settlement that terminated World War I rather than in U.S. policy actions thereafter.

One should not be too harsh in judging the U.S. conduct at this point. Needed to redress the balance, the United States participated in World War I, doing the right thing but with no clear understanding why. Frustrated and confused afterward, the United States then withdrew from close association and refused to coordinate its policies with other states with roughly parallel interests. This was no doubt a mistake, but it is worth pointing out that the mistakes made by the far more experienced British and French were much more serious — and ultimately disastrous.

One can also sympathize with the overly simplistic moral drawn by Americans from the coming of World War II and their tendency to elevate the effects of the Munich fiasco to a sacred general rule of international politics. We were at least on the right track about the main event, even if not necessarily so about its corollaries. We had absorbed an important strategic lesson, which was that we would have to play an active role in maintaining the balance of power if we did not want an early World War III. Unfortunately, we permitted the Versailles error to be repeated in the sense that we let a territorial settlement go into effect that was a continual thorn in the side of a stable European peace. That is, the Soviets were permitted a presence in Central Europe that prevents any real and permanent tranquillity.

Charles E. Bohlen has a different assessment. He says of the missed opportunity to pressure the Soviets before U.S. troops were pulled back:

Truman . . . left the decision on the movement of troops entirely to Eisenhower and the Joint Chiefs of Staff. This decision may have been a mistake, but it did follow the American tradition in the conduct of wars. Although I was not consulted, I certainly would not have disputed the President's decision at the end of the war to pull American troops back to our zones in Germany and Austria. I believe it would have been an egregious error to have followed Churchill's advice to hold on to our positions in Saxony and Thuringia. Such a standfast would have given the Kremlin a permanent reason for charging that relationships developed in the war had been torn up and discarded by the United States.[12]

Interestingly, a few pages later Bohlen recounts what Stalin said in late May 1945 when Harry Hopkins asked him whether the Soviet Union would honor the Yalta agreement and enter the Far Eastern war: "Stalin replied testily, 'The Soviet Union always honors its word.' Then he lowered his voice and added, 'except in case of extreme necessity.'"[13]

Once the Soviets were permitted an overextended influence in Central Europe, the United States had to keep a garrison year after year on its side of the Iron Curtain in order to redress the military balance. Thirty-seven years later it was still exhorting its NATO allies to make a greater conventional effort to overcome the Soviet advantage of an advanced position.

Since the Soviet blockade of Berlin and other such moves then raised the threshold of risk and tension, it is no wonder that the United States in its containment doctrine concentrated its efforts on keeping the balance from disintegrating further. Again, however, the formulation was very indirect and did not pinpoint the real problem. Instead containment spoke of preventing further Soviet advances. This was a highly desirable objective, of course, even if it did not represent a fully adequate strategic appraisal. Containment really argued that the problem was motivational (arising out of a Communist dynamic), whereas that was entirely a secondary strategic issue unless it led the Russians to some further overturn of the balance of power in Europe or elsewhere.

The policy of shoring up Western Europe through economic aid and a military alliance was, tactically speaking, an excellent and needed riposte to the Soviet overextension, even if it distracted attention from the main, or territorial, issue.

But hardly had the United States taken appropriate actions in Europe, even if based upon a strategic analysis that was not square on the central issue, than as fate (or Murphy's law) would have it, the Korean War broke out. Bohlen says that "the Korean war was interpreted by Acheson and most others in the State Department, as well as the Joint Chiefs of Staff, as ushering in a new phase of Soviet foreign policy. Their view, which Truman accepted, was that having launched an attack on Korea . . . the Soviet Union was likely to call on satellite armies elsewhere. . . ."[14] Bohlen sees that war as an isolated act, instigated by the North Koreans with Soviet knowledge. But, says Bohlen, because the official judgment erred, "the United States overinterpreted the Korean war and overextended our commitments."[15] Bohlen is right that these events led the United States to lump Asian communism in with European communism to form one worldwide, integrated Communist bloc, to be contained by the Free World. To call it overextending commitments is another question. Korea had to be defended, since Japan could not act in its own behalf and a change in the balance of power there would have produced difficulties, given the strategic importance of Korea.

Subsequently the United States made an alliance with Taiwan and put a half-million men on China's southeastern flank. The problem with these actions was not really that the United States was attempting too much, or even that it was playing too vigorous a role. The problem was that the strategic guidance that a worldwide containment model offered was anything but well suited to the policy problem the United States faced. It brought us into a costly war in Vietnam against an unimportant enemy, while continuing us necessarily in a friction with China (increased by such deployments). At the same time as it bogged down the United States, it liberated the Soviets to an unprecedented and completely unnecessary strategic freedom. This freedom for Russia was the inevitable counterpart of the U.S. action that necessarily forced Chinese moderation toward the Russians.

In short, the United States, when it came of age militarily at the turn of the twentieth century, made sequentially a choice in Asia of dubious quality (retaining the Philippines); followed by the highly appropriate choice of salvaging the sagging European balance in 1917; followed by an aloofness that was insufficiently discriminating; followed by a needed participation in the Second World War; followed by an inattention to geopolitical considerations that permitted Soviet overextension; followed by a highly intelligent tactical plan to prevent further losses, coupled with a problematic strategic concept that was effective so long as it was confined to Europe; followed by a proper response to the threat to the Asian balance represented by the North Korean assault; followed by an articulated anti-Chinese policy that not only deprived the United States of any strategic flexibility but gratuitously conferred strategic flexibility on its prime enemy.

This is not overextension; it is misdirection. The problem did not come from trying to do too much but from doing the wrong things. It pitted the United States against a third-rate enemy while freeing the primary enemy to do whatever it wished elsewhere.

The serious fault in the strategic models preferred by the United States does not stem primarily from their activist incitements, although this is potentially serious. More serious is the failure to rank threats by nations rather than categories. It is simply not true of the international system that threats acquire their importance by the flagrancy of the aggressions committed. A United States that acts as though that were so, instead of adhering to strict standards of setting priorities in enemies, is ever in danger of fighting counterproductive wars — wars that do not enhance the stability of the balance of power or U.S. security.

Lincoln P. Bloomfield concludes a thoughtful analysis of U.S. foreign policy by arguing that the United States must redefine its world role, for

what has to be confronted is to be found neither in cost-benefit calculations nor at the level of diplomatic style and maneuver where a Bismarck competes with Wilsonians. Beneath all that, the deepest tensions in our body politic concern conflicting beliefs about the nature of man and the meaning of morality in public policy.

Bloomfield thinks the failures stem from "an unresolved clash between values and power."[16] Certainly there is much evidence, in looking at choices of models on the part of the United States, of a definite preference for certain highly optimistic interpretations of human nature. Clearly also,

Americans continually grope to find the link between moral values and public policies, convinced that that link, when discovered, will be capable of being stated simply. Americans are far from believing what Reinhold Niebuhr spent a career arguing: that there are no political choices available between good and bad, that every action is tainted, and that at best the result of politics is a spectrum of choices with shades of increasing or decreasing moral content. Theodore White says at one point that General Stilwell

came of a tradition which [White thinks] has now all but vanished — the tradition of Americans who felt so strongly we were the good people that wherever they went they were convinced they, as Americans, brought virtue. Nor could Stilwell conceive that what was good for America could possibly be bad, or wrong, for other peoples.[17]

The quotation from Bloomfield shows little faith in the reformist possibilities of pursuing cost-benefit calculations or in examining "the level of diplomatic style and maneuver where a Bismarck competes with Wilsonians." Taking Bloomfield's words literally, one must agree. Cost-benefit calculations as such are only useful to the extent that the calculations are based on effective and meaningful choices in terms of the real world. But cost-benefit calculations are surely not irrelevant for a nation that has shown itself capable of incurring great costs for no noticeable benefits. And it is not Bismarck's style that we can profit from, compared with that of the Wilsonians. It is Bismarck's way of thinking about problems: the quality of his thought. The problem is not to try to convert Americans to the value of pursuing "amoral" policies but to ensure that the policies pursued, by their identification with positive and useful results, deserve to be coupled with the adjective "moral." What made the Vietnam War "immoral" for so many Americans, despite the moral justifications that accompanied it, was its separation from any result or outcome that could justify its bloodshed.

Chancellor von Bethmann-Hollweg's remarks to the Reichstag on August 4, 1914, seem especially poignant today. He announced that German troops, without provocation, had just crossed the Belgian frontier. He admitted it was "contrary to international law" and promised "to make good the injustice as soon as our military goal" was reached, but he added: "Who like we are fighting for the highest [possession] must only consider how victory can be gained."[18] On January 31, 1917, Germany, although not proud of a policy it felt forced to pursue, announced unrestricted submarine warfare. One German cabinet minister summed up German opinion when he said that "from a military point of view America is as nothing." The 1914 action helped net Germany an additional enemy in England; the 1917 action added the United States to the now formidable opposition. What makes all of it so poignant is that the outcome in no way justified these "wrong" actions. Whatever their moral or legal merit, practical merit they had none.

Admiral J. C. Wylie calls strategy a "plan of action designed in order to achieve some end; a purpose together with a system of measures for its accomplishment."[19] Political or foreign policy strategy is no different. It, too, must demonstrate a control over situations in the search to attain objectives. It, too, must represent a plan of action that relates purpose, method, and accomplishment. To produce national disaster with the very best (and even highly moral) intentions, as the United States did in Vietnam, is somehow not really much superior to producing national disaster through admittedly illegal and immoral actions, as the Germans did in beginning World War I. The moral pretensions of a policy do not automatically provide a post-mortem justification for action.

It should hardly require an extended argument to demonstrate that enmity is controllable, that it is only prudent to restrict the number of enemies confronted, and that to accomplish this requires systematic attention to enemies in the priority to which their "threat" entitles them. The conservation of enemies, expressed that way, is hardly more than common sense.

There are only two justifications for a book pointing out what is, in its larger outlines (if not detail) fairly obvious. First, there is no other book that addresses this topic in this way. Second, the United States, by its actions after World War II, rather clearly paid little attention to the fairly obvious. It embarked on a war in Vietnam that, before it was through, almost tore the nation apart.

Whether the advice not to neglect the conservation of enemies is considered "Bismarckian" can make little difference in how the advice works out. Of course, there are also those who truly believe that the United States cannot be relied on to follow the "subtle" advice to conserve enemies, but must rather blunder forward in some brash and uninhibited American native style. Let us hope that they remain a distinct minority and that the great majority will conclude instead that there is nothing wrong, morally or practically, with taking enemies seriously, on the prudent assumption that we will have some for many years to come.

NOTES

1. Thomas S. Kuhn, *The Structure of Scientific Revolutions*, 2d ed. (Chicago: University of Chicago Press, 1970), p. 64.

2. *Jen-min jih-pao* (People's Daily), August 17, 1971, as quoted in Franz Schurmann, *The Logic of World Power* (New York: Pantheon, 1974), p. 284.

3. Quoted in Kenneth W. Thompson and Roy C. Macridis, "The Comparative Study of Foreign Policy," in *Foreign Policy in World Politics*, 5th ed. (Englewood Cliffs, N.J.: Prentice-Hall, 1976), p. 4.

4. *Public Papers of President Lyndon B. Johnson, 1965* (Washington, D.C.: Government Printing Office, 1966), vol. I, p. 449.

5. Thomas Jefferson, letter to James Sullivan, 1808.

6. Quoted in Theo Aronson, *The Kaisers* (Indianapolis: Bobbs-Merrill, 1971), p. 56.

7. Quoted in Thomas A. Bailey and David Kennedy, *The American Pageant*, 6th ed. (Lexington, Mass.: Heath, 1979), p. 603.

8. See J. David Singer's related comment in "The Level-of-Analysis Problem in International Relations," in Klaus Knorr and Sidney Verba, eds., *The International System: Theoretical Essays* (Princeton, N.J.: Princeton University Press, 1961), p. 85.

9. Montesquieu, de la Brède et de, *The Spirit of Laws*, trans. Thomas Nugent, 2 vols. (London: George Bell, 1899), vol. 1, bk. IX, chap. 7, p. 141.

10. Russell F. Weigley, *The American Way of War* (New York: Macmillan, 1973), p. 201.

11. Text is in *Congressional Record*, 65th Cong., 2d sess., vol. 56, pp. 680-81.

12. Charles E. Bohlen, *Witness to History, 1929-1969* (New York: Norton, 1973), p. 226.

13. Ibid., p. 229.

14. Ibid., p. 309.

15. Ibid., p. 320.

16. Lincoln P. Bloomfield, *In Search of American Foreign Policy: The Humane Use of Power* (New York: Oxford University Press, 1974), p. 129.

17. Theodore H. White, *In Search of History* (New York: Harper, 1978), p. 178.

18. *The New York Times Current History, The European War*, vol. 1, (New York Times Co., 1915), pp. 221-22. Barbara Tuchman, *The Guns of August* (New York: Dell, 1971), pp. 152-53, has a convenient account of these events.

19. J. C. Wylie, *Military Strategy: A General Theory of Power Control* (New Brunswick, N.J.: Rutgers University Press, 1967), p. 13.

BIBLIOGRAPHY

Since the notes use complete citations, only those works most influential in affecting this book's content are also indicated here.

Allison, Graham T. *Essence of Decision: Explaining the Cuban Missile Crisis.* Boston: Little, Brown, 1971.

Ardrey, Robert. *The Territorial Imperative.* New York: Dell, 1971.

Art, Robert J. "Bureaucratic Politics and American Foreign Policy: A Critique." In John E. Endicott and Roy W. Stafford, Jr., eds., *American Defense Policy,* 4th ed. Baltimore: Johns Hopkins University Press, 1977.

Bismarck, Otto, Prince von. *Bismarck, The Man and the Statesman: Reflections and Reminiscences.* 2 vols. New York: Harper, 1899.

Bloomfield, Lincoln P. *In Search of American Foreign Policy: The Humane Use of Power.* New York: Oxford University Press, 1974.

Brodie, Bernard. *War and Politics.* New York: Macmillan, 1973.

Brogan, Dennis W. "The Illusion of American Omnipotence," *Harper's* 205 (December 1952), pp. 21-28.

Brougham, Henry, 1st Baron Brougham and Vaux. *Works.* 11 vols. Edinburgh, 1872-1873.

Bülow, Bernhard, Prince von. *Memoirs.* 4 vols. Boston: Little, Brown, 1931-32.

Carr, E. H. *The Twenty Years' Crisis, 1919-1939.* London: Macmillan Co., 1940.

Claude, Inis L., Jr. *Power and International Relations.* New York: Random House. 1962.

Clausewitz, Karl von. *On War.* Edited and translated by Michael Howard and Peter Paret. Princeton, N.J.: Princeton University Press, 1976.

Darwin, Charles. *The Origin of Species.* New York: Mentor Books, New American Library, 1958.

Dugdale, Blanche E. C. *Arthur James Balfour.* New York: Putnam, 1937.

Einstein, Albert, and Infeld, Leopold. *The Evolution of Physics.* New York: Simon & Schuster, 1950.

Falk, Richard A. *A Study of Future Worlds.* New York: Free Press, 1975.

Fisher, Roger. *Basic Negotiating Strategy.* London: Allen Lane, Penguin Press, 1971.

Frazer, James G. *The Golden Bough.* New York: Macmillan, 1922.

Fromm, Erich. *The Anatomy of Human Destructiveness.* New York: Fawcett Crest, 1973.

Gaddis, John Lewis. *The United States and the Origins of the Cold War, 1941-1947.* New York: Columbia University Press, 1972.

Gallucci, Robert L. *Neither Peace Nor Honor: The Politics of American Military Policy in Viet-Nam*. Baltimore: Johns Hopkins University Press, 1975.

George, Alexander, and Smoke, Richard. *Deterrence in American Foreign Policy: Theory and Practice*. New York: Columbia University Press, 1974.

Gray, Colin S. *The Geopolitics of the Nuclear Era*. National Strategy Information Center, Inc. New York: Crane, Russak, 1977.

Griffith, Samuel B., II. *In Defense of the Public Liberty*. Garden City, N.Y.: Doubleday, 1976.

Gulick, Edward Vose. *Europe's Classical Balance of Power*. New York: Norton, 1967.

Halberstam, David. *The Best and the Brightest*. Greenwich, Conn.: Fawcett, 1973.

Halperin, Morton H. *Bureaucratic Politics and Foreign Policy*. Washington, D.C.: Brookings Institution, 1974.

Hartmann, Frederick H. *The Swiss Press and Foreign Affairs in World War II*. Gainesville: University of Florida Monographs, Social Sciences No. 5, Winter 1960.

Holsti, Ole. "Individual Differences in 'Definition of the Situation,'" *Journal of Conflict Resolution* 14 (September 1970): pp. 303-10.

Hoopes, Townsend. *The Limits of Intervention*, rev. ed. New York: David McKay, 1973.

Howard, Michael. "The Classical Strategists," *Adelphi Papers* 54 (February 1969).

Jervis, Robert. *Perception and Misperception in International Politics*. Princeton, N.J.: Princeton University Press, 1976.

Kennan, George F. *Memoirs, 1925-1950*. Boston: Little, Brown, 1967.

Kissinger, Henry. *White House Years*. Boston: Little, Brown, 1979.

Klineberg, Otto. *The Human Dimension in International Relations*. New York: Holt, Rinehart, Winston, 1964.

Kuhn, Thomas S. *The Structure of Scientific Revolutions*, 2d ed. Chicago: University of Chicago Press, 1970.

Lebow, Richard Ned. *Between Peace and War: The Nature of International Crisis*. Baltimore: Johns Hopkins University Press, 1981.

Lewis, C. S. *The Discarded Image*. Cambridge: Cambridge University Press, 1967.

Lieber, Robert J. *Theory and World Politics*. London: George Allen & Unwin, 1973.

Lippmann, Walter. *The Cold War*. New York: Harper, 1947.

Lorenz, Konrad. *On Aggression*. New York: Harcourt, Brace & World, 1966.

Madariaga, Salvador de. *Englishmen, Frenchmen, Spaniards*. London: Oxford University Press, 1928.

May, Ernest R. *"Lessons of the Past": The Use and Misuse of History in American Foreign Policy*. New York: Oxford University Press, 1973.

Morgenthau, Hans J. *In Defense of the National Interest*. New York: Knopf, 1951.

Nicolson, Harold. *National Character and National Policy*. Montague Burton International Relations Lecture. Nottingham: University College, 1938.

Nixon, Richard. *The Memoirs of Richard Nixon*. New York: Grosset and Dunlap, 1978.

Reves, Emery. *The Anatomy of Peace*. New York: Harper, 1945.

Schelling, Thomas C. *The Strategy of Conflict*. Cambridge, Mass.: Harvard University Press, 1960.

Schilling, Warner R. "The Politics of National Defense: Fiscal 1950." In Warner R. Schilling, Paul T. Hammond, and Glenn H. Snyder, *Strategy, Politics, and Defense Budgets*. New York: Columbia University Press, 1962.

Seabury, Paul, ed. *Balance of Power*. San Francisco: Chandler, 1965.

Singer, J. David, and Small, Melvin. *The Wages of War, 1816-1965, A Statistical Handbook*. New York: Wiley, 1972.

Smith, Arthur H. *Chinese Characteristics*, 13th ed. New York: Fleming H. Revell, 1894.

Smith, Hedrick. *The Russians*. New York: Quadrangle, 1976.

Snyder, Glenn H., and Diesing, Paul. *Conflict among Nations: Bargaining, Decision Making, and System Structure in International Crises*. Princeton, N.J.: Princeton University Press, 1977.

Sondermann, Fred A. "The Concept of the National Interest," *Orbis* (Spring 1977).

Spykman, Nicholas J. *America's Strategy in World Politics*. New York: Harcourt, 1942.

Stromberg, Roland N. *Collective Security and American Foreign Policy*. New York: Praeger, 1963.

Thucydides. *The Peloponnesian War*. Translated by Rex Warner. Baltimore: Penguin Books, 1954.

Truman, Harry S. *Memoirs*. Vol. 2, *Years of Trial and Hope*. Garden City, N.Y.: Doubleday, 1956.

U.S., Congress, Senate. *Addresses of President Wilson*. 66th Cong., 1st sess. Senate Document no. 120. Washington, D.C.: Government Printing Office, 1919.

U.S., Department of Defense, Joint Chiefs of Staff. *Dictionary of Military and Associated Terms*. JCS Publication 1, September 3, 1974. Revised, June 1, 1979.

Watzlawick, Paul. *How Real Is Real? Confusion, Disinformation, Communication*. New York: Vintage Books, 1976.

White, Theodore H. *In Search of History*. New York: Harper, 1978.

Wolfers, Arnold. *Discord and Collaboration, Essays on International Politics*. Baltimore: Johns Hopkins University Press, 1962.

INDEX

About the Author

FREDERICK H. HARTMANN is Alfred Thayer Mahan Professor at the Naval War College in Newport, Rhode Island. His earlier books include *Germany Between East and West* and *The New Age in American Foreign Policy*.